For Caroline,

Emma and Susanna

and the memory of

Tim

July 27th 1978 - July 23rd 1995

Acknowledgements

The approach presented in this book has been tried and tested with managers and practitioners in many organisations. In the UK this has included staff in local authority social services and social work departments, from the National Health Service, and from national and local voluntary organisations and from service user groups. Senior, middle and first line managers, professional practitioners and people in service user organisations have been involved, both individually and as part of whole directorates or departmental and interagency teams.

The ideas and the research which underpins this approach are not limited to the 'human services'. The approach can be applied to introducing innovations into any social organisation.

This book is based on the Managing Change and Innovation Programme of the National Institute for Social Work. The work was funded by the Department of Health Social Services Inspectorate and the Social Work Inspectorate of the Scottish Office without whose support it could not have taken place. The ideas and opinions expressed in this book and the companion volumes are, however, those of the author and not of these departments.

This book is one of three published by The Stationery Office that draw on our experience of working with those managing change, particularly successful innovators. They are also based on a wide body of research on the diffusion of innovations and management literature focused on the management of change. This book describes the Managing Change Through Innovation approach, so called because it stresses that changing practice often requires innovations in management. The companion volume *Mapping Change and Innovation* is a practical guide that summarises the MCTI approach, and presents the questions that need to be addressed to build up plans, or 'maps', for managing change in local circumstances. The third book in the set, *Chance Favours the Prepared Mind* by John Brown, describes the development of services using the approach and relating it to a discussion of leadership and team building. All are published by The Stationery Office.

Our work on change and innovation management grew out of the work of the Practice and Development Exchange, PADE, at the National Institute for Social Work. This work was supported by grants from the Joseph Rowntree Foundation. The aim of the Exchange was to work with innovatory managers, practitioners and researchers to develop better models of practice and management based on the best available evidence. This started us on a series of development projects designed to implement research findings and to find better ways of supporting innovation and managing change. These included the Department of Health funded Community Social Work Exchange and Research into Practice: Residential Care of Elderly People programmes. Throughout this time I have had the privilege of working with many who have led change in their organisations and have been leaders in their fields. I would like to thank them all, particularly the many innovators of the PADE networks. My thanks go to all the members of the NISW/Kings Fund Consultancy Development Programme; staff from all levels in Warwickshire, Wigan, Westminster, Newcastle Social Services and many other social services departments and other agencies. I would also like to thank the students who participated in MCTI workshops as part of their management and advanced practice courses at the Universities of Southampton, Sussex, Stirling and Dundee. The members of the Scottish Network and workshops have been a constant source of stimulation and support throughout.

I would also like to thank colleagues in the US who have engaged with us and enriched our ideas. This includes those who participated through the federally funded Transfer of Technology Project on Community Based Practice in Cedar Rapids and at the University of Iowa; participants at the Wingspread Conference on Community Based Practice funded by the Johnson Foundation; the Transferring Human Services Technology to Pennsylvania Rural Counties Project funded by the Center for Rural Pennsylvania; the 1994 Obermann Seminar at the University of Iowa; and the National Association of Social Workers Conference on Effective Programme Replication and Adaptation in Washington DC. Special thanks go to John Zalenski of the National Resource

Center for Family Centered Practice and colleagues who participated in Managing Change Through Innovation workshops in Chicago, Vermont and Philadelphia.

I received exceptional support from the Management of Change and Innovations Advisory Group: Fabian Best, David Crosbie, Maneck Dalal, Lynette Domoney, Jeannette Eno, Chris Gostick, Jon Griffith, David Mason, Joyce Moseley, Stephen Osborne, John Starzewski and especially Robert Maxwell of the Kings Fund, who chaired the group and its parental predecessor for the Practice and Development Exchange. Barbara Stocking was a member of this group and made a key contribution, both personally through her own research and wisdom and by introducing me to the work of Everett Rogers.

Colleagues at NISW and from other organisations in the UK and US have been particularly helpful, including: Paul Adams, Alan Brawley, Nan Carle, Colin Cheesman, Bob Cohen, Mike Cooper, Christine Crosbie, Catherine Dobson, Gayle Foster, Sheila Gallagher, Raymond Green, John Griffiths, David Harrison, Emelia Martinez-Brawley, Wendy Macfarlane, Margo MacLellan, Wendy Mertens, Khristy Nelson, Roger Winter and Stan Witkin. Daphne Statham has provided particular support, as have my Development colleagues Giles Darvill, Trish Kearney and Gwen Rosen.

Barbara Hearn, now Director of Practice Development at the National Children's Bureau helped start Managing Change workshops at NISW. Jeanette Eno and Lynette Domoney provided crucial help by scaling the mountain of literature that exists on innovation and change and coming back with manageable information and useful insights. Their reviews of the literature and of models for managing change are available from NISW.

From the Department of Health Social Services Inspectorate and the Social Work Inspectorate of the Scottish Office I received particular encouragement from Don Brand, David Crosbie, Linda Hunt and Angus Skinner.

The project owed more than the usual debt to those who anchored the Unit when we were on the road as well as providing an essential contribution to the drafting of our publications: Nancy Dunlop, Dionne Mortley, Nnennaya Onyekwere, and Christine Greig who has administered the Managing Change and Innovation Network. Lynette Bolitho deserves special mention and gratitude for persevering with the manuscript, and tolerating its author.

I am indebted again to Margaret Hogan for her editorial work and her particular style of constructive feedback which I always read with some apprehension, and eventually, luckily, with relief.

Finally I owe a special debt to friends and colleagues who have been essential to this work. Nobody really writes books on their own. Individual authorship is a conventional way of punctuating events. Certainly all those mentioned will, I hope, recognise ideas that they had, or we had, or we have. This approach to managing change recognises that change takes place through a convergence of ideas, and that is certainly true of this book. Graham Tuson wrote a chapter on change management skills in an earlier working edition of this book which forms the foundation of Part Four of this edition. Mike Cooper sent missives from afar and the seeds of John Simmonds', of Sussex University, inspiration are still growing. John Brown and Mike Wardel provided essential suggestions and support when it was most needed. Many, have contributed generously of their ideas and time.

Contents

The Author

Gerry Smale trained in production management with the Ford Motor Company before joining the Probation Service. He has been director of a social work qualifying course for mature entrants at Sussex University, postgraduate management development programmes and founding director of the National Institute for Social Work's Practice and Development Exchange, PADE. He has carried out staff and management development programmes and consultancies throughout the UK and in the US. Recent work includes the transfer of technology on community based practice to the US and directing the Management of Innovations and Change programme. He is currently working on the Management and Development of Practice Expertise Programme supported by the Department of Health and a consortium of social services departments. Recent publications include *Empowerment, Assessment, Care Management and the Skilled Worker, Negotiating Care in the Community* and *Mapping Change and Innovation*, all published by HMSO / The Stationery Office.

PART ONE

Foundations of the MCTI Approach

Introduction

Many attempts to change practice, the day to day behaviour of staff as they carry out their work, simply do not work. Organisations are constantly reorganising, coming up with new mission statements, new strategies, changing their managers and staff and their job descriptions. But despite this whirl of activity many of the day to day practices of the staff, and the way that they relate to the public, stay much the same. Where change does take place it does not always have the desired impact: indeed it often seems to work in perverse ways and spark as many undesirable as intended consequences. Many managers are constantly confronted with the problems of managing change and yet have a limited repertoire of ways to tackle the problem. Staff often see how they could develop better services and the opportunity to be more responsive to the public but feel frustrated in their attempts to change practice from their position in the organisation.

Many are clear that they need to become much better at managing change. Paradoxically they also often feel that too much is happening, that they are having to cope with too much change to begin to tackle the management of change in a different way. Yet if they carry on with their old approaches they are doomed to repeat many of the change management mistakes of the past, and staff and management practice is likely to go on in much the same way as before. This book addresses the problem of how to be better at managing change, how to approach it in new ways, how to 'Manage Change Through Innovation' in management.

We are all, to a greater or lesser extent, managers of change in as much as we set out to change our circumstances and some dimension of the world around us. The phrases 'change manager' or 'change agent' are used in this book to refer to those people who set out to introduce a new way of working, a new method or new service: an innovation in their workplace. The innovation could involve new technology, such as the computerisation of the case record system. The innovation might be a new approach to working with the organisation's service users or customers, a new method of treatment such as 'family group conferencing', or a new approach to service delivery such as changing from direct provision to commissioning from others. Major changes in policy might involve many innovations: a new approach to management, for example, might involve changing the culture of the organisation towards 'a learning organisation'.

'Change managers', or 'change agents', are the people who take on the responsibility for introducing such innovations. They are not always managers, let alone senior managers: many innovations are discovered by and introduced into organisations by relatively junior staff. The term 'change agent' has a long history in the literature. It is typically used as a general term to apply to those people who consciously seek to introduce planned change into social situations (Bennis and others, 1985), either through a professional role such as management consultant, organisation developer, trainer; or because of the particular way they approach their formal organisational role as a manager (Schein, 1987) or practitioner (Smale and others, 1988). People using the approach set out in this book and its companion workbook *Mapping Change and Innovation* could be called *transactors* because they use the approach to guide them as they engage in a series of transactions with different people in their attempts to change practice, service delivery and the way that the organisation functions.

The Managing Change Through Innovation (MCTI) approach presented here has been tried and tested with managers and practitioners from both the social services and the health services, working in a variety of settings in the United Kingdom including social services departments, national and local voluntary organisations and health care trusts. It has also been used in transferring technology in the United States and developing community based practice (Martinez-Brawley, 1993; Adams and Nelson, 1995). Senior, middle and first line managers, professional practitioners and people in service user organisations have been involved, both individually and as part of whole directorates, departmental and inter-agency teams. However, the ideas and the research which underpins this approach are not limited to the 'human services'. *The approach can be applied to introducing innovations into any social organisation.*

This book has its roots in the experience of innovatory managers and practitioners working in many different settings. Development work carried out by the National Institute for Social Work brought many of these pioneers together through the Practice and Development Exchange (PADE), a programme designed to apply relevant research to practice and support innovators in developing new approaches to practice. Important lessons were particularly learnt from PADE's Community Social Work Exchange which brought together pioneers of 'Patch' and other approaches to community based practice from across the UK. This work continues in the US.

We noticed that many innovations, even the most effective ones, failed repeatedly to become mainstream practice, even when national and local policies supported them. By contrast other innovations seemed to be readily adopted, even if there was little evidence that they were more effective than the previous status quo. *Indeed it seems that many of the ways in which new forms of practice are developed and introduced actually inoculate the organisation against adoption, rather than leading to widespread implementation of new forms of work.*

We also found that a single common problem persisted no matter what area of practice or management we were involved in. Innovatory practitioners and managers alike felt that their organisations seemed to work against them changing practice, that they achieved change despite them. Although we were attempting to develop many different kinds of service, for example residential care of elderly people by applying recent research findings, or developing community based practice, a common question recurred: 'how do you change anything in this organisation and particularly the way people in it relate to the public and to other professionals?'

Throughout the text I have introduced examples from our direct experience but not as many as I might have used. Relevant examples have the benefit of clarifying the concrete application of an idea, but may prove relevant only to some readers. This approach to managing change stresses the need to reinvent innovations and to manage change in innovatory ways to meet the idiosyncratic needs of your particular circumstances. The concrete detail cannot often be applied from one situation to another. You will read that the idea of the wheel and axle are far more important than their replication: *we do have to reinvent wheels, but not the idea of the wheel*.

I have then attempted to illustrate ideas with what I hope are appropriate metaphors. Readers will recognise recurring ideas and images as our tour of the managing change territory unfolds. We are all at different stages in the process of managing different changes, and in different places in the development of our thinking. Until we write the interactive computer version of this text enabling you to start with your questions, we are stuck with our limitations in presenting the text in a coherent way, even if it suggests reality has a neat sequence to it that proves not to be there. I have great sympathy with Fritjof Capra (1996) who concludes the preface to his book *The Web of Life* by explaining the need to use many cross references within his text in his 'struggle to communicate a complex network of concepts and ideas within the linear constraints of written language'. This book also deliberately returns to key points and images, just as the different aspects of managing change overlap with each other.

CHAPTER ONE

How Do We Change Practice?

The way that change is managed, and specifically the way that new approaches to practice and service delivery are introduced, is crucial. Yet few managers or practitioners have explicit approaches to introducing innovations and many do not recognise the need for planned approaches to managing change. To be more precise, many managers have *implicit* ways in which they set about introducing change. Sometimes these rest on the ways in which the organisation typically sets about responding to new policies, for example reorganisations coupled with 'training' or replacement of staff. Sometimes they rest on 'instinct' and 'political acumen'. Increasingly, they are influenced by the theories of current management gurus. Often they act on a mixture of all three, focusing either on how the new practice or service should operate, at the expense of attention to the detailed process of getting there; or on global approaches to changing the culture of the organisation. Words of warning are appearing about such strategies. For example Schaffer and Thompson (1992) have criticised many popular corporate change programmes. They argue that managers adopting programmes such as 'Total Quality Management':

> '... will continue to spend vast resources on a variety of activities, only to watch cynicism grow in the ranks. And eventually management will discard many potentially useful improvement processes because it expected the impossible of them and came up empty handed.'
>
> (Schaffer and Thompson, 1992 p.18)

It is also clear that many of the approaches used do not work for all kinds of change, and worse, that some actually precipitate consequences that are the opposite to the intentions of the changes that are espoused. Common examples include 'decentralisations' that decrease local autonomy; 'needs-led' assessment procedures in community care that are more explicitly service driven than the service-led practice they replaced; and 'tailor made' services and products that quickly become a new range of 'off the peg' options. Some of the major fallacies in the management of change are discussed in chapter two. These are common approaches to changing practice that are not supported by evidence from research on the diffusion of innovations and the management of change, or from the experience of staff and managers we have worked with.

Common Perceptions of Innovation and Change

At the beginning of this project on the management of innovations and change a social services director was asked if he thought that managers from his department would participate. He said that they would really like to but they were:

> '...facing up to all the Community Care reforms and implementing the Children Act, new technology was about to be introduced and would radically affect working practices and local government reorganisations were on the horizon. With all this going on there would be no chance that staff would have time to get involved with the management of innovations.'

He was not the only director to respond in this way, and certainly not the only person to feel that faced with so many changes they did not have the space to look at how they might best manage them. Like many people under pressure he was tempted to do his job in the way that he always had, relying on tacit knowledge stored from his experience and any new quick clues he could readily pick up along the way. But our goal was to help him and the staff working in his organisation to manage these changes. It was also our aim to help staff to introduce innovations into the work of their departments, and we did not see any contradictions between the director's agenda, the policy reforms being introduced and our aims. For example, Sir Roy Griffiths' *Agenda for Action*, upon which the community care reforms were based, had said:

> 'The aim must be to provide structure and resources to support the initiatives, the innovation and the commitment at local level and to allow them to flourish; to encourage the success stories in one area to become the commonplace of achievement everywhere.'

> (Griffiths, 1988 p. iv)

Our first thought in response to the strange irony of the director's position was to assume that the response was caused by the language I had used. Perhaps I should have been talking about the management of 'change' and not mentioned 'innovation'. Perhaps his response was based on the assumption that 'innovation' meant inventing more new forms of practice and not adopting new methods such as those proposed by the reforms already on his agenda. It also quickly became clear that he assumed that policy changes inevitably meant reorganisation and that this was different from the processes involved in 'innovation'.

Understanding the relationship between *innovation* and *change* is important. Originally, it seemed as if there could be a clear distinction between 'the management of innovations' and 'the management of change'. 'Managing innovations' is used throughout the book to refer to the introduction of specific new practices, methods of work or pieces of technology. The primary focus of our work is on changing practice: the behaviour of front line staff in carrying out their work with the public and other professionals. In the human services this typically means the methods of practice that they use, but it could also mean the way that they use technology to achieve a better service.

'Managing change' is a wider concept applied to many kinds of change, including: restructuring organisations, changes in context within which agencies function, changes in the nature of the social problems that they confront, changes in the goals or mission of the enterprise, or significant changes in personnel. The distinction between 'managing change' and 'managing innovation' continues to be central to our approach, but we no longer see them as separate enterprises: *'managing change' involves 'managing the introduction and development of a series of innovations'*.

Most of the managers and practitioners whom we have worked with make a distinction between 'innovation' and 'change'. 'Innovation' is typically seen as 'good'. Most senior managers say that they want to run organisations that encourage staff to innovate, to be constantly developing better ways of tackling problems and improving service delivery. But innovation is also seen as a luxury that can be entered into at times of relative calm, and dropped when under pressure. This runs counter to many observations about innovations which frequently describe how they are the product of crisis or a solution to a previously insoluble problem (Domoney, 1989; Law, 1989; Green, 1989).

Change on the other hand is seen as inevitable and omnipresent. This has been especially true during recent times where managers and staff in many fields confront accelerating technological change and the globalisation of markets and social problems. The personal social services in the UK have been preoccupied with introducing wide ranging changes through the National Health Service and Community Care and the Children Acts. They will doubtless be confronted with a similar range of reforms by the current government and the next. The US has seen similar reforms of its human services, for example the development of family preservation and support programmes and the decategorisation of service funding. The rising profile of social problems such as ageing populations and the sharpening divisions caused by social exclusion make social policy reform, and the problems of implementation, key issues in many societies. This perception of change is the same in industry and commerce. Here changing markets and technology are seen as constantly driving accelerating change in products, forms of service delivery and the nature of organisations themselves.

Definitions of Innovation and Change Used in this Book

Throughout we have used the following definition of innovation, based on that used by Rogers:

> *'An innovation is an idea, practice, or object that is perceived as new by an individual or other unit of adoption. It matters little, so far as human behaviour is concerned, whether or not an idea is 'objectively' new as measured by the lapse of time since its first use or discovery. The perceived newness of the idea for the individual determines his or her reaction to it. If the idea seems new to the individual, it is an innovation.'*
>
> (Rogers, 1996 p. 11)

Thus the new idea may be:

> *a synthesis of old ideas;*
> *the adoption of an idea from others;*
> *the development of a unique approach.*
> *To some degree, it is a challenge to the present order.*

This definition deliberately separates innovation from originality, an association that we have found people commonly attach to the idea of innovation. For a new way of working to spread throughout an organisation or wider community or, to use the research jargon, for an 'innovation to diffuse', it has to become less and less 'original' as more people adopt it. The crucial issue is that it is 'new' to those adopting it. In practice, we have found that most innovations in the human services field need to be 'reinvented' to meet each new set of circumstances. However, to define 'innovation' so that it is synonymous with a completely new invention means that by definition innovations can never be adopted by others. By the definition of innovation used here the changes that the social services director was referring to above all include several 'innovations'.

Defining 'change' is to risk getting into deep philosophical water. We will follow the advice of Wittgenstein and not dwell on what the word 'really means' but describe how the word is used. This is also difficult because many of the writers in the field, like most people, vary the way that they use the word to fit the context within which they are using it.

When the word is being used in the context of the 'management of change' it often refers to the process of quite large scale transformations of organisations and their outputs: the introduction of market principles into the National Health Service, the implementation of the community care reforms and changes in child protection, for instance. In this book we will use the noun *'change'* to refer to such transformations.

'Change' is also often used as a verb to refer to actions throughout the process of the development and the adoption of a new idea, or to refer to altering practices and methods, and the 'reorganisation' or 'restructuring' of organisations. The terms 'reforming', 'revolutionising', and 'improving' may also be used in this sense, but have evaluative connotations and so will be avoided in this book where possible.

The word *'develop'* will be used to refer to processes where the activities build upon each other; where an innovation crystallises from loosely connected ideas into an identifiable process or product and matures as its use unfolds and as its application becomes more widespread. It is not implied that all development is good; cancer develops as do its cures.

Revisiting the Distinction Between Managing Innovation and Managing Change

Although a distinction between innovation and change can be useful, it describes a difference of scale if not essentially a different form of social process. In this book the main distinction is to see 'innovations' as discrete forms of practice or technologies, and as such the individual components of larger changes. To reorganise is to introduce innovations: the components that make up the new organisation. *The 'management of innovation' is then a way of approaching 'the management of change'.*

We refer to this approach as *'Managing Change Through Innovation' (MCTI)* to stress that *innovations in management are often required to produce innovations in the practice of staff.*

It is necessary to break down a change of policy and organisation into its component innovations. For instance within the community care 'changes' there are many innovations, such as preparing community care plans, introducing 'needs-led assessments' and care management, promoting user involvement in different situations, separating purchaser from provider functions, developing complaints procedures, devolving resource management, and so on. It is necessary to differentiate between the component innovations within broader changes because *different innovations have to be managed differently.*

Part Two of this book will introduce the 'Innovation Trinity' which will clarify the different approaches required for different innovations depending upon how an innovation compares to research based adoptability criteria; the mapping of the key people involved; and how the innovation relates to other events within the change agent's or change manager's work context.

Part Three will address the issues confronted by managers and policy makers, and development agencies, working to introduce changes in practice throughout an organisation or whole system.

About this Approach

'I wish that they would come and look at what we are doing now and find out why we do it this way before they sweep it all away again with the next round of change.'

(MCTI programme participant)

This plea came from a group of managers and practitioners confronted with their department's latest restructuring of management and front line teams. They had embraced the last set of 'reforms' and put considerable energy and commitment into implementing the then new procedures. Now a new agenda had been drawn up and another reorganisation proposed to introduce the latest policy on practice and service delivery. The plans for this round of reforms were drawn up on 'clean sheets of paper' elsewhere in the organisation. It was assumed that all would have to change to new work procedures and that staff would be regrouped into new teams designed to implement the revised policy. The policy was then communicated to staff through meetings, new job descriptions, procedures and practice guidelines accompanied by as much training as very limited resources allowed.

Confronted by major changes in national or local authority policy managers may feel that they have little option but to follow such a course. However, there are serious dangers in proceeding as if you can change the web of relationships within an organisation and between staff, the public they serve and people in other agencies they relate to, in the way that you design and build new machines. In chapter three the premises of a contrasting strategy are introduced. The approach described in this book invites change managers to constantly ask *'who sees what as a problem'*, to be clear about *'what needs to change'*, and to address the vital question *'what should stay the same'*. This is followed by Part Two of the book - chapters four, five and six - which lays out the core of the MCTI approach: the Innovation Trinity. This is made up of:

- *mapping the people*, to identify who needs to do what with whom;

- *analysing the innovation*, to identify how to manage a particular innovation or the specific, component changes in practice that make up large scale policy change, and to set realistic time scales; and

- *understanding the context*, to make use of compatible forces and avoid conflicts.

No management theory or practice can guarantee fixed outcomes: no one person, or group of people, can have that much control over the complex processes involved or the ever-changing context within which they work. But by making sure that the way you are managing change is consistent with the innovations that you are introducing, you may avoid the worst unintended consequences that are so often the result of our best intentions to reform practice. The analysis of the innovation or innovations involved in major reforms is crucial to matching change management behaviour to the intended changes in practice.

Managers and practitioners using the approach described in this book have found that it helps them to identify 'who they need to do what with'. It enables them to map their way through complex terrain and overcome obstacles as they try to change practice. For the experienced innovator the approach crystallises and 'legitimises' what they have done and adds to their repertoires as change agents.

Some managers and practitioners attempting to develop new approaches get stuck along the way. Conventional ideas about managing change enable them to recognise other people's 'resistance', without always suggesting how this might be 'overcome':

> *'We know exactly what we should be doing and everybody says that they agree that we should be working in that way but somehow we are always blocked and things stay much the same.'*

> (MCTI programme participant)

The approach described here has helped such managers understand why they are experiencing difficulties and how to find a path through them. While not denying that many people *appear* to be 'resistant to change', this approach invites you as a change agent or change manager to go beyond this interpretation of people's behaviour by developing your own plans for change in your own idiosyncratic circumstances by using the Innovation Trinity.

Other managers and staff feel that they are on the receiving end of change, that policy makers and change managers are ignoring them in the difficult processes of transition, yet at the end of the day, expect them to practice the new order. Even with the best intentions it is easy to do violence to some people and their work when introducing change. The approach described here of 'managing change *through* innovations' in management has helped change managers to recognise more of the consequences of their actions.

People using this approach have described it as 'street wise', perhaps because it rests on the experience of those who have been most successful in changing things. It has also been described as 'subversive'. Planning changes in the status quo often 'feels' subversive. This is an important feature of any innovation, not just this approach. Innovation involves departing from the status quo, what the geneticist Conrad Waddington called: *'the conventional wisdom of the dominant group' or 'COWDUNG' for short.* Whether this is seen as 'subversion', or some other kind of deviance, depends upon who is taking the initiative, and who is seen as maintaining the status quo. Change managers using this approach have found it useful to recognise that these dynamics are at play within the relationships they work in. They have found it helpful to consider the following:

> *If innovation is deviance from the status quo then:*
>
> *'delinquency' is deviance with authority organised against you;*
>
> *'leadership' is deviance with authority.*

'Why Not Tell Them What To Do?'

Many staff assume that they will be able to introduce new ways of working into their organisation if they can convince those at the top to adopt their ideas as policy and that change will then follow. However, senior managers often feel that their options are limited and that when they try to introduce change they are often confronted with staff 'resistance'. This book suggests how practitioners can initiate changes in practice from their position in the organisation. It also provides senior managers with alternative approaches that will improve on their chances of success. But first we should address a question which managers sometimes ask, particularly when confronted with the complex approach described in this book. Under pressure to achieve results quickly within arbitrary time-scales managers have said: *'why not just tell them what they should do and make sure that they do it?'*

This may be an appropriate approach where managers have the authority to make such demands; have the power to ensure obedience; and where they are confident that workers will comply as well as be seen to be obeying. However, it is also necessary to analyse what kind of innovation they are attempting to introduce in this way - and whether the desired practice can be prescribed in this way. A common reaction to this straightforward approach is obedience, which may be enough to achieve compliance, or it may be a mask covering passive opposition and minimal commitment.

Some innovations, for example those contained in statutory obligations placed upon local government organisations, are not negotiable. In as much as senior managers can ensure that they are being applied then workers can be instructed to follow orders, but if managers cannot be sure that staff are following orders then the process is more complicated. We have stressed that a recurring theme of this book is the need to recognise that different innovations need to be managed differently, particularly where the management approach could undermine the intended change. For example, in chapter five we analyse how we might approach change management if we want workers to exercise personal initiative and judgement - or even if we cannot stop them from applying policy in their own way. We will see that in these circumstances 'telling them' can cause serious complications and be self defeating. Similarly we will see that people who are gatekeepers of key resources, including the application of their own thought and effort, will have to be negotiated with for them to agree to release these resources, and this involves understanding how they make their decisions and direct their efforts.

The senior manager may open these negotiations with a clear command, but the wise manager will look and listen for feedback. He or she will see what workers do, hear what they say in response, and implicitly or explicitly negotiate - bargain over the way that the job is really going to be done. All the evidence is that there will be a convergence of thinking between the people involved. Even machines will only do what they are capable of doing when they are operating under optimum conditions. People are a little more complicated and their optimum performance depends upon many more variables, including the decisions that they make about how they are going to respond to the manager's communications and their ability to conform or deviate from commands. As we will see in chapter four the decisions of key people will be based on many things, including what the actions of others 'mean' to them: what it means to them to hang on to the status quo or to go with change. If a set of changes undermines a hard earned identity we can expect people to want to struggle to sustain their current status. If the innovation offers them a new favourable identity we can expect them to accept it.

Managers may have the authority to give orders but do they have the power to ensure compliance beyond superficial obedience? Where worker behaviour is the subject of the instruction, and where there is considerable scope for the worker to do something subtly or radically different from the instructed behaviour, that is where there is scope for innovation or deviance from the status quo, then 'orders' may do little more than reinforce the gap between the formal and informal organisation. Gaps may also open up between actual performance and action specified in job descriptions and procedures: between what people actually do and what their senior mangers and policy makers think they do.

Even ordering people to do what they want to do runs the risk of being objected to by those who do not find the authority credible or acceptable. This is the mirror image of the manager who rejects innovation because the initiative has come from below. Being blindly anti-authority has the same effect as being blindly authoritarian. 'Power struggles' always divert energies from the task.

Research on innovation and change, introduced in chapters two and three, makes it clear that the process of 'diffusion', the passing on of new methods and ideas from one person to another, or from one group or society to another, involves a process of 'convergence' of thinking. No matter how radical new ideas are, they never quite eradicate the old: Christianity replaced many old religions yet Christmas coincides with the Winter Solstice, Easter with the Rites of Spring and while some behaviour became sin, a few old traditions still persist.

This book is an attempt to make explicit many of the implicit assumptions and actions taken by successful managers of change. Many people intuitively negotiate their way towards a convergence of ideas as they present them to others. But many people also are taken by surprise at the seemingly irrational and negative responses. It will be argued throughout that in many situations the chances of successfully managing change are improved when the convergence, or divergence, of thinking is made more explicit rather than left implicit. This means that managers wanting to change the practice of others will encourage a climate where disagreements can be openly expressed so that all possible information available is put into the decision. Ironically, convergence of thinking is more likely to happen when there is open disagreement and a free sharing of alternative points of view. Such open negotiations can end in agreed action, or perhaps more commonly, agreement to follow a course of action whatever personal disagreements exist. This is not to say that change agents will go around spontaneously expressing their point of view. Timing and sensitivity to others' views is all important, throughout the exchanges that will take place. Negotiation needs to take place in a common language and the change agent will have to understand and learn to speak it, or work through a skilled interpreter, and be aware of the assumptions upon which the other person works. These issues and the skills and knowledge involved will be discussed in Part Four: chapters nine, ten and eleven.

The Managing Change Through Innovation approach is agnostic about whether managers 'should' manage by instructing staff or by developing consensus. However, readers will probably identify more examples of negotiation and consensus building than command and control strategies in talking about the implementation of innovations. There are four main reasons for this:

1. Change is not always introduced by senior managers. We have worked with many innovators at all levels of their organisation. This book is for all those who set out to change practice. You will see that being a 'change agent' or 'change manager', as we have called you, involves working with, and through, many people at all levels of an organisation, and frequently across organisational boundaries.

2. Where people can be told to adopt an innovation and they get on with it as a result there is not much more to say and change agents and managers will know what to do.

3. Many organisations involved in social change and people's problems, like the personal social services, do not typically operate in a world of such simplicity. It is recognised that you cannot simply issue instructions to people with very difficult problems, or who exhibit very difficult intransigent behaviour, such as perpetrators of child abuse, and expect them to change. The practice of staff, their work with these people, is inevitably difficult and although staff behaviour is typically not as 'pathological' it is also complex and often habitual. The fact that we are dealing with such complexity means that management strategies will need to be equally complex.

4. If we are wanting to increase the chances of an innovation being adopted, and reinvented to match local circumstances, then it helps if the convergence, or divergence, of ideas is transparent. This is consistent with the theories of many current management thinkers who have stressed that the innovative organisation is characterised by open communication across traditional groupings. They typically recommend flatter organisations that blur the formal distinctions between people not only across the organisation but also up and down it, and advocate replacing formal structures with a shared understanding of and commitment to the organisations

'vision' (Mintsberg, 1989; Peters and Waterman, 1982; Senge, 1990; Kotter, 1995). For example, we will see in chapter seven that Moss Kanter's (1985) research on commercial organisations led her to make a key distinction between 'integrative' organisations, that encourage and enable staff to innovate, and 'segregated' ones, that block initiative and communication and so stifle innovations. These ideas clearly expose the inherent difficulties of making hierarchical command and control structures sensitive and relevant to an ever changing world.

The spread of new ideas and ways of working proceeds through a process of convergence of thinking rather than through coercion. This book invites the reader to go beyond seeing the management of change as a struggle between those introducing new ideas or practices and those 'resistant' to change. It recognises the complexity of the processes involved and that in some circumstances instructions are required, while in others they could be counter productive. Problems come when the approach does not fit, or even contradicts the changes involved. To manage well the complex processes of change we need to recognise the position of all the people involved in a social interaction. Chapter four draws on innovations research to help you identify and map all the people, the 'key players', in the management of the changes that you are introducing.

Coercion is what those with authority or with the power to initiate do to those described as resistant. Coercion and resistance are essential parts of the same pattern. There can be no coercion without resistance. If the other party agreed and complied it would be called consensus; if they complied regardless of agreeing, it would be called obedience. If you initiate with coercion and others are going to fit in with your behaviour they will have to be obedient or resistant. Can you imagine one person arm wrestling while the other does not? If you fail to win a struggle with disobedient staff then you have to hope that their disobedience is right, because it will be difficult to direct it. If you 'win' and force their obedience you lose their initiative. The danger is that all initiative will rest with you: if you tell them to do something their first response will be to ask you to tell them how.

So are orders ever relevant? There is a scene in the film Zulu (starring Michael Caine) where the redcoats are in three lines - one loading - one aiming - and one firing. For this kind of warfare the individual soldier had to obey instantly so that the commanding officer could 'fire' by telling the sergeant major to issue the order to fire and then the NCO in charge of each line ordered 'Load - Aim - Fire'. This drill had to be followed precisely to achieve the required level of synchronised action. Drill sergeants drilled the mind out of recruits so that they would respond in the required way. This form of operation can still be seen as they Troop the Colour on the Queen's official birthday. In the first world war hundreds of thousands of lives were lost because the machine gun made such patterns of warfare lethally obsolete. To counter this innovation required an innovation in management and practice that did not immediately take place.

Contrast these scenes with the picture of a platoon of foot soldiers moving down a street in a counter terrorist situation such as we have seen on the streets of Belfast. Each soldier is thinking, taking account of his colleagues' positions and the ever changing landscape as they move down the street and turn corners into the next road. Each soldier has to judge the risks of danger and respond by constantly changing his position and actions. Each soldier is trained to take command at any time should they come under attack and the officer fall. They each know the rules of engagement. These 'orders' tell them when they can fire and when they cannot. Each has to judge whether the situation requires them to pull the trigger. Fire when you should not and you may end up in prison on a murder charge. Decide not to fire when you should and you and your comrades could be dead.

The key issue is who has to think and make judgements about what. Where behaviour has to be synchronised, standardised, uniform, that is carried out in a prescribed way, it can be directed by a single chain of command. In such situations a centralised command and control structure is relevant. It is not unimportant to note that the control was exercised by a sergeant who stood behind the rows of soldiers with orders to shoot anybody who broke ranks!

Where behaviour has to be constantly changing to meet changing circumstances on the ground, then the ever changing patterns of behaviour can only be maintained by co-ordinated individual judgements acting under broad policy directives. The co-ordination of these actions is itself in the hands of the practitioners, each of whom judges what to do based on the constant observation of terrain and colleagues' actions and each has to be capable of taking command of the situation if required.

This analysis suggests that senior managers should not decide on the degree of control they attempt to exercise based on ideological beliefs about authority or democracy in organisations, or based on philosophies of professional autonomy or some such criteria; nor should their approach be based on a particular theory of organisations. It suggests that they should fit their management approach to the nature of the task and how it is best carried out within the practical day to day politics of what they can actually do in practice. The professions may have defended the individual autonomy of their practitioners by powerful lobbying, but it is also true that a degree of autonomy and individual judgement is an integral part of the nature of many professional tasks. Large scale industrial processes have demanded the division of labour and high degrees of centralised control to produce standardised products. To apply the organisation of a professional practice to a factory, or that of a factory to a professional partnership, would quickly lead to crippling problems.

As a manager of others you may or may not want to see your organisation as a 'democracy' - but the important question is, can it operate with one mind? You may want to run a loose-knit collection of creative individuals – but where do they need to produce standardised performance? The crucial question is how should a particular task be managed, and more specifically how should the component innovations of major changes be introduced? These issues and how they relate to appropriate change management are essential dimensions of analysing the innovation, understanding its impact on significant relationships: mapping the contribution of key people and working with the forces within your own context.

Summary of Contents

In this opening discussion I have referred to some of the main themes discussed in Part One of the book: the discussion of the assumptions of the MCTI approach and common fallacies in managing change; and Part Two: the use of the Innovation Trinity to guide change management.

In Part Three there is a change of gear in as much as the major vantage point of the reader is assumed to be someone who is wanting to introduce change throughout the system or organisation that they are working with. This could be a team within an organisation identifying their training development needs and how they might by met. It will also inform senior managers and policy makers about when to negotiate with staff and when to introduce different approaches to staff development and training. It outlines the different activities that need to take place for a new form of practice to diffuse through the system: for it to move from an innovatory idea to mainstream practice.

Part Four of the book reflects on the main themes, identifying the skills and knowledge required to be an effective change agent, to further describe how change can be managed. Part Five concludes the book with an overview of the MCTI approach and a discussion of the need to change our change management in the light of feedback; the need to develop our ability to manage by consequences; and the crucial dimension of *time*.

But now I want to draw on research on the diffusion of innovations and the management of change and our experience of working with innovators and change agents to discuss common fallacies about the management of change.

CHAPTER TWO

Common Fallacies About Changing Practice

Recently a researcher was presenting to a national meeting for top managers and policy makers the conclusions of his well-known research on an experimental approach to case management. He was asked to comment on progress now that the senior management of a large local authority social services department had decided that case management based on the study should be adopted by the whole organisation. He explained that there were serious problems. This next stage in the process was not being researched but a few observations and possible explanations were mentioned in the subsequent discussion.

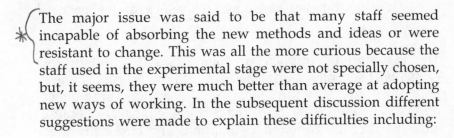

The major issue was said to be that many staff seemed incapable of absorbing the new methods and ideas or were resistant to change. This was all the more curious because the staff used in the experimental stage were not specially chosen, but, it seems, they were much better than average at adopting new ways of working. In the subsequent discussion different suggestions were made to explain these difficulties including:

- the 'Hawthorne Effect' seemed a likely explanation to many: this referred to experiments that took place in the 1930s that demonstrated that the presence of researchers evaluating new work procedures was itself likely to significantly improve performance (Roethlisberger and Dickson, 1939);
- the need for more training: the original staff had gone through a very different induction process from the way the 'new' ideas are being 'sold' to the rest of the workforce;
- the development of the innovatory method may have been dependent upon the 'charismatic' personalities of the originators: the failure of innovations to be translated into practice in different situations was cited as evidence of the significance of these 'special' people;

- the role of managers and their lack of clarity about the implementation of the new methods to be applied: a major part of this organisation's approach to widespread implementation had been to redefine middle management roles and recruit 'a new generation' of managers to replace 'the old guard'.

Implicit throughout this discussion was a simple linear model of research and development. This can be summarised as follows. A new method is first described, then tested by research; if it is shown to be effective and resources are available, and then if the method is politically compatible with current philosophy, it can be adopted by senior management and widespread implementation becomes the policy of the department. The method is then prescribed by all levels of management, and training given to staff who subsequently apply the new method by carrying out management policy. The Havelocks have pointed out that such approaches rely on a passive but rational consumer (Havelock and Havelock, 1973).

The assumptions implicit in such examples contain the elements of several major fallacies about how practice changes and develops. They are fallacies ('misleading arguments, mistaken beliefs': Oxford English Dictionary) because although they are common assumptions and frequently used approaches they are not supported by evidence. The first group of these fallacies I have called:

The Tell and Do Nothing Fallacies:
- *Cascade*
- *Anthropomorphic*
- *Natural Selection*
- *Trojan Horse or Start With A Pilot Project.*

The first of these myths is the assumption that information, and specifically prescriptions about how the organisation's tasks should be completed, 'cascade' down through the organisation.

The CASCADE Fallacy

The 'cascade principle' is a common metaphor used to describe how to transfer new ideas and policies to organisations. Top managers are introduced to the new idea and subsequently dissemination will occur down through their organisations. In partial acknowledgement of the noticeable failure of this process to follow the prescribed course in many organisations it is sometimes called the 'trickle-down effect'. A social services director participating in the conference just mentioned claimed that he and his senior management team had adopted the values of the Community Care Act but he thought that it would take another five years for it to filter down through the whole of 'his' department.

The cascade model or metaphor is consistent with a pyramidal organisation and the implicit or explicit assumption that innovation and change does, or should, emanate from the apex. As in the orthodox research and development model, it assumes that recipients are passive.

This view of organisations as waterfalls with a torrent of wisdom flowing from the top and dispersing outwards as it falls down through the organisation is, not surprisingly, very popular with politicians and senior managers. It maintains the image of themselves as the source of policy and change; it suggests that the depth of wisdom is greatest at the top and gets thinner as it falls. The illusion is perpetuated that there is a convenient natural motive force, a kind of organisational gravity that will promote diffusion and the acceptance of new methods. In this model the main task of the manager is to deal with resistance, to confront, counsel or move subordinates who resist saturation with the new wisdom or interrupt the flow through to others. Subordinates are at least stones who will be wetted with the new wisdom; better if they are sponges who soak up the falling enlightenment and, at best, new springs that will gush the new wisdom over their colleagues.

The widespread acceptance of this model or metaphor led us to assume that it would feature prominently in the research literature on innovations. We were surprised that computer searches failed to find many citations. Indeed we only uncovered two linked research studies which looked at the deliberate application of the model (Department of Education and Science, 1988; Morrison and others, 1989). This research does not demonstrate the effectiveness of the cascade method for disseminating new approaches to practice (Domoney, 1992).

Research on the diffusion of innovations suggests that the successful introduction, diffusion and adoption of innovations rests on a more complex set of relationships and social networks which will be discussed in chapter three (Rogers, 1995; Van de Ven, Angle and Pool, 1989). Even if the cascade approach were successful it would only be appropriate when applied to certain innovations. For example it might be appropriate to attempt to cascade simple information or instructions about standardised forms of practice. However, the use of orthodox authority to implement certain innovations can lead to bizarre and counter-productive consequences, as we will see when we discuss the problems caused by attempting to instruct staff to adopt 'empowerment' strategies with service users.

More and more management texts are challenging the place of rigid and extensive hierarchies in the management of successful companies. A major dimension of this review of orthodox relationships is the growing awareness that rigid internal boundaries and long hierarchies block communication and typically provide an inhospitable environment for the constant innovation companies need to achieve and sustain success. Flatter organisations, small, cross boundary task groups, flexibility and responsiveness are increasingly seen to be critical features. Stress in this literature is placed upon maximising the creativity of front line staff who are more likely to originate effective solutions to the problems that they are intimately involved in (Peters and Waterman, 1982; Peters, 1985, 1987, 1992; Kanter, 1989; Senge, 1990; Kotter, 1996).

A major motivating force for the Management of Change Through Innovations arose from a recurring question raised through our PADE experience: why was it that most innovations were initiated and developed *despite* the organisation that housed them? Against this there are findings that senior managers have a vital role to play in supporting innovations, both in providing or releasing resources (Crosbie and Vickery, 1989; Manz and others, 1989; Angle and Van de Ven, 1989) and in giving implicit or explicit support (see the discussion of 'minders' in chapter three). Much of the recent literature on the management of innovations and more general management literature emphasises the role leaders have to play in enabling others to innovate and their own role in initiating major reforms (Kanter, 1985, 1989; Peters, 1987; Beckhard and Pritchard, 1992; Manz and others, 1989; London, 1988).

Possibly these books display some pro-leadership bias: they are, after all, targeted on the management market. The relationship between leadership and performance is a complex and controversial area. Modern theorists (Smith and Peterson, 1988; Mintzberg, 1994; Senge, 1990) suggest that successful organisations cannot be understood by focusing just on leaders' behaviour. They stress that leaders are part of a complex set of interacting factors, all responding and contributing to the 'culture' of the organisation. From this perspective effectiveness depends upon the shared meanings which members of the organisation attribute to particular behaviours and activities. However, it also seems clear that effective innovation goes beyond the team, department or organisation and depends on relationships across organisational boundaries (Rogers and Kincaid, 1981). These are relationships which managers intent on protecting the team, department or the organisation's boundaries can stifle at birth. As one social services director put it, when asked to nominate staff for an interdepartmental group to develop child care practice: 'But if my staff join that group they will be contaminated by that bolshie lot from the next authority, and I'm not having that'. As we will see innovation depends upon contamination and mainstreaming them depends upon spreading the virus as far as possible.

What is crucial is to look at the ways key people behave and relate to each other within and across organisations. Often this is not a product of the formal structure of the organisation but of the communication networks which key staff participate in: who actually talks to whom is often more important than formal chains of accountability.

Organisational pyramids may be steep, but the use of the cascade metaphor for illustrating the nature of how communication should flow in organisations should not fool us into thinking that there is an organisational gravity that will be an effective motive force for transferring new ideas and methods of practice. There are also other fallacies that assume the existence of natural forces that will drive the adoption of innovations.

The ANTHROPOMORPHIC Fallacy

It is common to talk of 'new methods *developing*', of 'ideas *spreading*', of 'innovations *diffusing*' as if they somehow did this by themselves. The use of language in this way helps us to communicate but it can also mislead us into thinking that there is a force for change that does not require action from those who would have that change come about. J.K. Galbraith, in a discussion of forecasts for the end to the recent recession, has warned us against this phenomenon in the world of economics. Referring to the predictions of what 'the economy' was about to do he says:

'In all this, one central idea, or what could be so described, is foremost. The economic system has within itself a personified power for recovery. This is firmly stated: 'The economy,' one reads, 'is now wrestling with the final stages of recession'... The time has come to - has long since passed - for an end to this nonsense. The present recession is not an autonomous, self correcting economic drama. It is the wholly predictable response to the speculative extravagances and inanities (and the government policies) of the eighties.'

(Galbraith, 1991)

Another striking example nearer to the personal social services is recurring references to social networks or 'the community'. Many people support others and are supported through their social network in return, just as we will see that they are essential for communicating information about innovations. However, 'support' and the transfer of innovations does not happen just through the existence of the network or 'community', but through the actions of others within them.

A telephone system can be used as a metaphor for describing the working of social networks. It is a system that links people together and it lies dormant until activated by a person who succeeds in contacting one or more others. So it is with networks. People often, though not always, recognise that a considerable amount of work goes into the laying down of these networks. But sometimes they think that the process is so natural that it takes no effort at all. What many overlook is that the telephone system is connected to the electricity supply. Without this energy it would not work. In the same way people have to put energy into social networks if they are to serve their communication and support functions, as well as the energy they use to actually use them. The processes of diffusing innovations and other processes of change are the same: they cannot be left to energise themselves. Nor can they be directed simply by the 'force of truth'.

The NATURAL SELECTION Fallacy

Whoever coined the cascade metaphor certainly invented an adoptable 'innovation' even though research evidence suggests that it is but a myth. Many of us have an implicit belief that the march of innovation **is** progress, that the 'best' innovations are the ones adopted and the ineffective fall by the wayside. If the 'best' means those innovations supported by hard evidence that they achieve desired outcomes, then this is not the case. Unfortunately, good research evidence does not guarantee adoption.

In *1601* an English sea captain carried out an experiment and demonstrated that scurvy could be prevented by giving sailors three teaspoonful of lemon juice every day. Scurvy, at this time, killed more sailors on long sea voyages than warfare, accidents, and all other causes of death. *One hundred and fifty years later* a British Navy physician confirmed these findings, but it still took *another forty-eight years* before the British Navy eradicated scurvy by adopting the idea of supplying citrus fruits for scurvy prevention in *1795*. The merchant marine had to wait another *seventy years* and suffer an unknown number of deaths (probably between a half to two-thirds of all long voyage sailors), before the Board of Trade adopted a similar policy in *1865*. This was *two hundred and sixty four years* after the first empirical proof of the solution (Mosteller, 1981 quoted in Rogers, 1983).

There are also many similar examples in modern times of research having supported the efficacy of innovations which did not, however, come to be adopted: this is despite a more general acceptance of the usefulness of scientific evidence. Another relevant example is Coch and French's classic study which looked at the problems of resistance to change on the shop floor of a clothing factory. It was necessary in the nature of the company's operation to change frequently the methods used by employees and switch them to different tasks. This led to a marked resistance to change which was seen as expressing itself as:

'...grievances about the piece rates that went with the new methods, high turnover, very low efficiency, restriction of output and marked aggression to management.'

(Coch and French, 1948 p.512)

After a period of action research the authors concluded:

'It is possible for management to modify or to remove completely group resistance to changes in methods of work and the ensuing piece rates. This change can be accomplished by the use of group meetings in which management effectively communicates the need for change and stimulates group participation in planning the changes.'

(Coch and French, 1948 p.534)

In this conclusion it is clear that it is not the change itself, the innovation, that is resisted but the imposition of management designed solutions to the problem. When the action researchers worked with the managers to change their **behaviour** when introducing new ways of working, the resistance largely disappeared. Of course the innovation in management behaviour has to be the right one. The company had already tried solving the problem by use of a special monetary allowance for transfers, trying to enlist the co-operation and aid of the union, by making necessary layoffs on the basis of efficiency and so on.

Despite repeated injunctions in management texts consistent with these findings, this research has had very little impact on the way many manage change. Note that it was published in **1948**. Innovators do not change things by being written up in learned journals (though of course it is the case that had they not done so this research could not have been quoted here!).

Relevant research is overlooked in many areas of activity, including fields usually associated with scientific progress such as medicine. (It is also true that innovations are adopted before their efficacy has been empirically established.) Indeed, the dissemination of research results has a limited impact on the innovation process. The review of the research evidence on the diffusion of innovations leaves us in a somewhat paradoxical position. The evidence suggests that evidence is not enough either to promote or to stop the progress of an innovation, or for that matter, the persistence of myths about the transfer of innovations and the dissemination of research results! (Stocking, 1985; Angle and Van de Ven, 1989; Rogers, 1995).

The TROJAN HORSE or START WITH A PILOT PROJECT Fallacy

Another rational common sense approach to the introduction of innovations that turns out to be at best only partially true is the belief that innovations can be introduced into agencies through pilot projects. Although pilot projects can play an important role in the *development* of an innovation, they are not a good way of spreading new ways of working: indeed they can be counterproductive. The fallacy is in believing that the good elements of the pilot project's experience will be naturally retained and adopted by others while the bad fall into disuse.

In the Trojan wars the Greeks were laying siege to Troy. They built the Trojan Horse as a gift to the citizens who made the mistake of taking it into the city. Unbeknown to them Greek soldiers were hidden inside the horse. Many organisations adopt pilot projects as a way of testing and developing a new approach to practice as if, like the Trojan Horse, they will infiltrate the organisation and lead eventually to widespread change.

Our experience of working with staff from many community social work and other innovatory practice sites during the last fifteen years demonstrated that setting up special projects to develop innovatory practice was very successful in terms of the development of the innovation. Indeed many examples of such practice would not have existed had they not been able to protect their resources because of their 'special' status (Smale and Bennett, 1989; Darvill and Smale, 1990). Mike Cooper, a leading pioneer in the field, has described how he used the fact that his work was being researched by Professor Roger Hadley's team (Hadley and McGrath, 1984) to ward off attempts to reduce his staff (Cooper, 1992). Such devices were particularly important to some teams as their success in reducing numbers of children on at risk registers and receptions into care caused senior managers to want to move staff to teams maintaining high caseloads (Darvill and Smale, 1990).

However, there is a danger that the success of these pilot projects is never translated into mainstream practice. Projects can be constantly marginalised: the 'It's all right for them' syndrome applied to any differences between the conditions of the project to other teams. If the project takes place in a highly segmentalised organisation, then other people in the organisation will see its subsequent introduction to their team in the same way as they view externally generated innovations. The 'Not Invented Here', NIH, syndrome (Marcus and Weber, 1989) is likely to be become a significant factor.

'Special' projects attract considerable resentment from others in the mainstream of the organisation, especially if they are released from normal, routine duties or given extra resources. For example Newburn (1992, 1993) describes how the teams set up to respond to the Hillsborough disaster experienced growing resentment from former colleagues and managers the longer their separate work went on. We suspect that these feelings make it more difficult for mainstream staff to learn from the experience of others, particularly prophets in their own country.

Our experience of working with innovatory practitioners in situations such as these first led us to recognise that organisations can be inoculated against innovation. While pilot projects are developing their new form of practice, others in the organisation are working out how they are going to resist working in the same way. Managers, whose commitment to the innovation is vital for widespread adoption (Angle and Van de Ven, 1989; Crosbie and Vickery, 1989), can appear to be giving approval to the innovation without working through the implications of committing the organisation to full adoption. When managers get to the point where they attempt to generalise from the experience of the pilot project, others in the organisation are ready with their counter arguments. In short, those introducing Trojan Horses have to be careful that they do not prove to be operating a process best described by a different metaphor, that of vaccination.

The Minnesota Management of Innovations Research Programme came to similar conclusions. Lindquest and Mauriel (1989) compared two alternative strategies for adopting and implementing an innovation: a 'depth strategy' using demonstration sites or pilot projects to 'debug' the innovation before it was disseminated to other operational units; and a 'breadth strategy' in which the innovation is introduced to people at all levels across the organisation. They found that those using the 'breadth' strategy were less isolated and achieved more widespread adoption of new ways of working. As Angle and Van de Ven (1989) point out:

'This finding is contrary to conventional wisdom that successfully implemented innovations start small and spread incrementally with success.'

(p. 686)

The implications of this research and of our PADE experience is that pilot projects have an important place in the development of an innovation but they only work as sources of dissemination if they are part of a wider strategy of adoption. The Greeks did not beat the Trojans just by putting their horse inside the walls: they also successfully planned how the hidden soldiers would leave the horse at night and open the city gates, allowing the main army to enter the city and win the subsequent conflicts.

We should recognise that experiments, or pilot projects, in new ways of working will be necessary but may carry the danger of 'inoculating' people against the new ideas. Managers wanting an organisation to learn from a pilot project will need to build in a constant exchange of information between the isolated practice and those involved in mainstream workings of the organisation. Even then, the dangers of this fuelling better informed counter measures may suggest a completely different dissemination strategy. We will see in subsequent chapters that it is the process of development within a pilot project that is often crucial, rather than the end result.

The research literature referred to so far does not distinguish between different kinds of innovation. But different innovations are adopted in different ways, and where pilot studies can demonstrate advantages for employees they may aid adoption.

Giving one group of staff new word processors that make their task much easier without threat to jobs may provoke others to want the improved machinery themselves. But where the task is high status, often unintentionally implied through extra resources of various kinds or through the selection of staff, and contrasts between 'special projects' and 'bread and butter work' develop, or complex structures leading to communication being difficult, they may hinder the process, as argued above.

The nature of the innovation may introduce another consideration. We have referred to PADE's Community Social Work Exchange and work with special projects. We started off with the assumption that a goal was to promote practice typically found in projects, or social services department teams that operated as if they were separate projects. By the end of that work we had come to the conclusion that this assumption should be turned on its head. Because of the nature of the innovation, community social work, the issue that needs to be addressed is 'how can we operate all social services activities as if they were special projects?' (Smale and Tuson, 1990). In short some innovations require change that cannot be produced within the assumptions of the 'mainstream' of the organisation.

Several of the dimensions of the current Children Act and Community Care reforms that are consistent with community social work are of this order. The devolved resource management envisaged in the original Community Care white paper was a step towards reform at this level. But other issues, such as enabling people to exercise greater choice through 'needs-led' assessments and involving service users in planning services, also required fundamental changes in who makes decisions and with whom. Many of those changes have not been made. We will return to these distinctions when we discuss the analysis of the innovation as a crucial dimension of change management.

I have called the above fallacies the *Tell and Do Nothing* fallacies because in each there is an erroneous, if implicit, assumption that there is some natural force that promotes the innovation. They are, at best, only half truths because although some elements may work, further action is required to *make* changes happen rather than relying on the hidden forces assumed in the model. Obviously this action has to come from people. It is a commonly held view that the success of the innovation rests on the 'charismatic' personalities of the originators. This leads us into a discussion of common fallacies based on erroneous assumptions about the people involved.

The People Fallacies:

- *Charismatic Individuals Cause Success - or Failure Is The Fault Of Resistant Villains*
- *People Want To Avoid Re-Inventing The Wheel*
- *To Know Is To Act Differently.*

The CHARISMATIC INDIVIDUALS FALLACY; and its Corollary - FAILURE IS CAUSED BY RESISTANT VILLAINS

The credit for a new method is often ascribed to individual heroines or heroes. It is common for a failure to replicate innovations to be attributed to the absence of the charismatic inventors. Somewhat tautologically, the absence of such people in failed attempts to innovate is often cited as evidence of the significance of these 'special' people. It is beyond the scope of this paper to discuss the nature of charisma but long ago, Freud (1970), describing *Civilisation and its Discontents*, drew attention to the dangers of believing that 'charisma' was a characteristic of particular individuals. He suggested that it was a socially constructed shared characteristic of the beholders rather than a personal attribute of the subject. Mark Twain has a telling insight on the subject as related to innovators:

'A person with a new idea is a crank, until the idea succeeds.'

In the charisma model those who obstruct the adoption of a good idea must be villains, or, if not actively malignant, then at least ignorant, or stupid, or dominated by self interest or all three. Although he has reservations about the term, Everett Rogers (1995) continues to refer to those who are last to adopt an innovation as 'laggards'. However, he has also argued that it is wrong to simply see these people as personally responsible for their lack of openness to innovation. His further analysis of the diffusion research leads him to conclude that the failure of 'laggards' to adopt a beneficial innovation is a product of the diffusion *system*: the result of their position in the communication networks that transmit the innovation.

Angle and Van de Ven (1989), in the culmination of the Minnesota research studies on the management of innovations (MIRP), come to a similar conclusion, leading them to state:

'... *over the course of the MIRP studies we often encountered top managers who expressed frustration with the 'unwillingness,' 'narrow-mindedness,' or NIH (not invented here) syndrome of their subordinate unit or subsidiary managers in adopting changes they were requested to implement. For example, one corporate executive stated, 'If I could only get them to take a broader view, they would see the need for change'. The MIRP innovation adoption findings suggest it may be more productive to direct this frustration at corporate executives and public policy makers who fail to appreciate the logical consequences of their top-down or externally-imposed mandates on the behaviour and performance of organisational sub-units.'*

(Angle and Van de Ven, 1989 p. 687-8)

In our own PADE experience of working with innovatory practitioners and managers we found people who some would see as 'laggards' being perceived by others as innovators of an alternative approach. Systems thinkers from organisation research and family therapy would see the attribution of individual blame within patterns of interaction involving the reciprocal behaviour of several, if not many people, as a matter of 'punctuation' (Minuchin and Fishman, 1981; Watzlawick and others, 1974). By this they mean that cause and effect were being attributed to one person or another and would be seen as being dependent upon the position of the person making the attribution. This can be illustrated by the following diagram:

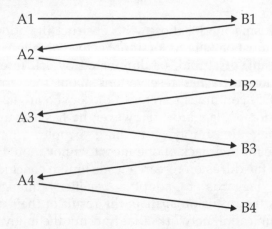

In this interaction between A and B, action A.1 leads to the response B.1 which leads to A.2 and so on. However, it is common for A to make sense of the other's behaviour by focusing on the sequence B.1, B.2, B.3 and so on, and for B to focus on A.1, A.2, A.3. To say B.3 was caused by A.3 is to 'punctuate' the interaction in a certain way, just as it is an alternative punctuation to say that A.2 was caused by B.2.

Watzlawick drew attention to the fact that in understanding human relationships, as in modern physics, the point of view of the observer is decisive:

'In contrast to objects, however, human relationships are not phenomena that exist objectively, in their own right as it were, nor is it possible to have a consensus about their properties. Above all, if there are differences of opinion about the characteristics of a human relationship, it cannot be proved that one of the partners is right and the other wrong, or, to anticipate one of our main topics (the author is applying systems theory to understanding mental health problems), that one partner is 'normal' and the other is 'crazy'. Relationships, the contents of our interpersonal, pragmatic reality, are not real in the same sense as objects are; they have their 'reality' only in the perception of the partners, and even this is shared only partially by the partners.'

(Watzlawick, 1990 p.16)

It is now widely recognised (we should perhaps say 'amongst those who share a systemic perspective') that our perception of reality is either the result of interpersonal agreements or the outcome of the cultural, racial, social class and family contexts that we are born into and predispose us to punctuate events in a particular way:

*'Real **is**, after all, what is **called** real by a sufficiently large number of people. In this extreme sense, reality is an interpersonal convention, just as use of language depends on the unspoken and mostly quite unconscious agreement that certain sounds and signs have specific meanings. The 'reality' of a banknote, for example, does not lie primarily in the fact that it is a printed, multicoloured piece of paper, but in the interpersonal agreement that this object represents a specific value.'*

(Watzlawick, 1990 p.19)

These quotations come from professionals focusing on mental health issues where the consequences of the processes described can be serious. Who gets defined as 'mad' or 'bad' often has long term consequences for their lives. But they can also be dramatic and grave for people caught up in innovation and change in their employment. The disposable employee is becoming a feature of our organisational lives. For example consider the attitude of Dr John Nicholson, business psychologist and adviser to the government on the Citizen's Charter:

> *'Frankly, I haven't come across any organisation where there isn't a rump of managers who simply wouldn't be able to adapt to a new way of doing things. You have to sack them.'*
>
> (Nicholson, 1992)

Whose responsibility is it that an organisation and its staff become entrenched in obsolete behaviour? Senior managers know that organisations, like the individuals they are composed of, are constantly caught up in ever present change. The innovation manager should always ask: Is it possible that 'resistance' is a response to bad innovation management? Is Dr Nicholson revealing an insight into the consequences of his approach to introducing change? A more benign version of the same processes are found in Kanter's recent work on how to maintain innovation and so effectiveness in large organisations, **When Giants Learn to Dance: Mastering the Challenges of Strategy, Management, and Careers in the 1990s** (1989). She emphasises the need for constant staff development to keep people at the cutting edge of their competence and to prepare them for moving on to other employment as the organisation requires different skills to keep pace with change.

The removal of those who 'resist' change can have severe consequences for their lives, and also in terms of the loss to the organisation of their experience, and the additional redundancy and replacement costs. Everett Rogers' (1983) advice to apportion blame for so called 'laggard' behaviour to the nature of the system is particularly pertinent. It needs to be stressed that the part played by key actors is crucial at certain stages in the processes of a new method spreading. But in chapter four we will see it is necessary to identify with some precision the people taking up certain roles in relationship to others, and recognise that their actions are not entirely based on personal competence and motivation; nor do they always correspond to those whose formal position within an organisation suggests that they should fulfil the function.

Managers should distinguish between those who are resistant to, that is opposing, the actual innovation that is being introduced; those whose persistent actions make the new way of working impossible; and those people who are *resisting, that is opposing the way* that changes are being introduced.

All change will involve a degree of loss (Marris, 1974) and this will need to be taken into account, but the manager needs to be able to distinguish between the expression of pain, which may be transformed into positive experience if handled appropriately; and opposition, which escalates if managed badly.

As a first reaction, innovation managers would be wise to see resistance as feedback to their own interventions, and adjust their behaviour to increase support for the innovation. There are two main reasons for adopting this approach:

- they have more control over what they do than they have over the attitudes and behaviour of others;
- they have limited time and space and it is probably best to assume that they should spend what time is available building on strengths in the situation rather than focusing on the so called 'pathology'.

Elsewhere attention has been drawn to the dangers of focusing only on pathology in personal relationships and when tackling social problems (Smale, 1977, 1984). The approach presented here attempts to illustrate how the innovation manager can identify the ingredients of positive change. If we adopt a gardening metaphor and assume an ecological perspective, we should focus on fertilising growth without damage to the environment and mobilising the natural forces at our disposal. We do not immediately reach for the weed killer any more than we would introduce trees in pots to replace the ones we tore down in our haste to change the landscape, as if it were a machine to be redesigned.

The action required to follow this prescription is described in subsequent chapters. The management of innovation and change is a complex, sensitive business. From this perspective 'agree with me or go' is the major symptom of what we might call 'laggard innovation management', characterised by a lack of management innovativeness, a poverty of ideas and intervention repertoire on the part of would-be change agents.

The PEOPLE WANT TO AVOID RE-INVENTING THE WHEEL Fallacy

The National Institute for Social Work's Practice and Development Exchange was established to exchange information between innovatory practitioners, managers and researchers and develop better models of practice and management through a synthesis of their knowledge. A basic assumption made at the beginning of our work was that there were many people attempting to develop solutions to the same practice and management problems.

We also assumed that it would help them if we set up mechanisms so that people do not have 'to reinvent the wheel', especially at times of major change. This common sense assumption was subsequently endorsed by Sir Roy Griffiths in his *Agenda for Action* on Community Care:

> 'Central government has a responsibility for identifying and disseminating examples of good practice. This may be particularly important during the implementation period, as there is a danger of effort being wasted in the identification of identical solutions. This role should support rather than constrain the development of imaginative and entrepreneurial solutions at the local level.'
>
> (Griffiths, 1988 p.23)

The 'reinvention of the wheel' cliché appeared in most of our early reports and publicity to help explain the purpose of practice exchange. Conventional wisdom suggested that people reinvented wheels because they lacked access to relevant information and knowledge about who was doing what where. Both of the factors are important elements but we quickly found that the transfer of information was considerably more complex (Smale, 1985), and that the simple belief that people wanted to avoid reinventing the wheel was a fallacy.

The following example illustrates some of the issues. At an early PADE event over a hundred participants had been working in small groups to identify the major issues confronting them in making changes in practice. The results of their work was displayed around the room on flip charts. The information from each group had been summarised and put in reasonable order. Representatives from the groups met over lunch to identify major common themes across these groups and to prioritise the afternoon's agenda. They sat in a huddle and started to have the mornings discussions all over again, repeating the points they had made in their original groups and arguing over the 'most important' issues. When it was pointed out to them that they did not need to repeat the morning's work, that the information was all around them, they started to look around the room and record the recurring themes, but it was not long before they slipped back into their own discussion. The afternoon's agenda reflected *their own* small groups 'common themes' rather than those of the wider group.

Information based on the experience of others was often seen as less significant than participants' own experience. *We needed to do more than provide people with access to information from others.* Other early PADE activities included work with many organisations who provided information relevant to the personal social services (Smale, 1985; SWING, 1988). There are a variety of reasons why people do not typically get information on an area of development before embarking on their own endeavours. This is partly due to the problems of finding the right information at the exact time it is required. A crucial factor in gaining usable access was contact with a person who knew, or could provide the right kind of information at the moment it was felt to be needed. People were either swamped with information they felt they could not use or starved of what they desperately wanted, when they needed it (Smale, 1985).

But many people do not even look for relevant information. In many of these early discussions it seemed as if people felt they would be 'cheating' if they got help, an observation since supported by research (Bernard, 1990). Many also seemed to want to invent their own 'wheels' and enjoyed breaking new ground.

Many of the assumptions that we made about the development of practice and the dissemination of research needed to be reviewed. It became clear that a model for *exchanging* information and practice experience needed to be more complex than providing access to information or just putting people together.

A critical finding from a variety of research areas on the adoption of new practice is that not only do *people want to reinvent the wheel* but that *reinvention is often necessary*. For example Everett Rogers says:

'...an innovation may be somewhat like a toothbrush in that people do not like to borrow it from someone else. They want their own. Or at least they want to put their own 'bells and whistles' on the basic innovation. A strong psychological need to re-invent seems to exist for many individuals...

'Recognition of the existence of reinvention brings into focus a different view of adoption behaviour. Instead of simply accepting or rejecting an innovation as a fixed idea, potential adopters on many occasions are active participants in the adoption and diffusion process, struggling to give their own unique meaning to the innovation as it is applied in their local context. Adoption of an innovation is thus a process of social construction. This conception of adoption behaviour, involving reinvention, is more in line with what respondents in diffusion research have been trying to tell researchers for many years.'

(Rogers, 1995, p. 179-180)

The TO KNOW IS TO ACT DIFFERENTLY Fallacy

In the personal social services many professionals recognise the complexities involved in changing certain clients' behaviour, for example perpetrators of child abuse or juvenile delinquency. They also recognise how difficult it is to change relationships within these people's families and their immediate social networks. All staff are well aware of how difficult it is to forge collaborative working relationships with other professionals and other agencies in such a way that they are routinely sustained in practice. It is clear in many of these situations that simple statements of how people should behave or policies and practice guidance on working in partnership fail to have a significant impact on what many people do. These obvious facts are not always borne in mind when the people in question change from being 'clients' or other professionals and become our colleagues above or below us in the organisation. It is as if we believe that 'they', the clientele, are difficult by definition, whereas 'we', our colleagues, should be reasonable and accept changes readily. All too often when colleagues, that is staff at any level, do not accept the changes proposed, they cease to be 'one of us' and are seen as 'difficult' and put in a quasi client position. Their 'resistance' is seen as a problem located in them without which they would be reasonable, become 'one of us' and change in the way proposed. Although many people introducing change may say they recognise the complexities involved in changing their own and other people's behaviour, they often act as if it were simple. The belief that people should and will do what they are told to do is not only based on simple assumptions about the way in which authority works within organisations, it is also based on the *naïve assumption that people can always do what they want or intend to do.*

These simplistic ideas surface as problems in the management of change when those introducing innovations and managers making changes in policy assume that once a change in ideas has been communicated or a decision made to adopt a new policy, then a new approach to practice will follow. Many managers would probably agree, at least in principle, that it is important to get their staff to 'own' a new way of working and that it is necessary to be clear what is required of them to practice in a different way. They might think that this is enough. Many managers underestimate the difficulties involved in changing what people do. Practitioners may also drastically underestimate what is involved in changing their practice. For example Marsh and Fisher (1992) found that the DATA effect (were 'Doing All That Already') often undermined practitioners' good intentions when attempting new approaches to practising in partnership with service users. Although they believed that they practised in an appropriate way, observation of their practice demonstrated that they did not.

Consider the relationship between the availability of staff development and expectations of subsequent practice changes. Staff are often expected to be able to practice new, complex forms of practice after only a few days training, or even in response to a new set of procedures or practice guidelines (Smale, 1991). In some situations short training courses will work and co-operative staff will be able to comply with new directives. However, evidence suggests that practice cannot always change in this way, and that more extensive staff development activities are required (Schon, 1983; Schon, 1987; Argyris, 1982; Smale, 1983, 1987).

Argyris, for example, in his work on improving individual and organisational behaviour illustrated that trainee consultants found it difficult not to practise the opposite of what they preached. He set up a situation where they were invited to comment on the way that a supervisor was commenting on a member of staff's performance. When criticising the supervisor they frequently replicated the behaviour they were critical of: it was indeed common for people to demonstrate that they operated on a 'do as I say, not do as I do', basis (Argyris, 1982).

Some people always expect to be able to change their own behaviour, because they have changed their ideas. Consider the following passage from *Educating the Reflective Practitioner* by Donald Schon (1987). He is describing how students attempted to put their new learning into practice :

> '.... it was clear from their expressions of frustration and discouragement that they not only expected to make complete interventions that incorporated everything they had discovered through analysis but also expected to get them right first trial. Their unrealistically high aspirations reinforced their feelings of incompetence, increased their sense of vulnerability to failure, and produced a level of stress that made on-line reflection more difficult.'

> (Schon, 1987 p.267)

We will return to the work of Schon and Argyris when we discuss the different tactics needed to introduce different orders of innovation in chapter five.

Such beliefs are a major contribution to ways in which departments are inoculated against an innovation. It is assumed that practice has changed after new management prescriptions, brief training, and/or the best intentions of staff. Staff themselves may believe that their own intention to behave in a different way is translated into practice. The innovation is subsequently judged without having actually been applied.

As we have stressed before with other myths, there is also some truth in the 'to know is to act differently' fallacy. It is important to be able to distinguish between those innovations that can be introduced through a new prescription and those that cannot. The next group of fallacies, *the innovation fallacies*, illustrate the necessity for analysing the nature of the change being introduced.

> *The 'Innovation' Fallacies:*
> - *Innovation Is Always Progress*
> - *All Innovations Are Additions*
> - *More Of The Same*
> - *New Ways Of Working Have To Be Led By Restructuring.*

The INNOVATION IS ALWAYS PROGRESS Fallacy

The pro-innovation bias is a term used by Rogers to describe the implications of most diffusion research: that an innovation should be diffused and adopted by all members of a social system; that it should be diffused more rapidly; and that the innovation should be neither reinvented nor rejected. This he describes as 'especially troublesome and potentially dangerous in an intellectual sense'. As a result, more is known about the spread of rapidly diffusing innovations than about the take up of slowly diffusing innovations; more about adoption than rejection; and more about continued use than about discontinuance. Diffusion of bottle-feeding among poor mothers in the Third World is an example of an innovation that, while advantageous for some, has had disastrous consequences for the majority of adopters. As we have seen the diffusion of innovations research has traditionally referred to those who are very slow to adopt an innovation as 'laggards'. It is important to recognise that rather than being open to criticism for their lack of vision, such *'laggards' may actually be right, having perceived the disadvantages of the proposed innovation.*

The pro-innovation bias, says Rogers, may result in social problems being defined in terms of individual-blame, rather than examining deficiencies of systems, or system-blame. Examples include exhortations to parents to prevent children from eating lead paint, to drivers to change their behaviour and to parents in developing countries to restrict family size. More effective solutions acknowledging system-blame were, respectively, legislation regarding use of lead paint, modifications to vehicles and highways, and improvements to agricultural and social security systems.

The ALL INNOVATIONS ARE ADDITIONS Fallacy

It is common to assume that all new approaches to practice and service delivery can only be introduced if new resources can be found to add on the new form of practice to existing work. In the UK we might have called this the 'What about the statutory work?' syndrome in social services departments. This occurs where an area of practice and service delivery is defined as a duty by government statute. There is often an implicit, erroneous assumption that these can only be carried out in a conventional way. The syndrome also overlooks the fact that duty is often interpreted in a particularly narrow, conservative way, ignoring equally important areas of practice covered by the same policy. The 1989 Children Act illustrates this particular problem where selective implementation led to a focus on child protection at the expense of family support (Department of Health, 1995) which has led to calls to 're-focus children's services'.

Innovatory work is often seen as a 'luxury' compared to the routine, established practice of organisations. These attitudes are sustained even when the definition of statutory work is selective in favour of traditional work patterns (Bennett, 1987) or when the work is obviously extremely demanding and stressful (Newburn, 1992).

It is true that new responsibilities are placed on departments and that new areas of work arise. But of course many innovations are replacements for current ways of working.

This sometimes requires extra resources for the management of the transition period (Beckhard and Pritchard, 1992). This applies when old and new systems run in parallel, as the new is developed to a point where it can take over. This often happens with new machinery where space permits. Another example is the introduction of new 10p pieces while the old are being collected and phased out. Some changes cannot be phased in: a new exchange rate for example.

However, the need for transition management should not obscure the fact that many innovations mean giving up the current way of doing things and 'unlearning' existing practice responses (Smale, 1987). Peter Marris (1974) has drawn attention to the significance of loss in all change processes. This is likened to the grief of bereavement, described as the expression of a profound conflict between contradictory impulses to consolidate all that is still valuable and important in the past and preserve it from loss, and at the same time to re-establish a meaningful pattern of relationships in which the loss is accepted. So in management of change, the changes need to be identified where a sense of bereavement is likely to be provoked (Marris, 1974). Rosabeth Moss Kanter (1989), discussing the issues involved in major organisational changes, points out that:

> 'Commitment-building management practices involve the active recognition that the way the transition phase of restructuring is handled makes a major difference in whether the new structure produces the desired results. Issue number one in managing a difficult transition smoothly is to allow employees to mourn the past, to grieve over their losses.'

The MORE OF THE SAME Fallacy

Just as managers may assume that innovations are additions to the status quo, so they may think that they can always be added on to the organisation by using more of the same adoption procedures that they have used in the past. People understandably attempt to solve problems with 'more of the same' solutions that they believe to have worked in the past. Often this works but there are significant exceptions. We have said that there is some truth in most of the fallacies outlined here and that they are flawed by oversimplifying complex processes. The Minnesota Management of Innovation (MIRP) studies suggest that managers attribute innovation success to a variety of factors that differ from hard evidence (Angle and Van de Ven, 1989). Managers can assume that they are successful in introducing innovations through any of the processes that we have identified as fallacies; indeed they would not persist if this were not so. Oversimplifications can be misleading, causing important factors to be overlooked. But it is more serious when the way that an innovation is introduced undermines its own adoption. We will see in chapter five that some innovations are particularly prone to this confusion, for example changes in the nature of the relationships within the organisation such as devolved resource management; or between the organisation and others, including user participation in decision making.

Watzlawick describes how people draw on their own experience to apply solutions to problems that have worked before: to respond to a problem with 'more of the same' solution. He points out that this approach to problem solving is applied even if it does not produce solutions. Faced with failure people escalate the application of the failed solution, applying even more of the same. If the failed solution adds to the problem rather than resolving it such strategies can prove disastrous. The application of force to counter violence leading to greater violence is a typical example. More of the same becomes a problem when the solution is obsolete. The management of innovations is prone to such obsolescence, making it likely that the belief in more of the same management strategies to introduce change will be fallacious. In chapter five we will analyse an example of this fallacy in action that is particularly relevant to the implementation of the Community Care reforms. We will describe a social services director attempting to manage changes in the relationships between senior managers and others, devolving decision making, in the same way as he has managed hitherto. We suspect that many departments will go down the same road in reorganising their departments in an attempt to initiate new forms of relationships between staff and the public and professionals in other agencies. We expect that a response to the constant round of reorganisations will soon lead to a call to 'reorganise for stability'.

The NEW WAYS OF WORKING HAVE TO BE LED BY RESTRUCTURING Fallacy

Reorganisations are perhaps the most common way in which many organisations are inoculated against the adoption of innovatory forms of practice. Managers struggle to change structure at the expense of attention to practice: the completion of the task of the organisation. In this unstable state practitioners cling on to the security of their known ways of working and fit them into the new structure. The reorganisation is then completed, but with much of the old practice in place.

Major reorganisation and wholesale restructuring has become a continual fact of life in many organisations, particularly large companies and in the social and health services. There are many reasons why some of these changes take place. Some are undertaken through choice, others are forced on the organisation through changing circumstances or new government policy. Reorganisation can be a rational response to a major problem such as rising costs set against fixed or diminishing income, changes in the market, or revolutions in the means of production and service delivery. Some reorganisations are attempts to clarify lines of accountability and confusion that have occurred as an organisation has grown or taken on different responsibilities and tasks.

However, sometimes they are not undertaken to address clear problems but for less tangible and more controversial reasons. These include the 'new wallpaper' reorganisations which often follow the arrival of a new chief executive or senior manager and the implementation of new management theories. All too often reorganisations stem from the mistaken assumption that they are an inevitable part of the process of implementing policy and initiating changes in front line practice. More often than not reorganisation is simply assumed to be *the only way* of achieving change. If a reorganisation fails to make a difference the most common response seems to be 'more of the same', that is further reorganisation.

In chapter one we referred to Schaffer and Thompson's (1992) criticism of many popular corporate change programmes. In 1995 John Kotter published an article that was to rapidly become the most requested reprint from the Harvard Business Review's lists. 'Leading Change: Why Transformation Efforts Fail' (Kotter, 1995) was based on an analysis of many initiatives over fifteen years to produce significant change in organisations via 'restructuring, re-engineering, restrategising, acquisitions, downsizing, quality programs, and cultural renewal'. He concluded that:

> *'To date, major change efforts have helped some organisations adapt significantly to shifting conditions, have improved the competitive standing of others, and have positioned a few for a better future. But in too many situations the improvements have been disappointing and the carnage has been appalling, with wasted resources and burned-out, scared, or frustrated employees.'*

(Kotter, 1996, p.3-4)

Kotter (1996) goes on to provide his own analysis of the errors made and how to rectify them. Schaffer and Thompson advocate that managers adopt a 'Results Driven Improvements Process'. This involves identifying specific targets to be achieved in introducing particular changes. Distinguishing between the different innovations involved in major changes of policy has the same advantage of reducing global changes to identifiable areas of work or 'innovations'. The approach presented in the subsequent chapters also differentiates between different characteristics of innovations and the different actions required as a result. Compared to these approaches reorganisations are a crude approach to change management, provoking many problems. Some of the key issues we have encountered include:

- *clean sheet reorganisations and the destruction of aimed-for practice;*
- *disruption, practice led organisations and practitioners tunnelling through;*
- *loss of trust when it is needed most.*

Clean sheet reorganisations and the destruction of aimed-for practice

Reorganisations often seem to be based on the misguided principle that you can somehow start all over again with an organisation, the way one might knock down a building and start again. We have come across few examples where senior managers have successfully identified and promoted practice within their organisations consistent with proposed reforms. For example in the UK a key aim of the Community Care and Children Services reforms initiated in the early 1990s was the development of needs-led assessments and partnerships between professionals and parents and between agencies. We have yet to come across an agency that approached these reforms by auditing their staff to identify who was already working in these ways: which staff carried out service centred assessments or which teams had developed partnerships with local service users, other agencies and community resources.

We know of many examples where such work has been dismantled through reorganisations ostensibly designed to introduce these new ways of working. This was often not deliberate but an accidental consequence of restructuring staff and management by dismantling locality based teams to regroup staff to focus on adult or children services. The short term effect on many was like attempting to change the course of a river while the water still flowed: many things got washed away by accident as staff clung on for survival. The consequences include a focus on emergency work at the expense of long term support (Department of Health, 1995) and finding that old partnerships had been left high and dry. The evidence suggests that assessments are still service driven and partnership between services and agencies is still the unattainable Holy Grail that will probably provoke the next round of major reorganisations.

What is constantly overlooked is that most organisations have many different approaches to practice within them and that the innovatory ideas that lead to policy change are often being applied somewhere in the organisation. In chapters four and seven it will be seen that these people are the vital seed corn for the growth of new practice: without them to influence the rest of the organisation it is doubtful that changes in the mainstream of practice can ever take place. It seems that in their haste to achieve change through reorganisation *many managers plough up the lawn to turn the whole garden over to grass.*

Gareth Morgan (1986) has pointed out that we have different metaphors for organisations. Some see them as organisms, as brains, as cultures, as political systems, as psychic prisons, as flux and transformation, as instruments of domination and as machines. It is, it seems, this latter image that implicitly or explicitly is in people's minds when they instinctively reorganise to produce change. It is as if they see individuals as cogs or machines to be moved, and told or informed as if they were being re-programmed. They are not treated as sentient beings who need to be convinced, persuaded, enthused or otherwise negotiated with. The diffusion of innovations research emphasises that new ideas and practices come about through a convergence of ideas, not through treating people or organisations like blank sheets of paper. These issues will be introduced in the next chapter and expanded upon in Part Four of the book.

Disruption, practice led organisations and practitioners tunnelling through

Organisations should be practice led: they should be designed to achieve their fundamental tasks and not determined by the need to maintain or enlarge the organisation, nor should they be run primarily for the convenience of the people within them. The literature on the management of change reinforces the view that reorganisation is not an effective strategy to improve practice. For example Rosabeth Moss Kanter's (1989) research into the impact of corporate take-overs identifies major problems caused by large scale reorganisations. These include what she calls *the 'three D's'*:

- *Discontinuity: gaps between what was once appropriate and what will now be appropriate - until the next change;*
- *Disorder: uncertainty about what should be done and the standards to apply;*
- *Distraction: the diversion of people's attention from the tasks of the organisation.*

Managers have important immediate tasks to perform and decisions to make, but during reorganisations they are called away for meetings and are often caught up in secret deliberations. At the same time leaders may be less available to counter the 'three D's'. They are so swamped by decisions about what to do that they simply do not have the time or attention for process matters such as the observation of how things are going. I have already referred to the managers who cannot get involved in developing their ability to manage change and innovation because they are in the middle of a reorganisation. It is in these circumstances that front line staff carry on their practice, for good or ill, regardless of the changes going on around them.

A team leader neatly summarised this approach during the early stages of recent major policy change when he said that he and his team were 'extremely busy working out how they were going to get round all these new changes'. Managers too busy to monitor the actions of staff are often only too pleased that they can delegate practice direction, even if it is unintentional. Perhaps organisations are a little like computers in as much as they return to default positions if you try to stop and start them again. If basic practice is sound and the aim of the reorganisation was cost saving or improving management systems, the costs may be inevitable and worth carrying. If practice is poor and its improvement or radical reform is the target of change the whole exercise is counter productive.

Loss of trust when it is needed most

It is especially ironic that more commitment is needed at the very time when the basis for commitment itself is temporarily weakened. The difficulties restructuring can make for the organisation to retain its old values, and the threats to current productivity, have been described by Kanter (1989) as follows:

- *The cost of confusion*: from small details such as people not being able to find things, not knowing their own telephone extensions, to staff not understanding their new roles and how they relate to others.

- *Misinformation*: communication is haphazard; some managers do a better job than others of keeping their people informed. Rumours are created and take on a life of their own, especially when it is not clear what was the 'right' information, and some of the rumours are potentially destructive.

- *Emotional leakage*: managers are so focused on the tasks to be done and decisions to be made that they neglect or ignore the emotional reactions engendered by the changes. But the reactions leak out anyway, sometimes in unusual behaviour.

- *Loss of energy:* any change consumes emotional energy - especially if the restructuring is perceived negatively. People become preoccupied with the current situation. They feel guilt about the people who are losing something. The mood becomes sombre, morale sinks, and it is hard to maintain the usual pace of work. For example:

'It's very hard to work when you have no idea what will happen next. 'Final' changes are replaced by new ones every other week. So even when you're told you survived a 'final' round of cuts, you know you can still get another turn next month. No one can really know what's coming down at his level until they settle who's where on the top floors...

'Right now it's so chaotic you can be demoted if you stay on, but also called disloyal if you go for the exit package. Most of the people leaving looked relaxed, like now they can stop worrying about what's happening here. The ones who can't get out or want to stay anyway are the most nervous and upset.'

The ghosts of false reassurances can come back to haunt senior managers. Kanter warns that the sheer amount of change with which companies are dealing today makes in-house competition more likely to arise from a variety of sources and for them to be compounded by reorganisations. She refers to research that has found performance to be lower in internally competitive groups and demonstrated a negative correlation between individual competition and achievement by executives and managers. She goes on to point out that creativity requires a measure of security, not the constant insecurity brought about by competitive dynamics:

'One of the costs of reorganisation is the loss of staff who do not like the way the change is managed and leave. Those who are good at their job are often the ones who can get another job easily. This 'cost' to the organisation is often underestimated. Major reorganisation also stops innovation not only because

senior management is too preoccupied with the reorganisation, but also because key people who promote innovations have been moved elsewhere, leaving vacancies which cannot be filled because of the uncertainty of the reorganisation.'

It seems particularly strange to come across organisations 're-engineering' to develop themselves as a 'learning organisation' by getting rid of staff with much experience and expertise. Do learning organisations really 'learn' by wiping the memory of the organisation and starting again?

✳ All change involves risk: as we will argue in the next chapter, staff have to be prepared to put faith into a new idea, a new way of working and the people who are introducing change. In Part Four we will see that the skills and personal attributes that a change agent requires are those that will engender the confidence of others. The scenario deduced by Kanter is not compatible with this environment. We have already drawn attention to the inevitability of loss accompanying change (Marris, 1974; Kanter, 1989). People need to discover the gains in the new situation and to accept the losses involved. To do this they need to be able to rely on some stability within the situation. In the next chapter we will discuss the importance of distinguishing between *persistence and change*: between those things that stay the same and those that change in the introduction of any innovation. The relationship between persistence and change is a crucial one for change agents.

The potential for loss of commitment in restructuring, whether from what Kanter calls 'cowboy competition', the struggle for position, or status detached from task performance, from poor management of innovation and change is, on this evidence, a serious threat to any company or organisation. Furthermore it is possible that the organisation will lose the very people it needs to build future success.

Effectiveness cannot be achieved unless staff maintain their commitment to the task. Transitions have to be managed so that a new synergy between people has the opportunity to develop, that is relationships between similar activities which can contribute to each other's development even though they are not directly, causally related.

We can then understand the reaction of the director involved in many changes but rejecting the idea of paying attention to managing innovations, if in his mind changing practice means reorganisation. He is aware that this leads to inevitable disruption which in turn halts or hinders 'innovation', defined as the creativity of the staff. Starting from his assumptions his fears are well founded. This would not be a serious long term problem if innovation was only concerned with the inventiveness of the workforce to come up with original ideas. The problem is serious however, because *all change involves the creativity required to reinvent an innovation to suit local circumstances:* the adoption of new ways of working always involves a degree of reinvention. This is particularly true of services designed through partnerships between participating service users and providers: 'designing packages of services tailored to meet the assessed needs of individuals and their carers' (Department of Health, 1989 p.17) requires such creativity.

The director's response could be called the 'Reorganisation Above Task Syndrome', or *RATS in the system.* Managers can be so swamped by urgent decisions about the reorganisation and interviewing for new posts, they simply do not have time to give attention to how things are going, let alone reflect on what they are doing.

Some of these problems are inevitable, like the way you have to dig up a road and so make it narrower in the process of adding a new lane to make it wider. But some major disruptions are avoidable and all transitions need to be managed effectively. Adequate resources are required for 'transition management' for successful change in organisations (Beckhard and Pritchard, 1992). Attempting major change without the knowledge and resources to manage the process adequately is like surgery without sterilisation and anaesthetics.

This is not to argue that organisations should never be restructured. Some innovations are in themselves 'reorganisations', for example devolved resource management. Many innovations will have organisational consequences that provoke reorganisation. The issue is that *new forms of practice and service delivery have to be implemented and worked out in detail and then the organisation changed to accommodate them.* It has been argued that managers should be constantly changing their organisations in the way that the gardener tends her land and living plants. This metaphor contrasts with the more common mechanistic metaphor of organisations in the minds of many managers and suggests that alternatives may be more helpful (Smale and others, 1988; Morgan, 1986). *Restructuring does not of itself lead to new practices although it typically disrupts current practice and its management.*

We do not have evidence that a specific way of working follows a particular form of organisation. Even where there is some evidence that some structures have particular consequences it is clear that there is no simple causal relationship. Hadley and McGrath (1984) demonstrated that 'Patch' teams can achieve many of their stated aims, but it is also true that many teams organised in this way did not change their practice and operated as if they were still in the town hall (Smale and others, 1988). The crucial issue is for the form of management of change to match the form of change, the innovation being introduced. Reorganisation can be a very blunt instrument, like digging up a plant to see if its roots are still healthy.

Final Thoughts

All of the 'models' that we have described as fallacies have elements of truth in them and will sometimes lead to desired outcomes. A rain dance is sometimes followed by rain. No model for managing change can enable managers always to obtain the desired results: there will always be factors beyond the control of the major actors that will change the course of planned change. But a model for the management of change should increase the probability of change in the desired direction, improve on chance and reduce some of the counter-productive consequences outlined above. A model for managing changes in practice should not inoculate the organisation against the innovation it is intended to introduce, just as surgery should not kill the patient.

The directorate and senior management team of one organisation we worked with crystallised the problem. They all declared that they were engaged in managing change in their organisation, but only one said that she was involved in changing practice. As the director said at the time: 'Then what on earth are the rest of us doing it for?'

Conclusion

We have pointed out that there is a pro-innovation bias in the literature and in most of our minds. To counter this and to summarise the major points of this chapter, change agents and managers may want to consider the following. Participants in our development programmes have agreed that when confronted with an innovation they do not want to implement a useful approach is to 'STALL':

To Inoculate Your Organisation Against an Innovation:

STALL:
S ET UP A PILOT PROJECT to DEBUG THE INNOVATION
T ELL THEM TO CHANGE IN WRITING
A DD THE INNOVATION TO CUSTOM AND PRACTICE
L EAVE DISSEMINATION TO NATURAL FORCES
L EAD THROUGH REORGANISATION

S ET UP A PILOT PROJECT to DEBUG THE INNOVATION:
This buys time, and enables you either to evaluate before the innovation could prove effective, or to wait for results until the innovation is obsolete. The main advantage, however, is that it enables the bulk of the organisation to work out why the innovation cannot be adopted by them.

T ELL THEM TO CHANGE IN WRITING:
Draft new guidelines/procedures/instructions. You demonstrate on paper that you have adopted the innovation and that failure is their fault, or the innovation's, or both. You are protected from criticisms and it is rarely enough to get them to change their practice even if they want to: change what you say but not what you do.

A DD THE INNOVATION TO CUSTOM AND PRACTICE:
Do not introduce new resources, but even if you do they are likely to be absorbed by the status quo unless you stop old practices.

L EAVE DISSEMINATION TO NATURAL FORCES:
Either through the formal channels of communication down the hierarchy or the logic of the innovation's advantages; keep training short and based on individuals; don't give staff time to exchange ideas.

L EAD THROUGH REORGANISATION:
This also buys considerable time. It has the added advantages of providing you with the opportunity of getting rid of difficult staff and giving the others an example of what could happen to them if they forget who's boss.

This chapter has discussed major fallacies used in the management of change; the next chapter moves on to describe the building blocks for an alternative approach based on research on the diffusion of innovations and our understanding of how adults learn and change their practice.

CHAPTER THREE

Towards An Alternative Approach

Introduction

This approach guides change agents and change managers towards critical activities that have to be undertaken to improve the chances of successfully developing, implementing and mainstreaming changes in practice. Drawing on the experience of managers and practitioners who have been successful in implementing new forms of practice and relevant research on the diffusion of innovations and the management of change, we have attempted to identify the key issues which have to be addressed to manage change effectively. This is not a blueprint or model that can be applied in a step-by-step fashion to managing change in your organisation. Managers and practitioners can develop their own plan of action by addressing these issues. The specific questions to be addressed are spelt out in the companion workbook *Mapping Change and Innovation* (Smale, 1996). In our experience, managers and practitioners who negotiate successfully with the key people involved to answer these questions radically improve the chances of successfully changing practice.

Our approach is based on an awareness of the complexity of social situations and the impossibility, even undesirability, of any one person or small group of people being in control of all the variables that affect and direct change. The recognition that change takes place relative to other changes in the social system and physical context is central to this approach. The aim is to go with compatible changes and not to constantly struggle against resistance. This approach involves analysing the major changes taking place to identify the discrete innovations involved. This not only makes thinking about the total problem more manageable but highlights how different parts of the change have to be handled, or managed differently. This is not a recommendation to split up complex changes by segmentalising organisations into specialist units. It is a prescription for detailed planning and differentiated action based on a better understanding of what needs to be done.

This chapter opens with a discussion of the basic assumptions underpinning this approach for the management of innovation and change, and discusses what a model or approach to managing change can do. We begin by continuing our discussion of the difference between the convergence of ideas versus the linear process view of communication between change managers and potential adopters. This is followed by a discussion of the distinction between innovation and change and the importance of identifying *what changes and what stays the same*. Effective innovation managers do not help themselves or others by approaching some change as 'all change', by changing more than is required to introduce the new way of working. We then describe the limitations of any model for managing change. Finally we discuss the value of seeing all innovations as solutions to problems.

CONVERGENCE VERSUS LINEAR PROCESSES

What Is the Problem?

The opening transactions between those managing innovations and others will be to initiate a 'convergence' of thinking about the nature of the problem that the innovation is an attempt to resolve.

In introducing the innovation fallacies we pointed out that many people assume that the transfer of ideas is a *'simple linear'*, or *'direction and compliance'* process of development. However evidence from the diffusion of innovations literature and adult education demonstrates that the communication of new ideas is a complex *'convergence' process.*

Ideas, new methods of work, and even new policies, rarely follow the straightforward linear path (Rogers, 1983; Rogers and Kincaid, 1981; Angle and Van de Ven, 1989). The road taken by a new method, from idea to widespread implementation, is often a route full of bumps, twists and bends, brick walls, U-turns and tangential changes of direction. It would not matter if the failure of simple linear or direction-compliance models meant that life was more complex than elegant ideas. The main problem of the fallacies is that appropriate action is not planned and managed, and people are encouraged to identify the wrong causes when the assumed path of change is interrupted. The consequences can be extremely costly.

A Convergence Model for Communication

The 'simple linear' model for the dissemination of a new method of practice assumes that the information passes from its source, typically from an 'expert' or from the policy makers at the top of an organisation, to others who are either open to information and instructions or 'resistant' to change. Rogers and Kincaid, analysing communication networks, argue that:

> '...communication..(is)..a two-way process of convergence, rather than a one-way, linear act in which one individual seeks to transfer a message to another.'
>
> (Rogers and Kincaid, 1981)

This argument has much in common with the body of knowledge built up on adult learning. Paulo Freire's now classic work on adult literacy and education in Latin America is recognised as having far wider relevance (Freire, 1972; Shaull, 1972). Criticising orthodox approaches to education where the teacher relates to students as if the latter were 'receptacles to be filled by the teacher', Freire points out that:

> 'Instead of communicating, the teacher issues communiqués and 'makes deposits' which the students patiently receive, memorise, and repeat. This is the 'banking' concept of education, in which the scope of action allowed to the students extends only as far as receiving, filing, and storing the deposits.'

Freire argues that:

> 'Knowledge emerges only through invention and re-invention, through the restless, impatient, continuing, hopeful inquiry men (sic) pursue in the world, with the world, and with each other.'
>
> (Friere, 1972 p.45-6)

People have their own ideas, beliefs and knowledge; they are not passive or neutral receivers waiting for messages. The communicators, in practice, enter into dialogues with people who interpret messages in accordance with their own assumptions and beliefs which may or may not be the same as the communicators'. Those sending communications may be clear about what they intend to say, but they should never prejudge what the other person receives. In their 'own mind' those receiving a message will hear what the message means to them: they will understand or not, agree or disagree with the communication, and then react, which may or may not be overtly consistent with what they think. Communication across ethnic, racial, class, professional or other cultural boundaries needs particular care if preconceived assumptions and prejudices are not going to lead to misunderstanding or worse.

The experience of PADE, and research on how new technologies spread, suggests that the 'simple linear' model is inadequate; that it not only over simplifies reality: it distorts it (Havelock and Havelock, 1973; Tornatzky and others, 1980; Webb and Dawson, 1991; Drazin, 1990; Stocking, 1985). Although researchers have disagreed as to the wisdom of modifying innovations (Calsyn, Tornatzky and Dittmar, 1977; Glasser and Backer, 1977), most recognise that adaptation is not only inevitable, it is desirable and even essential. The benefit of reinvention may be that rather than simply accepting or rejecting an innovation, potential adopters actively strive to give the innovation meaning in a local context (Rice and Rogers, 1980). The distinction between invention and adopting innovations produced elsewhere is then blurred, the latter also requiring creative thought and management. We have said that we suspect that much so-called 'resistance to change' is not people fighting the proposed new method to blindly maintain the status quo. Those opposing a change are often just as keenly aware of a need for reform as others but often have their own ideas about how it should be done. Often their 'resistance' is the natural reaction of excluded people to managerial or change agent activity based on a 'simple linear' model of change where solutions are being introduced without collaboration and debate allowing an overt convergence of ideas.

These issues have to be placed in a wider context by looking at the strategies and methods used by those introducing change and the behaviour of those accepting or resisting it. In previous chapters attention has been drawn to many people's lack of explicit strategy for implementing new policies or methods of practice other than 'in-service training' and the common knee-jerk reflex: 'reorganisation', or 're-reorganisation' which is often nothing more than a middle management reshuffle. There seems to be little awareness of the following:

- *Change is a process that needs to be 'managed'.* Like any successful journey it needs to be deliberately planned, continuously monitored so that changes in course can be made as required, and with a conscious allocation of staff effort to complete essential tasks and solve problems that come along the way.

- It is not enough to state what should happen in policy statements and procedures and to expect subordinates to behave differently.

- All management should be open to constant innovation and change in its own performance as well as in what is expected of others.

Agreement to change without compliance is a very difficult problem for change managers to overcome. But it is easier to confront staff who have 'agreed' than to work with people whose agreement, or disagreement, has not been sought. New practice will be vulnerable to covert or overt sabotage where the process of convergence, or divergence, is hidden, where compliance depends upon tacit assumptions about common understandings and the avoidance of overt conflict between change agents and potential adopters, or between managers and staff.

The work of PADE and the Management of Change Through Innovation programme has been based on an awareness of the need to develop a satisfactory explicit approach for the initiation and spread of new methods of practice and management: for development and the transfer of innovations. A common feature of many books on change and change management is their focus on what to change and how to do it. *Many change agents and change managers only look at what they want to change. In this there is a danger that we behave like musicians who are only concerned with producing notes and not the gaps between them: the sound they make may be impressive but it will never be music and put together it will be a cacophony of noise.*

Conservation is a key dimension of effective change management. This theme is woven into the MCTI approach to change management. In chapter one the distinction between innovation and change was discussed and working definitions proposed. Reference was made to growing criticism of popular corporate change programmes (Kotter, 1995) and Schaffer and Thompson's (1992) advocacy of a 'Results Driven Improvements Process'. This involves identifying specific targets to be achieved in introducing particular changes. Distinguishing between the different innovations involved in major changes of policy has the same advantage of reducing global changes to identifiable areas of work or 'innovations'. In the MCTI approach a fundamental distinction is made between what should change, and what needs to stay the same.

Persistence and Change

All things change but some things are more stable than others.

Bennis, Benne and Chin begin their discussion of planned change as follows:

> *'Richard Weaver once remarked that the ultimate term in contemporary rhetoric, the 'god term', is 'progress' or 'change': the world, as Oppenheimer remarks, alters as we walk in it. It would appear, then, that we are beyond debating the inevitability of change; most students of our society agree that the one major invariant is the tendency toward movement, growth, development, process: change. The contemporary debate has swung from change versus no change to the methods employed in controlling and directing forces in change.... The predicament we confront, then, concerns method: methods that maximise freedom and limit as little as possible the potentialities of growth; methods that will realise man's (sic) dignity as well as bring into fruition desirable social goals.*
> (Bennis, Benne and Chin, 1961; 1985)

This paragraph appears in the first edition of *The Planning of Change* in 1961, and in the fourth and latest, in 1985. This reflects the continuing relevance of the statement, and the length of time that this awareness of the issues has been in existence in the social sciences applied to organisational and social change. Two issues should be underlined.

First: the paradoxical idea of the inevitable persistence of change is not new. It is the central theme of the I Ching written over three thousand years ago (I Ching, 1951). The awareness certainly does not then originate with the latest generation of management gurus (Peters, 1987; Kanter, 1989). However, the awareness of the need for managers to consciously respond and actively contribute to the 'management' of change is more recent. Beckhard and Pritchard (1992) place this in context, writing:

> 'In the past few years, many organisation theorists and writers have paid increasing attention to leadership as a basic factor in the fully functioning organisation. Much attention has also been paid to the impact of the organisation's culture on its performance and potential. A third subject receiving increased attention is the management of change. Each of these valuable contributions focuses on one aspect of the three interdependent factors: leadership, culture, and change. Their objective is to help the reader understand the future and its implication for managerial action.'
>
> (Beckhard and Pritchard, 1992 p.xii)

Second: the fact that the statement appears in all four editions of the book over twenty four years means that it has persisted, or not changed. As predicted by the statement, the book has changed through four editions and is part of the changing literature on organisational development. The co-existence of such 'persistence' and 'constant change' is commonplace. It is important to draw attention to it here because many writers now talk of change in global terms and we will be developing an approach which turns away from this tendency. The story is told of how Einstein gained his inspiration for the theory of relativity through imagining a man jumping from the top of a tall building. As he falls he takes his wallet out of his pocket and watches it fall beside him. The wallet appears stationary to the man; both man and wallet are stationary and in motion. Just as an innovation is 'an innovation' relevant to the experience of those adopting it, so change in anything is relative to its context. Through this example we can see that the change in the man's attitude is a problem that urgently needs a solution, a parachute perhaps. It may be a fact, but irrelevant if the wallet's position relative to the man changes gradually due to wind resistance.

It is misleading and unhelpful to constantly stress that everything changes all the time. It may well be true that a butterfly beating its wings in one part of the globe sets off a chain of linked events that leads to a hurricane in another, but this knowledge, or rather theory, does not yet lead to practical intervention. It is also true that all is flux and that nothing stays the same but as we have seen above, the relativity of change is all important.

The relationship between persistence and change is of the utmost importance in the management of the process. The following incident illustrates the issues.

A person was invited to dinner by a friend who, following an operation for throat cancer, could no longer swallow food. The person was curious to know how the host would manage the situation but assumed that if he stayed for the meal he would just talk to his friends as they ate. In fact, the host took food into his mouth, chewed and discreetly deposited it in a napkin with a skill that made it look as if he was simply wiping his lips. In a subsequent discussion he explained that at first he had given up all contact with food, going to great lengths to avoid seeing, and most of all, smelling it. This had major implications for the rest of the family who all had to give up meal times and avoid preparing or even talking about food in his presence. Gradually it dawned on him that his avoidance was making his loss worse; instead of enabling him to come to terms with his new state, he remained obsessed with the old and the loss of eating. He worked out that there was only one thing that he had to give up, swallowing. His operation did not require him to give up smelling, tasting, feeling or chewing food. Nor did it impose on him isolation and the company of friends at dinner. So he took up his current habits. The family were able to return to many of their old ways. But they, like him, had to come to terms with a new 'normal' situation, and one which had taken the guest by surprise.

Have you, reading this, felt some discomfort or even disgust at the thought of eating dinner sitting next to a person spitting food into his napkin? If so, then it will be clear to you that such an innovation has implications for all the people involved and that others have to be prepared to change the rules to allow an innovation such as this to take place. It is perhaps not surprising that faced with the same problems many would individualise this problem, leave it with 'the patient', and compound his loss, and perhaps in so doing lose more themselves.

A crucial question the manager has to ask of all innovations and of all widespread changes is: what changes and what stays the same. It is necessary to counter the natural tendency to think and talk as if everything must change at the same rate and so provoke uncertainty and anxiety beyond that needed to mobilise action.

Outcomes and Consequences Changing the Way that Change is Introduced

In chapter two we drew attention to the fallacy of the pro innovation bias. It seems that it is almost impossible to read and write about change and innovation, especially now that they are such buzz words in the management literature and the media, without implying a pro change, pro innovation bias. It may be assumed that to set out to 'manage' innovation is to assume that innovation is 'a good thing'. This is not so. It is clear that many innovations have disastrous consequences, either because they fail like the Titanic, or perhaps just as often are disastrous as a result of their rampant success, like taking rabbits to Australia. A major argument for improving our capacity to manage these processes is to reduce the harm that unplanned, uncontrolled, or mindless innovation can cause through unintended consequences, such as the unrestricted introduction of new ways of burning fossil fuels.

To be partially successful in introducing an innovation it is necessary, but not sufficient, to have the new idea in place, being used by those who are supposed to use it, for it to have the intended impact. To be successful the innovation has still to be relevant by the time that it is adopted and not causing or precipitating significant counter-productive, harmful, unintended consequences. The successful management of innovation cannot be done by the management of objectives alone: it has to include active observation of, and response to, the consequences of change. This is not to say that the process of innovation can always be painless. We are aware that there is some truth in the old saying 'you cannot make omelettes without breaking eggs', but good cooks make sure they don't kill people with salmonella. The cook with a greater repertoire of skills may also blow the eggs when required and use the shells for Easter decorations. The history of innovations in many fields is the story of unintended consequences (Burke, 1978). Rogers illustrates this by demonstrating how the 'successful' introduction of metal axes led to child prostitution amongst the native people of Australia, and the 'successful' introduction of machines to the Lapps destroyed the livelihood of the majority of the population (Rogers, 1996).

A visiting American professor recently asked a social services director keen to promote the transfer of social services from the public to the independent sector, what she would do when some of her best staff left to set up small independent agencies to undertake their current work under contract? While still pondering this she was asked if she realised that other good staff were likely to be recruited by these independent organisations contracting for the specialist services and able to give their staff greater scope for professional development and status than the grind and risks of 'statutory work'. The American professor was simply predicting unintended consequences of such change, drawing on what has happened in the US where the public services are low status occupations passed over or evacuated by the majority of professionally qualified social workers and entrepreneurial managers.

There are many problems associated with the transfer of innovations that go beyond the obvious difficulties of getting people to change their practice. A major issue concerns the unintended consequences of an innovation, a particularly disastrous form of which is the production of the problem that the innovation is designed to solve.

The Community Care reforms are in part an attempt to undo a past innovation: the use of social security payments to fund residential care for elderly people. In addition to the original intentions these began to be used to preserve social services departments' budgets and to expand private residential care with the unintended consequence of increasing the numbers of people entering residential care against their wishes and a huge increase in expenditure (Audit Commission, 1986). We can predict that the recent reforms in the UK of Community Care services for adults and services for children will also have unintended consequences. One example is emerging from the introduction of care management to rationalise and increase the cost effectiveness of resource allocation. These innovations, devised to counter the fragmentation of service provision as in the US (Netting, 1992), could have the unintended consequences of fragmenting service provision previously co-ordinated within one organisation, making service planning and monitoring more difficult.

Crucially in the UK many departments which initiated structural purchaser-provider splits are constructing bridges between them so they can plan future services more effectively. They found that the split made service planning and monitoring more difficult. Doubt has also been expressed about the wisdom of introducing financial payments to replace 'informal' care arrangements (Smale and others, 1994) and the consequences of changing a person's role from 'social worker', associated with problem solving with people, to 'purchaser', associated with buying and paying for services (Smale, Tuson and Statham, in press). Introducing a solution to a problem that does not exist is dangerous: the 'solution' can contribute to the creation of the problem. This somewhat theoretical prediction, discussed further in chapter nine, should be considered in the light of the serious warnings that were given of the dangers of following North American experience (Schorr, 1992; Sturges, 1992), and the evidence coming out of some early evaluations (Hadley and Clough, 1996).

In short all innovations, and all changes, should be judged by their impact on all those that they affect and not simply by whether they happen or not. New industrial technologies are no longer judged simply by their effectiveness and efficiency. Their impact on the environment has also to be taken into consideration. The management of change and innovation should be a reflective and a self reflective process: it should include monitoring the impact of the innovation on people; and also monitoring the consequences of the management process itself. If a method does not work an innovation is called for to replace it. If the innovation does not have all the desired consequences then it will need to be reinvented, or replaced in its turn by new innovation. If the way in which changes are introduced has undesirable consequences, that too has to be replaced by a different way of introducing innovations. This theme will be discussed further in Part Five where it will be suggested that we should move away from management by objectives towards management by consequences.

WHAT A MODEL OF CHANGE MANAGEMENT CAN DO

Two dimensions of this issue need to be addressed: the kind of information that is useful and the limitations that any model for the management of change will have.

The Limitations of 'Information' Dissemination in Innovation Transfer

We started PADE with a question: how could we provide people with information about innovatory practice so that they do not have to waste valuable time, energy and resources reinventing the wheel? Since then we have revised many of our ideas through reviewing research on how innovations are transferred from one organisation to another, and our experience of working with practitioners and managers developing new forms of practice and service delivery across Britain. We now assume that not only do people want to adapt the wheel to their own purposes, but working in partnership with service users means involving others in the process of inventing a unique 'wheel' to fit the idiosyncratic circumstances of all the different groups of people that they are working with.

The discussion of care management above illustrated that changes can be counter productive where they are attempts to introduce innovations that are other people's solutions to different problems. We will see in the next chapter that one of the reasons that the course of many innovations is so convoluted is that people use inventions for alternative purposes and often they have consequences far beyond the innovator's original intentions (Burke, 1978). For many innovations that do not involve technical hardware, it is more important that ideas and concepts are communicated rather than full prescriptions for practice. The ideas of roundness and axles may be more helpful than fully designed wheels.

Reinvention, or adaptation, should be the norm, as Watzlawick has pointed out:

'...there is no idea more murderous than the delusion of having found the final solution.'

(Watzlawick, 1990 p.166)

The Limitations of Models for Managing Change

No model for the management of change could ensure that innovations were adopted. Angle and Van de Ven (1989), drawing out the implications of the Minnesota Management of Innovations programme, say:

> *'At the outset we emphasise that we do not propose to offer a set of management principles that, if followed, will ensure innovation success. On the contrary, our experience in MIRP has convinced us that many factors that influence the success of an innovation are not within the control of the innovators. Accordingly, rather than offering a formula for successful organisational innovation, we instead suggest some approaches that we believe will increase the **likelihood** of success.'*
>
> (Angle and Van de Ven, 1989 p.664)

A model for the management of change should increase the probability of change in the desired direction, improve on chance and reduce counter productive consequences. A model for managing changes in practice should not inoculate the organisation against the innovation it is intended to introduce. Managers meeting resistance to change should assume that this is feedback to them on the way that they are managing the process. This may not be literally true, but they are not able to retrospectively change the feelings, attitudes and motivations of others who are already hostile. They are able to modify their own behaviour which may influence others' feelings and behaviour in the future. If they change what they do they may increase the chances of success and reduce the negative consequences of the way that the change takes place.

The approach to managing change described here is based on an awareness of the complexity of social situations and the impossibility, even undesirability, of any one person or small group of people being in control of all the variables that affect and direct change. Recognising that change takes place relative to other changes in the social and physical context is central to this model. The art is to go with compatible changes and not to constantly struggle against opposition. Many things change without our deliberate intervention. Angle, Van de Ven and colleagues (1989) have noted that managers attribute successful change to their own actions and tend to blame external consequences on others.

We will see in the next chapter that the approach involves analysing major changes to identify the discrete innovations involved. This not only makes thinking about the total problem more manageable but highlights how different parts of the change have to be handled, or managed differently. This is an analytical not an organisational recommendation; it is not a recommendation for specialisation and literally attempting to split up complex changes by segmentalising organisations. This can be a disastrous strategy as the unintended consequences of restructuring ripple out through the system. It is a prescription for detailed planning and differentiated action based on a better understanding of what needs to be done.

Change, Innovation and Problem Solving

It is helpful to frame innovations as solutions to problems. This enables us to go beyond seeing the reactions of some people to change as 'resistance'. We need to be able to recognise whether the problem addressed by the innovation is, or is not, a high priority problem for key people, or even a problem at all for some of the major actors in the situation. It also helps us recognise that the solution may not be other people's chosen solution, even if they agree with the definition of the problem.

Not everybody will see the status quo as a problem. Indeed some will see the innovation as 'a problem'. This is made more likely if an innovation is introduced ahead of a consensus about the nature of 'the problem'. We are reminded here of Handy's first injunction to managers introducing change:

'Create an awareness of the need for change. Preferably not by argument or rationale but by exposure to objective fact.'
(Handy, 1981)

In chapter two we saw that we have had good research evidence since 1948 that full consultation, starting with sharing the problem rather than a chosen solution, pays dividends in the management of change (Coch and French, 1948). This approach recognises that all the people involved in the situation into which an innovation, or solution, is being introduced can be seen as problem solving at some level. Some may recognise the same problem that you, the change manager, want to address and agree with the solution you think will work. We will see in the next chapter that these are crucial people to work with and that you have no choice but to do some work with *all* those involved. Others will be preoccupied with other problems or other solutions: they may even see the status quo as the solution to many of these problems and their solution may be to sustain it for as long as possible. *It is important to recognise that much so called resistance to change can be understood as negative feedback to change agents about:*

- *their definition of the problem;*
- *their chosen solution; and*
- *the way that they are managing change.*

To introduce 'solutions' to people who do not perceive themselves as having a problem will not unreasonably be seen as imposing a gratuitous burden, or at least an inconvenient interruption in their work.

To introduce a solution that is not seen as related to the problem as the people involved define it themselves, is reasonably seen as an irrelevance.

To introduce a solution without people being able to see how it will solve the problem requires people to trust the innovation and/or the innovator.

Trust is an important commodity in the management of change. Nobody can be certain that an innovation will 'work'. If we know anything about the processes of innovation and change it is that they are unpredictable and cause anxiety. It is then vital that those managing change do everything that they can to establish their credibility to develop the trust of those who need to put faith in the innovation.

The fact that many will want change, even when they have different definitions of the problems that need to be addressed and competing solutions, enables us to recognise the possibilities for *'convergence'* in thinking between the change agent and others. It also helps us to assess the potential for *'divergence'* between significant people. Another way of framing this is to recognise *'allies'* and *'opponents'* and the potential for building 'synergy' with complementary innovations and directions of change.

Framing innovation as a problem solving process also has the following consequences:

- It enables the innovator to *keep the purpose of changing things in the forefront of their minds, rather than just 'the innovation'*. It is unhelpful to focus on the innovation alone and judge success only in terms of the adoption or application of the innovation. It is dangerous if the innovation becomes a cause in its own right. *'Success' is not the adoption of an 'innovation'. Success lies in finding effective solutions to our problems.* It is necessary for the evaluation of 'change' or of 'an innovation' to consider the consequences of our interventions, not just the short term objective of applying a particular solution.

- It encourages us to focus on the purpose of change. Keeping it tightly defined helps us *avoid changing more than necessary.*

- *It helps us to recognise that negotiation over 'what needs to change and how' is a better starting point than assuming a certain definition of the problem and attempting to sell a pre-chosen solution, or even consulting about a set of potential options or change.*

Seen as solutions to problems innovations can be:

- *a better solution, an improvement on existing practices or equipment;*
- *a new solution to an old problem;*
- *a new solution to a new problem;*
- *a solution to an old problem that does not have so many harmful, unintended consequences; or*

- *some combination of all these different descriptions.*

Innovations are often seen as one kind of solution to some of those involved and have another purpose for others.

The innovation of opening community based accommodation for mental health patients and closing large mental hospitals was a professional solution to the side effects of institutionalisation to some; the resolution of a human rights issues for those who advocated 'normalisation' in living arrangements for people previously excluded from the community; and a cost saving exercise for others. For some at the heart of these processes they represented a massive, unnecessary disruption - and were seen as major problems and not as solutions at all.

The video recorder was seen by some as a way of introducing low budget television recording for many purposes such as skills training and as a new form of photography. Others saw it as an extension of the domestic television giving the viewer more control of their watching. Then others recognised the potential for film hire, and a potential competitor and threat to the cinema became a massive boost to the cinema industry.

Addressing the Right Problem

The status quo can also be seen as the way in which problems are being solved.

Recognising this enables us to see that *where all innovation addresses the unintended consequences of an existing solution, it must also address the original problem to succeed.* To effectively introduce innovatory alternatives to residential care we have to be clear how we are solving the problems that residential care was a solution to, that is the anxiety of those who recognised the risks to people under-supported in the community.

Many of our most difficult, persistent problems are perpetuated because some people get the benefits of the problems solved by maintaining the status quo, and it is others who suffer from the unintended consequences. It is often not difficult to find motivation for change amongst those who are suffering. But why should we expect those whose problems are being solved to change?

Many managers and practitioners have 'the innovation' chosen for them by policy makers. They then have to work out how to apply the innovation in their situation. This will include considering the degree to which it is both necessary and possible to reinvent the innovation, and the direction such reinvention should take. This will depend upon their initial mapping of their circumstances (see chapter four).

Whenever possible, the change manager will review and change the solutions to be applied, making sure that they:

- address 'the problem' as defined by the key players;
- build on and, where possible, marry up with the solutions that all players would see as possible and desirable;
- build on and dovetail with the old solutions that you need to keep in place.

Wherever possible you should add to the 'normal' way of solving problems for the people involved. To introduce 'foreign' solutions from a different problem solving culture is either to be avoided or entered into consciously and then managed appropriately. It is necessary to understand and learn from others to engage in a 'convergence' of ideas across cultural boundaries. To assume that one culture should simply replace another is to risk the dangers of colonisation at the expense of creative convergence.

First Steps

The opening transactions between those managing innovations and others will be to initiate a convergence of thinking about the nature of the problem that the innovation is an attempt to resolve. The first questions that the change agent or transactor should address with those directly involved is:

- *For whom is the status quo a problem?*
- *Who wants the innovation and for what reason?*
- *What problems does the innovation solve, and for whom?*

- *How do service users or customers see the problem?*

Change managers will find it useful to look at *all* the people in the path of the innovation, attempting to identify and reconcile different definitions of the problem and its possible solutions, that is appropriate innovations. Service users, whether social service users, health service patients or commercial companies' customers, are crucial key players. There are two reasons for underlining this when managing change. The first and obvious one is that the service has to be relevant to the people it is designed to serve. If they do not see the innovation as a solution to their problems we have to question the validity of its introduction. In the health and social services this is the relatively new area of service user participation. In the commercial world there is a longer tradition of market research. The second reason for identifying this dimension is because the service user can also be an agent for innovation and change.

Major ideas change when a new piece of information enters into a field and does not fit with the conventional wisdom. In science, a new discovery may add new knowledge but occasionally the new observation does not fit existing theory. The old knowledge and the new observation can only fit if the underlying theory - the paradigm - shifts. The growing voice of the service user is often such an agent of change. They are outside of the provider system and so they will see problems and potential solutions from a 'new' perspective. The mobilisation of this voice by change managers is often an important part of introducing change in the system. The convergence of thinking between the ideas of the would-be innovator and the service user is a crucial dimension of making sure that the innovations introduced are appropriate, that is relevant to the resolution of the problems that the organisation exists to serve.

Addressing the questions above enables the change manager to identify:

- *the changes that need to take place;*
- *the different innovations included in these changes;*
- *what changes and what stays the same.*

The choice of changes to be made and innovations to be adopted will also depend upon the purpose of the organisation within which the change manager and other major actors work. Thus those involved will need to be working on the relationship between the proposed changes and the policies directing the organisation.

Working with the Vision and the Mission of the Organisation

Many of the most successful innovators had a clear vision of what kind of service they wanted to deliver. In our experience of working with innovatory managers and practitioners this is true even if, maybe especially where, the organisation does not have a good idea about what it is about. It may be that the 'badly' managed organisation is a playground for innovators while the tightly run ship is far harder for them to operate in and stifles initiative. This certainly relates to the idea of innovation as deviance from the status quo. The tighter the organisation the nearer any innovation will be to delinquency; whereas in a loose organisation a challenge to the status quo will be seen as deviation at most or even just an idiosyncratic way of solving the problems of how to deliver services and carry out the organisation's tasks. This has led some management writers to talk about the need for 'loose-tight organisations'. This means that they are appropriately tight around some issues, for example budgetary control, while being loose over others, for example enabling workers to use their initiative to seek better ways of doing their jobs. Our experience was that during the 1970s and 1980s there was far more innovation within the personal social services in the UK than there has been in the 1990s. It is not clear whether this is a result of tighter management resulting from more management development, or the consequence of a government driven change agenda that has pushed aside practitioner and management led initiatives.

In the personal social services, the community social work pioneers of the 1980s were a good example of such innovators. They were markedly different from their colleagues for three major reasons.

First, they held a certain group of clear, shared principles. In addition to more widely held values about good practice they believed that:

- services had to be accessible to people in terms of the times of the day and week, and as near as possible to where they lived;

- services should not be stigmatising: people should not have to be labelled as 'clients' before they receive help and support;

- all people in the neighbourhood, including those traditionally only seen as 'clients', were seen as potential sources of support;

- the role of the professional was to link up those with resources to those with particular needs at a particular time, rather than assume that they would themselves always provide the service;

- social situations, that is family and neighbourhood networks, were seen as the focus of help, support, problem resolution or management and change, and not just as individuals who 'had' or 'were' problems;

- service users were to be involved in decision making about their lives as fully as possible and also involved in service planning;

- team work, both within the agency and across agency boundaries, was seen as essential: just as the 'problems' were recognised as involving the relationships between identified service users and others, so the relationships between people attempting to help were seen as crucial to problem resolution or management.

The second difference was the way they applied these values. They took them literally and went out into their community looking for ways to apply them - to use some of the jargon of the day, *they were 'proactive' rather than 'reactive'*. A key example of this difference was the way that they would encourage people to tell them of those who had problems, and find ways of helping others to respond. They would also regularly visit schools to see if there were families that needed help, but had not yet reached the point of formal referral. They would then seek to link them up to people who could help without formally taking them on as 'clients'.

The third difference was that these innovators applied these solutions in many different ways. They used them as 'guiding principles' around which they constantly improvised. They seemed to constantly change their practice to fit the specific circumstances they found themselves in, rather than follow prescriptions for practice such as particular methods of intervention, for example family therapy or task centred casework. *They were problem solving: innovating, or re-innovating rather than applying a particular innovation no matter what the circumstances.*

It is worth noting in passing that we have worked with many practitioners and leading change managers for the last fifteen years without 'stress' and 'burnout' ever appearing as issues of concern. Overwork was often a problem. But it seems that seeking out and addressing problems, even if you find too many, is better than waiting and being bombarded by them. We discuss the importance of initiative for change agents in chapter four, but we should never forget that *those taking the initiative find change more palatable than those being changed by others.*

For large scale innovations the change managers and the senior management team will need to demonstrate their commitment to the vision of change. This does not mean that the vision is a fixed, detailed set of prescriptions, but that managers will demonstrate a clear sense of direction, working out the complete vision with others as changes progress.

Change managers should consider:

- *How does the innovation fulfil the organisation's mission and contribute to its major aims?*
- *How does it fit with the change manager's vision of good practice?*
- *How does this vision 'fit' with the prevailing conventional wisdom about good practice?*
- *How does it match service users' perceptions of what they want and need?*

Final Thoughts

This chapter has reviewed some of the major assumptions of the MCTI approach and outlined the foundations, or 'first steps' in the process of managing change. In our early work we assumed that there was a rational sequence to these events: that you could start with understanding the problem then move on to plan the required action, using the analysis of the Innovation Trinity described in the next part of the book. This is still a rational way of presenting the material, but that is all. It becomes clear when these ideas are put into practice that the sequential approach was our tacit belief in a 'simple rational' model of development, and that elegant though this is, it does not fit to real world situations. In practice the managers and practitioners we work with find that all these issues come at them at once, and all the time. In your head it may be possible to analyse a problem and then apply a solution, but in practice are you not often expected to apply a solution before proper analysis can be undertaken? In this chapter we have suggested sharing the problem, exposing staff to the evidence. But we know that you are probably having to manage changes defined by others based on their perception of the problems that should be addressed. However it is still the case that what will take place is some kind of convergence between 'their' definition of the problem and its solution and yours. People do have degrees of choice over their own behaviour and the way that they do their work: even when they agree they may not comply; even when they comply they may find an opportunity to deviate from the defined path. You, and others, will have to judge whether such innovation is leadership or delinquency.

I assume that you are not going to read this book and abandon all that you ever believed about the management of change and replace it with what you read here. Are you not reading it and matching it to what you already know, hopefully accepting some useful ideas and rejecting others that diverge from your way of thinking?

Effective change managers and change agents will constantly return to the basic, first step questions. They need to re-address them because staff change, both the people and their ideas. Being alive to this, to feedback from all those around you, is a key part of the change agent's repertoire described in Parts Four and Five of this book. The next phase involves developing a plan for managing the implementation of new ideas, the invention, the adoption and the adaptation of innovations, by understanding the Innovation Trinity.

PART TWO

The Innovation Trinity

Introducing the Innovation Trinity

Practitioners, policy makers, senior managers and other agents of change wishing to initiate practice development or introduce new methods of work need to confront three major issues:

- *mapping all the significant people*
- *analysing the nature of the innovation*
- *understanding the context*

and relate all three to the *problems* being addressed; and where possible *develop a convergence of thinking and action* between the key people about *what changes*, and *what stays the same.*

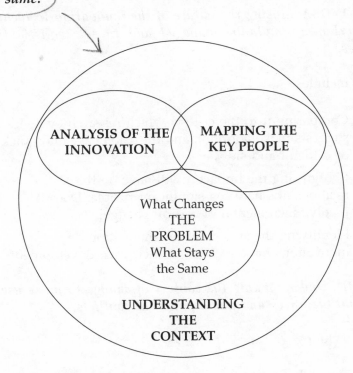

Fig 1: The Innovation Trinity

FIRST: Mapping all the significant people involved to identify who should do what with whom.

The central dimension of this approach is the recognition of the part played by all the significant people involved. We begin by comparing them to the roles identified as crucial by the diffusion of innovations literature, research on the management of change in organisations and our own experience of working with innovatory managers and practitioners. This is then followed by identifying:

- Who has to do what differently?
- How are significant people responding to change?
- Who is initiating change - who is it 'being done to'?
- Who experiences what losses and what gains?
- Who are the 'change agents' and what is their support?

SECOND: Analysing the nature of the innovation to identify how change should be managed and to set realistic time scales.

This includes:

- Comparing it to the criteria which research evidence suggests make adoption and diffusion easy and quick or difficult and slow.
- Recognising the impact it will have on the relationships between significant people. Does it involve incremental or radical change?
- Identifying the stage that the innovation or innovations have reached in their own development.

THIRD: Understanding the context of change to make use of compatible forces and avoid potential conflicts.

This includes:

- The 'culture' of the organisations within which the innovations are to be located.

- The relationship between these organisations and their environment.
- The relationship between significant people within and without the organisation.
- The direction of other changes.

We begin our discussion of the Innovation Trinity by looking at mapping the people.

CHAPTER FOUR

Mapping The People

Switching on new pieces of technology and learning to use them may seem difficult for the technologically illiterate, but most of us recognise that learning about the hardware is easy compared to getting people to use it. Research on the diffusion of innovations and the literature on managing change confirms any would-be change manager's experience: it is 'the people' that are the problem. Fortunately they are also the solution, but the change agent's key activity is to distinguish between those people who are a problem and those who are part of the solution: indeed to identify who will play all of the key roles involved in any change process. We have already introduced this analysis by inviting you to discover who sees what as a problem and what solutions would they adopt. Now we need to be more specific and identify all the key players. It is important to identify people by name wherever possible. The thoughts and motivations of key players in the field are as dependent upon their individual positions as they are upon their titles and job descriptions. We have to get beyond the stereotyped notions we might have about categories of people and begin to understand why people are reacting in a particular way, whether positively or negatively, to a proposed innovation.

During one of the many workshops run during the development of this approach to managing change, a senior manager expressed his interest in the ideas presented. He said that they helped him understand why change management went wrong in his organisation, but he feared that the approach was not practical. His reason for this was that the ideas presented in this chapter for mapping the people involved meant that 'to adopt this approach you would really have to know your staff'. We have found that there is no easy answer to this criticism. Just as we have admitted that it would have been nice to have arrived at a simple elegant model that fitted in with managers' existing ideas so that it was eminently adoptable, so we would have liked to have helped the hard pressed manager with an approach to change that meant that it could be achieved from the drawing board, without engaging with the many people involved. The evidence suggests that the majority of people change their practice, their ideas and behaviour through engaging with other people. This inevitably means that the would-be change agent has to get in there, relate to people themselves and, as we will see, work on the relationships between others. Policy statements and books can articulate important information just as maps and directions can describe a possible journey. But on their own they are unlikely to produce changes in behaviour.

It is significant that the people who found the working edition of this book most useful were successful innovators. They said they found it extremely helpful in spelling out what they had done; what they, in a sense, already knew even if they had never put it into words. We found it more effective to give workshop participants written material *after* they had been working on the ideas and applying them to their work situations. People have different learning styles (Kolb, 1981) but with this material most participants appreciated reflecting on their own experience and considering a problem that the innovation addressed; then being introduced to new ideas and attempting to apply them to their own situation and experience of managing change; then reading the book. We will pick up on these themes in chapter seven when we consider the impact of change on the individual: now we will explore the key players in the process.

Mapping People: Lessons from Research on the Diffusion of Innovations

Research on the diffusion of innovations has taken place over the last forty years at an accelerating pace. By 1995 Rogers was able to draw on over 3,890 separate studies for his authoritative review (Rogers, 1995). Research has looked at many kinds of innovations, from hard technology to changes in behaviour, from new forms of seed corn to birth control, in many settings from the great plains of the US to developments in the so-called Third World.

Rogers points out that:

> '...the diffusion of an innovation takes place as information about it passes through the relevant social systems so that

individuals, groups or organisations can decide to adopt or reject that innovation.'

He emphasises the importance of communication and the convergence of ideas:

*'**Diffusion** is the process by which an innovation is communicated through certain channels over time among the members of a social system. It is a special type of communication, in that the messages are concerned with new ideas. **Communication** is a process in which participants create and share information with one another in order to reach a mutual understanding. This definition implies that communication is a process of convergence (or divergence) as two or more individuals exchange information in order to move toward each other (or apart) in the meanings they give to certain events.'*

(Rogers, 1995 p. 5-6, emphasis original)

Barbara Stocking's (1985) research on the spread of innovations in the Nation Health Service endorsed many of Rogers' conclusions, and provides us with the nearest relevant evidence for application to the personal social services in the UK. The adoption of an innovation can be illustrated by drawing an 'S-shaped' diffusion curve (Fig. II), the steepness of the curve reflecting the rate of adoption.

Fig. II: The Diffusion of Innovations Curve

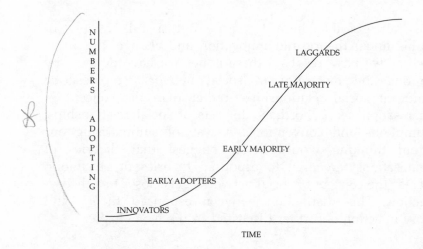

(Adapted from Rogers, 1983 p.11)

We can see from this curve that Rogers has indicated that there are different categories of people involved at each stage. He synthesises the research to identify the characteristics of the people in each category. This leads us to the first stage in this approach to the management of innovations: the need to look at the significant actors, those people whose actions will determine whether an innovation is adopted. From this analysis the change agent will be able to identify what sort of action needs to be taken with whom, to plan the transactions that have to be undertaken to manage the adoption of the innovation.

Identifying the Significant People: Planning Transactions for Change

The identification of the major significant actors begins with a review of the importance of social networks. These are the channels through which information flows, or stops. They are also the arena for much of the innovator's action. As the approach has developed we have become increasingly aware of the inadequacy of orthodox explanations of behaviour 'within organisations' for understanding why and how innovations develop. The diffusion of innovations literature constantly refers to the significance of transactions across organisational boundaries. But contemporary management theory and much research on the organisational dimensions of innovation and change tend to assume that the significant arena for action is within the boundary that it is assumed exists around the organisation.

It is not possible here to carry out a full review of organisational theory and innovation and change. But in as much as we have resolved these issues we have done so by adopting the metaphor of social networks to describe significant social relationships, rather than the concept of 'organisation' as a shorthand for sets of social relationships, assumptions and conventions. A way of summarising our current thinking would be to suggest that theories of 'organisations' are akin to espoused theories of behaviour, whereas the concept of social networks gets closer to a theory-in-action. This distinction between espoused theory and theory-in-action is further discussed in the next chapter.

Support for Innovators: Networking Innovation and Change

In chapter one we drew attention to the relationship between innovation and deviance. Throughout the workshops we have run in developing this approach, we have found it helpful for participants to reflect on this relationship to help them understand the social processes they are involved in when they attempt to introduce change, when they innovate. One crucial dimension of the dynamics of deviance is that the 'deviant' is typically treated as an 'outsider' (Becker, 1973). It is endemic in the processes of introducing new ideas and new forms of practice that innovators will be, to some extent, isolated from their peers and managers. Our experience of working with many practitioners and managers at all levels endorses Tom Peters' comment:

> *'...that you can tell who the trail blazers are; they are the people up ahead with the arrows in their backs.'*

Given the opportunity, these people identify with, gain support and encouragement from, and multiply their knowledge and experience through contact with other people engaged in similar work in different organisations.

There is an old saying that 'all problems are a shortage of ideas'. Innovation requires the changing of ideas. A person thinking of a new way of doing things often has to step outside of the way in which the problem is normally tackled (Kuhn, 1970). Within certain situations this is normal and perfectly acceptable to all. The innovator is said to be someone with greater experience, wisdom or ingenuity. However, there are other times when the new thinking challenges central beliefs and values held by most others in an organisation, family or group.

A person challenging conventional wisdom can be seen as more of a threat than a help. Their position is more that of a deviant than a conformist. The more the innovator *behaves* as well as thinks differently the clearer this becomes. The history of the development of science and technology is full of examples. For example Charles Darwin's theory of natural selection was certainly seen as a threat, while the early anatomists, acting on their belief that the human body could be understood scientifically, often had to break the law to carry out their investigations.

This analysis highlights some of the problems experienced by many of the individuals who participated in the exchange networks that we have organised through the National Institute for Social Work's Practice and Development Exchange. As innovators they are often relatively isolated from their peers and others in the organisation. Typically, they may have identified with a small group of sympathetically minded people. This group may be seen by both others and themselves to be 'subversive', their success in achieving change being 'despite the organisation'. The frustration for the innovators comes from their ambivalent position within the organisation. They often identify with its aims, but set about achieving them in different ways. They may be both 'conformist' and 'deviant', so they can often not be rejected as simply 'delinquent' but also not accepted as 'one of us' by the majority.

The innovator may, on the other hand, be a new manager or group of managers at the top of an organisation. The labels attached to such people are different. Instead of being thought 'difficult' and possibly censured by authority for their nonconformity, they have the organisational authority to define those resisting change as 'conservative', 'reactionary', 'laggards' or even 'deviant'. But although some things change, the pattern remains very similar. The innovator still runs the risk of being marginalised: being defined by the majority as 'unrealistic', 'impractical', 'crazy' or 'out of touch'. Similarly the innovatory motives may be challenged through such labels as 'careerist', 'authoritarian' or 'anti professional'. Innovators may be some or all of these things, but labelling the innovator obscures what is happening in the processes of change generally, and specifically distorts perceptions of the impact that the change is having on the relationships between people.

The innovator, like the deviant, delinquent or 'outsider', often has special support needs which need to be met to sustain her or him through the risky business of change. This has been acknowledged by companies which attach great significance to innovation, such as 3M (Mitchell, 1991). To give up and conform, to be re-absorbed by the group, is always a temptation if no other form of support is available. It is also necessary to have somebody, somewhere, with whom you can 'check your sanity'.

Set against this analysis of the close relationship between deviance and innovation it is not surprising that the interpersonal relationships of innovators, and their *networks*, have been found to be a crucial variable in research on the diffusion of innovations (for example Albrecht and Hall, 1991; Rogers and Kincaid, 1981; Eveland, Rogers and Klepper, 1977).

Rogers emphasises that the diffusion research clearly shows that 'early adopters' are part of extensive professional networks which inform them, and that later adopters rely almost exclusively on interpersonal contact for their information about innovations. He stresses the crucial significance of *social networks* for the diffusion of innovations. Indeed, Rogers' own research has concentrated on the nature of networks and what variables promote or inhibit diffusion (Rogers and Kincaid, 1981). These findings are echoed throughout a diverse literature on innovation and change. Thomas Kuhn's classic work on *The Structure of Scientific Revolutions*, for example, discusses the essential role played by 'invisible colleges' in the development of new paradigms (Kuhn, 1970). We will return to this issue in chapter seven.

Networks are therefore crucial channels for communication and they contain people who stimulate and support the development of an innovation. But this is not the whole story about the web of human contacts described by using the network metaphor. There are many people involved in any person's or group of people's social networks. In common with other dimensions of the MCTI approach it is necessary to differentiate between these people to identify the nature of specific actions. We need to identify the major actors to identify who needs to do what with whom to produce changes in practice. Readers will recognise that some key people will be in more than one of these roles. They will also see that they will be in different roles relative to different innovations: a person might be an advocate of one kind of change and hostile to another.

The Major Players in the Transfer of Innovations

Rogers (1983) categorises the five groups of people named on the diffusion curve illustrated in Fig. II as: Innovators; Early Adopters; Later Adopters; Later Majority and Laggards. Drawing on a variety of research studies, he suggested that in very general terms they displayed certain characteristics:

Innovators. Rogers describes these people as 'venturesome', pointing out that:

> *'Venturesomeness is almost an obsession with innovators. This interest in new ideas leads them out of a local circle of peer networks and into more cosmopolitan social relationships.'*
>
> (Rogers, 1995 p. 263)

The 'original' innovators are, by definition, the inventors, either researchers or practitioners who develop a new 'technology' which may be a form of service delivery or method of intervention. However, we have stressed that the term 'innovation' refers to 'an idea, practice, or object that is perceived as new by an individual or another unit of adoption', and stressed the importance of recognising that an idea or practice does not have to be 'original' to be an innovation. The S-shaped curve (Fig. II) shows how an 'innovation' becomes less and less 'original' as it passes through time and up the curve, whilst still being an 'innovation' to the next group of people yet to adopt it. It follows from this definition that an 'innovator' is somebody introducing a idea new to the recipients, but which does not have to be 'original'.

Early Adopters. They tend to be innovators themselves and actively seek information about new ideas. In many fields, from farming to medicine, they tend to differ from later adopters in having higher social status and more education; in having more favourable attitudes towards change and a greater ability to cope with uncertainty and risk. They tend to be part of a more highly interconnected social system, with their networks extending outside their own immediate professional and social circle as well as having greater exposure to the mass media. Communication through the mass media about new ideas influences these early adopters. They are also persuaded by direct personal contact with innovators and other early adopters through visits and attendance at conferences and professional meetings (Rogers, 1983).

Later Adopters are mainly influenced by local experience and by interpersonal contacts within a more restricted network of peers. Mass media, including 'the literature', seem to have far less impact upon later adopters.

Laggards are the most parochial people of the adopter groups and tend to take the past as their point of reference. It has already been mentioned that Rogers expresses reservations about the use of the term laggards, pointing out that 'it is a mistake to imply that laggards are somehow at fault for being relatively late to adopt'. He goes on to say that it is all too easy to blame the individual where 'system-blame' may more accurately describe much of the reality of the laggards' situation (Rogers, 1995 p.266). Rogers argues that the negative connotation would probably be attached no matter what language is applied. This and the positive connotations applied to 'innovators' is part of the strong pro-innovation bias. This issue is related to two of the fallacies described in the beginning. The process that Rogers is describing, of attributing blame, is essentially the same as we saw in attributing credit to the so-called charismatic individual. The 'praise-blame' dimensions illustrate the pro-innovation bias - if innovations are by definition 'good', then those promoting them are heroes, and those blocking them villains. The fallacy is clearly illustrated through our growing awareness of green issues - of the harmful consequences of innovations seen only as examples of 'progress'.

The following major roles are identified in the literature (Rogers, 1995; Stocking, 1985; Angle and Van de Ven, 1989) and through our experience of working with innovatory practitioners and managers through NISW's Practice and Development Exchange.

Product Champions. It is significant that Stocking (1985) named 'Identifiable Enthusiasts' at the top of her list of factors influencing the rate of adoption of any innovation (see chapter five). Research evidence has some influence on these early adopters, but it seems to play little part in the decisions of those in the 'majority' categories. 'Product champions' are crucial early adopters, being the people who not only adopt new methods, but take up the cause of spreading the message to others (Howell and Higgens, 1990). Handy (1981) has also stressed that managers wanting to introduce change should:

'Select an appropriate initiating person or group: appropriate in this context refers to sources of power as perceived by the recipients of the strategy.'

As we have seen, the diffusion research makes it clear that the social and professional networks of product champions are crucial for spreading new ideas and methods.

Opinion Leaders are those people within an organisation or profession who have an influence on the methods used by others. They are 'role models', whether intentionally or not: others tend to copy their behaviour and the solutions they adopt to problems. They are often the most crucial people in the system for the change agent or change manager to identify and work with. Just as product champions are essential to provide the energy to promote an innovation through the system, so opinion leaders are, by definition, those who lead the opinion of those who will, or will not, adopt the innovation. If indigenous opinion leaders oppose the innovation then the change agent has to provide alternatives who will overcome their influence. Thinking of many failed change management attempts as organisations and social systems being inoculated against innovation, we see product champions and opinion leaders in favour of the innovation as the *virulent viruses* most likely to infect the main body with the new ideas and practices.

The discussion of the relationship between innovation and deviance illustrated how the innovator, or change agent, becomes marginal to the system through deviating from the status quo by beginning to push for change. (In Part Four we will see that it is important for the effective change agent to consciously take on and maintain this marginality.) The relationship between the change agent and the opinion leaders in respect to each separate innovation is central. The opinion leaders can support or kill a change proposal by virtue of their position, their status or their influence. If the opinion leaders are unconvinced, they will express their lack of conviction towards a change agent's proposal (irrespective of its objective value); and it is the opinion leaders who form the major links in the chain between the early adopters, the early majority and the later majority - the opinion leader literally 'spreads the work' through the target system.

Therefore a critical early task is to identify the opinion leaders. If organisations are perceived as networks of social relationships, and if we pursue the anthropology and sociology underpinnings of some of the research on diffusion, then opinion leaders are 'big chiefs' in their tribes or villages, and change agents are those who have come 'over the hill' from visiting another village or another tribe and have discovered new practice or new solutions. It is essential to understand that by endorsing an innovation an opinion leader risks losing status and credibility, should the innovation fail. The opinion leader holds this position by virtue of greater knowledge, wisdom, experience, and so on. If an opinion leader gives endorsement to a change agent's project, product or idea, then it must be worthy of consideration because the opinion leader 'knows best' about local conditions, and the change agent frequently does not. Alternatively, the opinion leader can often have a wider view, and the change agent may not. The innovation will need to be perceived by the opinion leader as 'solving a problem' that the opinion leader perceives. It is this transmission and diffusion theme that similarly explains the failure of practitioners to pick up research findings. Researchers need to understand that they are external to target systems, and that the local network will not accept the application of findings made in another area. Research findings often have to be reinvented locally by locals, and then related to national findings: this is why reinvention is necessary. The local people do have to reinvent the wheel.

Brown (1996) outlines how this understanding is applied to the diffusion of adolescent crisis family support teams in the UK. Over a five year period, these new services have mushroomed throughout the UK in response to 'a problem' in the target system - the need to reduce residential children's homes - that was well recognised by the 'chiefs' or opinion leaders in each locality.

Recently Larkin and Larkin (1996) have drawn on their own research and that of other communication experts to point out that front line managers and supervisors are the 'real opinion leaders' for front line staff, rather than 'charismatic executives'. They also point out that the best way to communicate major changes to the front line workforce is through face to face communications rather than any form of publication or use of video presentation at large scale meetings. The commercial world of advertising has long recognised the value of endorsement of their products by significant opinion leaders: from the long tradition of royal appointments of certain suppliers through to the huge sums paid to sports stars and others to become associated with a particular brand name or product.

Gatekeepers are those who control the allocation or the distribution of resources. The MIRP research included areas of innovation which involved large capital investment. In these circumstances the role of top management and investors as sponsors is crucial (Angle and Van de Ven, 1989). In social services area teams the area director also often plays a significant role in providing, or at least legitimising, the use of resources in a particular way (Crosbie and Vickery, 1989).

However, there are many other gatekeepers of resources. *Each person is to some extent the gatekeeper of their own resources of time, thought and energy*. Innovators in social work practice have often turned outside their organisation to develop resources when faced with little hope of increased finance from their agencies (Smale and Bennett, 1989; Darvill and Smale, 1990). It is also the case that changes in practice can be stalled by the way that resources are released, or not, by relatively low-status administrators. These people can be effective gatekeepers, operating procedures which are frequently obsolete, in such a way that it is actually difficult to acquire the resources senior managers have released. These actions powerfully reinforce would-be early adopters' sense of 'it can't be done here'.

Change Agents are those 'formally or informally employed to implement innovation or to introduce new methods to others' (Rogers, 1983). The broad scope of this definition and the widespread emphasis on the need for a person, or people, to consciously manage the 'process' of introducing an innovation has led us to use this term throughout the text, sometimes using 'change manager' interchangeably with 'change agent' to avoid constant repetition. We have made the assumption throughout that you the reader are wanting to manage change, that you are a change agent-change manager.

We have referred to the use of the term 'transactors' for change agents who consciously use the MCTI approach, although we fear this may be one piece of jargon too far. Such a change manager is an agent of change who sets out deliberately to introduce an innovation through a series of planned negotiations with people, based on an analysis of the nature of the innovation and an understanding of the context within which the innovation is taking place. The negotiations are conscious interventions into complex relationships between people, both within organisations and across organisational boundaries. These transactions (hence the term) will usually be aiming to 'bring people together' in as much as they need to share ideas and assumptions and to develop their relationships, so that they can behave in new reciprocal ways to enable a change in practice to take place.

Producing a convergence of ideas is a critical, continuing task for the change manager. This involves 'bringing people together' to form a shared direction, if not physically to clarify which 'problem' any innovation is being introduced to solve. Where there is wide agreement about the way that problems are being framed, then the innovation (and the innovator) has a clearer field in which to operate. This process is one that needs to be negotiated and accepted both within and across the network groups. The change manager is not only a transactor, but also a problem-identifier and problem-solving collaborator, while also bringing people together. The 'solutionist-thinking' manager, on the other hand, brings people together to inform them of pre-ordained solutions in a linear or dictate-conformist approach. All too often this implicitly discourages the critical commitment of people and fails to encourage discussions of constructive alternatives to the manager's preferred solutions.

Change managers or transactors will work through relationships with people in social networks, some of which will be recognisable organisational entities or formal relationships within an organisation. But much networking may involve linking up people or their actions in order to promote new ways of working. It could be said that most, if not all people are change agents of some kind (Waddington, 1977) and that everybody operates through transactions with others (Watzlawick, 1990), but we intend to use the term to identify those who deliberately do so. By definition 'transactors' are people using the approach presented in this book - people who analyse the innovation and attempt to understand the organisational context and its relationship to the nature of the proposed change, in order to identify what kind of transactions they need to have and with which people so as to take specific steps in the development of a particular innovation.

Process Consultants. Many management writers have pointed out that external consultants can help introduce change (Schein, 1987) and they have become an accepted part of the management scene for a variety of reasons. They are particularly valuable in those situations where the participants in an organisation or social situation are stuck in their current position and unable to perceive, or act on, alternative perceptions or solutions to the problem. This is seen in its most intransigent form when relationships get stuck in a fixed pattern which disables one or both parties from responding appropriately. We will see examples of this in the next chapter when we discuss the impact of innovations on relationships. Another common area where patterns of relationships can become fixed and precipitate problems can be seen in the work of family therapists, who are a specialist form of process consultant.

This need is graphically described by Angle and Van de Ven in their suggestions for the management of the innovation journey. They point out that:

'Along the innovation journey, setbacks and mistakes are frequently encountered, either because plans go awry or unanticipated environmental events occur which significantly alter the ground assumptions of the innovation. As setbacks occur, resource and development time-lines diverge. Initially, resource and schedule adjustments are made and provide a grace period for adopting the innovation. But with time,

unattended problems often snowball into vicious cycles. Because of learning disabilities, these vicious cycles are seldom broken without outside intervention.'

(Angle and Van de Ven, 1989)

However, there are many situations where outside consultants are either unavailable or where their introduction will be blocked by others in the organisation. It is also the case that many interventions need to take place in the space between organisations, the relationships between people from different organisations, or between different sections of an organisation, that are not the responsibility of any one party. If these different participants could agree on who should pay for a consultant they may well have overcome major dimensions of their problems.

To deliberately manage the development and adoption of an innovation is to act as a process consultant. A transactor, like most agents of change, has to be able to carry out some of the crucial dimensions of a process consultant's functions. Acting on what Argyris and Schon would call Approach II, or Watzlawick and family therapists would call a 'meta level', the transactor will be 'marginal' to the interaction (Smale and others, 1988; 1992). As we have defined it, a transactor will be part of the essential action required to introduce an innovation, consciously using this approach to plan and guide appropriate action. To be deliberately 'marginal' is to participate while maintaining enough intellectual and emotional distance to act consciously in the knowledge of what it means to be in the position of the other actors. The concept of marginality will be discussed further in Part Four.

The experience of working with innovatory practitioners and managers through the work of the Practice and Development Exchange has led us to add to this list five further categories of actors who are not typically identified in the literature.

Legitimate Initiators. We have found that in some organisations it is not possible to introduce bottom up innovation without senior managers rejecting initiatives from those they feel should only respond to initiatives from the top. There are also some staff whose attitude to authority is such that they will reject initiatives because they come from the top. There are also situations where class, gender, cultural or ethnic differences make the acceptance of new ideas difficult. In all of these situations the initiating change agent will look for indigenous people who can legitimately introduce innovations in the eyes of those they want to adopt change. Our attention was drawn to this area by some women participating in change management workshops. They explained how in their organisation they were not supposed to initiate change, partly because of their position in the organisation and partly because of their gender. They took the view that they needed to press for equal recognition and opportunities within the organisation, but meanwhile they still wanted to achieve other changes. This they did by getting more senior male colleagues to take up the initiative on their behalf.

Minders. Many practitioners and managers who innovate within their organisations come into conflict with their peers and senior colleagues. Often those who are successful have a 'minder', someone in a senior management position who supports them when the going gets tough. Angle and Van de Ven (1989) have pointed out that senior managers are often involved throughout the process and play four different roles: sponsor, critic, mentor and institutional leader. The role of minder is compatible with these functions but has the specific dimension of protecting the innovator from others in the organisation. Typically it is middle managers who try to stop the development of many innovations, because often one of their functions is to ensure that policy is applied, which often means maintaining a status quo. We have already drawn attention to the hostility sometimes shown towards 'path-finders' and the tight rope early innovators walk between acceptable deviance and 'delinquency'. The minder protects the innovator from those who would define innovation as delinquency and penalise the innovator. This leads us to the next category.

Opponents. Much of the literature gives the impression that the field contains active positive agents on the side of change and other people who are the object of their persuasive or 'therapeutic' attentions: those who are recalcitrant for a variety of reasons who need to be addressed by strategies for 'overcoming resistance to change'. In our experience, in many organisations there are very few people happy with the status quo. There are those who, while advocating change, are hostile to the particular innovation under consideration. We suspect some so-called 'laggards' fall into this category. Such people resist the innovation because they are the product champions of an alternative innovation. Their existence is one of the reasons why it is necessary to go beyond the usual strategies of 'training' and 'restructuring' to develop an adequate approach for developing new methods of practice.

Close Collaborators. These are the people change agents need to work with to introduce innovations and with whom they can openly discuss analysis, strategies and tactics. We have referred above to the dynamics of deviance, and conformity being a part of the processes involved in challenging the status quo and attempting to change it. Individuals doing this on their own can begin to question their own sanity when others consistently tell them they have got it wrong. Close collaborators are essential and they are often found outside the organisation, which is one reason why diffusion networks are so crucial to change processes.

Network Entrepreneurs. This final category of actor is of critical significance, because of the central role performed by social networks as a medium for information and action. There is a tendency to talk of networks, be they diffusion networks, 'invisible colleges', 'natural helping networks' or neighbourhood relationships as if they were totally spontaneous phenomena. In our experience networks are natural, even inevitable, but they do require energy to initiate and maintain them (Smale and others, 1988; Crosbie and others, 1989). We have called the people who work at linking people to others, those who initiate and maintain links between people and so 'make networks happen', network entrepreneurs.

Finally we would draw your attention to a recurring problem. It is easy to assume that people not enthusiastic about the adoption of your chosen innovation are 'resistant' or some form of opponent. In fact, these people, especially those who seem to agree but fail to act as if they do, are often simply *'Busy Doing Something Else'* (or BDSE). We should not underestimate how significant this is in diverting people from adopting an innovation or implementing their part of an adoption process. The need to have identifiable enthusiasts or 'product champions' is directly related to this basic problem. *We need their energy to overcome the natural inertia of people slipping back to their habitual forms of practice: the most common form of BDSE.*

From Identification to Action

By identifying the major actors and assessing their role through the above categories it should be clear what the change agent, change manager, or transactor needs to do to progress a specific change: gatekeepers need to be negotiated with; the support of opinion leaders won; minders sought out to give protection and so on. The analysis of the innovation discussed in the next chapter will make some of these tasks more specific, and Part Four of the book will describe the skills, knowledge and behaviour of the change manager or change agent in a way which describes how these tasks might be carried out. Here I want to review some of the major questions the change manager will need to address about these key people. Then we will briefly consider the impact of all these changes on the individuals concerned and how the change manager should respond.

Beckhard and Pritchard (1992) suggest that change agents should identify three major dimensions of each of the major actors:

'Do we need them to:

- *make it happen;*
- *help it to happen, by providing resources;*
- *let it happen, by not blocking the process?'*

(Beckhard and Pritchard, 1992 p.76)

We have found it helpful to expand on this and ask the following sets of questions:

Who needs to make it happen and take action for change:

- bring product champions and the next adopters together;
- help it happen: release resources;
- support innovators and change agents;

- change their behaviour in their practice;
- change their behaviour so that their relationship with significant others changes?

Who has to let it happen: keep out of the way?

Who has to give their consent?

Who could sabotage the innovation?

Who has to not block resources?

Who has to refrain from diverting resources?

Who has to avoid taking counter-action?

All the questions to be addressed are detailed in the companion volume *Mapping Change and Innovation*.

This leads us to a major dimension of working with the people involved. People's reactions and behaviour will depend upon how they feel about the changes being proposed, the people introducing them, how the proposed changes make them feel about themselves and about their relationship to others. So far we have drawn attention to the need for the change manager to draw up a map of the people and their positions on that map in terms of the *roles* they might play in its progress or demise. In the next chapter we turn to the ways that you might begin to **map the feelings of the key people involved in the process**, and how you might begin to work with these feelings rather than ignore them.

CHAPTER FIVE

Understanding 'Self' In The Sea Of Change

The processes of change are a minefield of people's feelings. The change manager's or change agent's ability to understand them and respond appropriately will influence success and the impact of undesirable, unintended consequences. But imagine a marine minefield where the mines float at the whim of currents and wind, for people's emotions do not explode at fixed points along the way. It has long been recognised that all change involves a degree of loss. In many reorganisations people lose their jobs, but even when this does not happen loss features in all change and has to be addressed by the effective change manager.

This is not to say that every change agent or change manager has to become a bereavement counsellor. But you do need to know where you are sailing in the minefield, and what you are going to do when you hit mines, as you surely will, just as sailors hit storms. If you can employ a 'mine sweeper' so much the better. Where change means loss of employment many commercial organisations make use of 'mine clearance' in the form of career counselling. Some lead the way with pre-retirement courses, and by offering opportunities through staff development for future careers (Handy, 1995). But all managers will have to deal with feelings generated by changes in practice. Addressing some of the following questions will help to identify the issues generated by some of these feelings. We stressed in the above chapters that the change manager may see the chosen innovation as a good solution to their problems but that others will see it differently. Now we can consider how many of the different feelings generated by change revolve around the different meanings the change has for other people.

What Does the Innovation 'Mean' to Significant Players?

It has been our experience that people's reaction to change will depend on at least three major interrelated dimensions:

1. Are they active or passive?
2. Does the innovation change their identity?
3. Do they perceive themselves as winning or losing?

1.   Are they active or passive in the process: are they proactive initiators or passive objects, or even victims of change?

The degree of initiative and perceived control people have in the process of managing change is crucial. A frequent exercise used in our innovation workshops and consultancy is to get people to place themselves in a line to represent a continuum from 'a person enthusiastically leading innovation' to 'a person having change imposed upon them'. Typically the former are keen to learn all they can to further the cause of their innovation; while the latter have a marked tendency to exhibit the signs of learned helplessness described vividly by Seligman (1975). If they were simply rendered passive then they might be easier for the change manager to work with. In practice, many people implicitly oppose change without declaring their opposition, but also without demonstrating acceptance. Others will simply be obedient, agreeing with the changes and implementing all that they are told to do without using any initiative or adding personal commitment. At worst they will work to rule; at best they will simply do what they are told and delegate decision making and thinking upwards. Of course some innovations and some change managers require this kind of response.

Change agents and managers should consider that:

To have the rug pulled from under you is a very different experience from coming to a decision to reject the old flooring and choose a new carpet, or to move to another room.

Those who only care if they have their hands on the rug and want to achieve change in the quickest possible way can expect to get into a mess, to meet with great opposition, and take a long time to get through or over it.

2.   Does the innovation produce a change of identity?

The Luddites were not only being driven out of work, but, arguably more importantly, their skills and prestige as craftsmen were made obsolete. The history of technological change is littered with examples of the disastrous consequences of change agents who overlooked the significance of the meaning of the status quo for key participants and, intentionally or not, undermined their position. Technology is prone to these problems as smarter machines replace individual skills, machines that can be operated by less trained hands or no hands and no minds at all. This is becoming clear to a new class of workers as IT machines take over educated, middle class jobs. But other innovations are more subtle in reframing, and in the eyes of some participants, degrading or upgrading their task.

Underestimating the meaning of innovations has caused particular problems when technology is transferred to different cultures where the meanings attributed to the same objects and actions will be very different. In the diffusion of innovations literature there are classic examples, such as the way that the introduction of steel axes undermined aboriginal culture in Australia. The missionaries only saw the axe as a tool, while the aborigines saw the stone axe as a symbol of status and wisdom amongst the elders who were the only people who owned them. Introducing steel axes, rapidly taken up by the young men, undermined the authority of the elders and the relationships within the community began to fall apart (Rogers, 1995). The differences in the cultures involved in the personal social services may be less obvious, such as the difference between 'management' and 'professional' cultures in many organisations. In the UK it is to be expected, for example, that home care organisers would see 'care management' as a promotion, while professionally qualified social workers who do not aspire to be 'managers' may see the same role as a dilution of their position. This analysis needs to go beyond what the change manager sees as being in the interests of the people concerned. It is the way that the people define their interests and what the status quo and the proposed change means to them that is crucial.

The degree to which the task changes will determine the amount of learning and unlearning that staff have to do. Some staff will welcome the upgrading and reject the downgrading of tasks, just as others will want them to be easier. Few welcome less rewards from their work, but money is only one of the rewards people expect, and to be rewarded you need to value what you are given. Some will see more money with less respect as a poor deal. It should be stressed that it is the subjective experience of the people concerned that is of crucial significance. We have come across situations where managers intended to promote people, giving them more money and organisational authority, but have actually diminished the professional role and undermined the significance of the job as perceived by participants. Attempting to change occupational therapists into 'care managers' is one such example that led to all the OTs leaving one authority, despite increased pay and grading. Morale can plummet in an organisation where staff are kept in employment and retain their salaries but their jobs are demoted. Some managers and staff will move to have more autonomy and status in a smaller organisation with inferior conditions of service.

Change managers will find it helpful to consider the following questions:

> *What meaning does the status quo and the innovation have for all the key people involved?*

Specifically the change manager can be guided by recognising:

> *What symbolic significance is attached to the status quo by key players?*

> *Who sees the innovation as what kind of symbol?*

> *For whom does the innovation change the purpose of the task?*

> *Who will experience a change in status or image of themselves?*

> *How does the innovation change the motivation of significant people?*

Note we are suggesting that these questions should be considered and the answers sought, not necessarily asked directly unless the change agent can be confident of a direct response. The skills involved in managing the relationships involved will be discussed further in Part Four.

3. What do key people win or lose?

Peter Marris (1974) has drawn attention to the significance of loss in all change processes, likening it to the grief of bereavement. This he describes as the expression of a profound conflict between contradictory impulses to consolidate all that is still valuable and important in the past and preserve it from loss, and at the same time to re-establish a meaningful pattern of relationships in which the loss is accepted. So in the management of change we need to identify where a sense of bereavement is likely to be provoked. Winning for some is experienced as loss of the struggle. It is not just that there are winners and losers, but that all lose something and potentially gain something too. Kanter, discussing the acute disruption involved in major reorganisations caused by corporate take-overs, warns managers that:

> 'Issue number one in managing a difficult transition smoothly is to allow employees to mourn the past, to grieve over their losses.'

To which she adds:

> 'The second key to commitment building during the restructuring process is getting the survivors excited about the future - offering positive vision to compensate for their loss.'

> (Kanter, 1989)

The idea that opposition to change is an irrational response comes from the psychoanalytic interpretation of such behaviour. In this framework people's 'resistance' is seen as being caused by their anticipated loss through change (Marris, 1974). This formulation suggests that the proposed change is good, probably by defining all change as progress, or inevitable, like death; and like denial, 'resistance' to it is a product of the psychology of the resister. However, as stressed elsewhere, this interpretation does not help you, the change agent, to understand the opposition you are dealing with. But you will be helped by understanding exactly who experiences what kind of loss. It has already been suggested that losses are often compounded and sometimes caused by the way change is mismanaged, rather than a response to the innovation itself: that is, when the lawn is ripped up to make way for grass. The innovation manager will only be provoking avoidable disruption by making wholesale changes in the name of introducing new policies and practice. As we have seen from our discussion of innovation myths, reorganisation is often a good example of using a sledgehammer to crack a walnut; or deliberately to mix metaphors, more like using a sledgehammer to re-mix a cocktail.

While accepting that all change will involve a degree of loss, the change manager needs to be able to distinguish between the expression of pain, which may be overcome or even transformed into positive experience if handled appropriately; and opposition, which escalates if managed badly.

As a first reaction, change managers would be wise to see resistance as negative feedback to their own interventions, and adapt their behaviour to increase support for the innovation. There are two main reasons for adopting this approach:

- change managers have more control over their own behaviour than they have over the attitudes and behaviour of others;
- they have limited time and space and it is probably best to assume that they should spend what is available building on strengths in the situation rather than focusing on the so-called 'pathology'.

Using the gardening metaphor again, we could say that change managers should focus on fertilising growth without damage to the environment and mobilising the natural forces at their disposal. We do not immediately reach for the weed killer any more than we would introduce trees in pots to replace the ones we tore down in our haste to change the landscape.

Loss and bereavement theory (Murry-Parks, 1996) suggests that with all loss eventually there are also gains. These also need to be understood, explored and recognised. But the change manager needs to beware of two dangers. First, losses may well outweigh gains, at least in the short term. Although there is loss in all change, and always gains to be made, there are winners and losers in many situations: *putting up with the loss of a problem is much better than gaining one.* Secondly,

Moss Kanter's recommendation that managers should *allow employees to mourn the past, to grieve over their losses'* is presumably well meant but suggests that managers may have more control over other's feelings than they could ever have. In practice this means recognising that it is inevitable that staff will take time to mourn the past and grieve over their losses whether it is given to them or not, and that more time may be required where loss is denied. Trying to argue people into recognising the benefits of change prematurely reinforces any suspicion that staff may have that they are either misunderstood or not cared about, and is thus a major source of management induced so called 'resistance' to change. This should not be interpreted as evidence of resistance, but recognised as negative feedback to change management behaviour and responded to appropriately.

Because of these considerations *the change manager should reflect* on the people on their maps and attempt to understand *the impact of change on all individuals, working groups and the wider social system.* And specifically:

> *Who experiences what as 'gain' or 'winning'?*
> *Who experiences what as 'loss'?*
> *How can you make sure that people have space to mourn their losses?*
> *What can you do to help people recognise real gains and build commitment to the new solutions and new situations?*

In the introduction to this book in chapter one I said that the MCTI approach to managing change is agnostic about any one general style of management. Indeed it is argued throughout that a good change manager will need a wide repertoire of management behaviours because different innovations have to be managed differently. But managers should seriously consider the impact on all their staff of loss. They should be especially attentive when initiating culls of unwanted personnel and how they will be seen to manage them. All people in the organisation, and all those they relate to, will experience something of the crisis. All will see something of its management, and what they do not see they will make sense of some other way, through second hand information or rumour. Cutting staff may be inevitable, regrettable and understandable to anybody who has all the facts. But the manner of their going can be well managed, for many kinds of pain can be well managed. Or it can be avoided, and like any untended wound its consequences can be dire. Change managers who do not look after staff in crisis can expect those staff to make sure they look after themselves before they tend to the needs of the organisation.

CHAPTER SIX

Analysing The Innovation

Introduction

Different innovations need to be managed differently

Common sense tells us that it is obvious that major changes will be more difficult to implement than minor ones. But identifying the difference between a major and a minor change is by no means a matter of size or simple common sense. In this chapter we will explain why different innovations have to be managed in different ways and how you can identify appropriate action and time scales for the changes you are managing.

To plan for and implement the effective management of change we need to analyse three different dimensions of the innovations and changes proposed.

The First Dimension: how 'adoptable' are they?

The research on the diffusion of innovations gives clear indications of the characteristics that make some innovations more adoptable than others. Comparing your innovations and changes with these enables you to have realistic expectations about the likely time scale, and to begin to clarify all the tasks.

The Second Dimension: the order of change in relationships involved

This looks at whether introducing the innovation can be done within existing relationships or requires a change in the nature of the relationships between significant people. Understanding this enables you to see who needs to change what behaviour - crucial for identifying appropriate innovation management.

The Third Dimension: innovation and time

This helps you to identify the action required to move from 'a good idea', to a new way of working or technology.

The First Dimension: The Characteristics of the Easily Adopted Innovation

The attributes of innovations, like the attributes of adopters, contain a range of significant variables which affect the speed of adoption. Five major attributes affecting the rate of adoption of a wide range of innovations drawn from many fields of study were identified in the classic work of Rogers and his colleagues (Rogers, 1995; Rogers and Kincaid, 1981). Rogers concludes that there are five key attributes:

- *Relative advantage*: the degree to which an innovation is perceived by the potential adopters as better than the idea it supersedes.

- *Compatibility:* the degree to which an innovation is perceived as consistent with the existing values, past experiences and needs of potential adopters.

- *Complexity:* the degree to which an innovation is perceived as relatively difficult to understand and use.

- *Trialability:* the degree to which an innovation may be experimented with on a limited basis.

- *Observability:* the degree to which the results of an innovation are visible to others.

Rogers (1995) goes on to demonstrate how other key factors effect the rate of an innovation's adoption. These include:

- the type of innovation-decision that needs to be made, whether: optional; collective; or made by those in authority;

- the communication channels available: for example mass media, interpersonal;

- the nature of the social system, for example its norms, degree of network interconnectedness etc.

We will return to these issues when we look at the context within which change is taking place: the third leg of the Innovation Trinity.

Stocking's research on innovations within the NHS employed Rogers' model of innovation diffusion. She concluded that for an innovation to diffuse rapidly in this context it would need to be exhibit some or all of the following features:

- *The existence of identifiable enthusiasts:* those who invented or discovered the idea, who are keen to disseminate it, who have reasonable status in their profession or speciality groups, and who are prepared to put in considerable time and energy into promoting it. Everett Rogers (1983) names these people *'product champions'*.

- *The innovation should not be in conflict with current* national or organisational *policies* or *established climates of opinion* among professionals and other groupings.

- *It needs to have local appeal* to those who have the power to promote change.

- *It has to meet the perceived needs of patients or of staff, must 'add-on' and not require major role or attitude changes, and be simple to organise.*

- *It should be adaptable* to suit local circumstances.

- *Little finance or other resource is required* unless such requirements can be hidden, or increased resources be made available. (Stocking, 1985)

It has to be stressed that *these are **not** the characteristics of 'good or 'relevant' innovations. They are simply those which 'diffuse rapidly'. When innovations are perceived in this way they are then relatively easy for people to adopt, and so for change agents to introduce.*

Managers and practitioners participating in the MCTI development programme have found it helpful to match each of these criteria against the new form of practice or innovations they are working on (see chapter seven in *Mapping Change and Innovation*. This enables them to identify a realistic time scale for their change management. They can see that a complex innovation that runs counter to prevailing ideas and policy will take longer than a simple adjustment to current custom and practice. One of the useful products of this analysis is that it helps change agents to tease out the hidden or tacit assumptions that approaches to practice are often based upon. In our experience *it is always more difficult to introduce changes that run against taken for granted assumptions and tacit knowledge.*

Often the change agent has to bring to the surface these assumptions, and challenge practices that have become habitual. This will often appear to be an unreasonable thing to do, for they are ideas and behaviour that are not based on clear, remembered reasons. We can see why this should be so when we reflect upon the discussion in chapter three on the need to recognise who sees what as a problem. People who are not aware of why they do things, either because they are the unspoken custom and practice of the organisation, or because they are based on their own tacit knowledge, may know that they have a problem, but not easily identify it, or the possible solutions.

Stocking notes that her study tends to confirm that within the NHS, equipment-related technologies diffuse more readily than changes in organisational behaviour such as hospital meal times. Further discussion of the nature of the innovation may help to explain this and the observation that innovations diffuse more rapidly if they 'add-on' to existing behaviour and do not require 'major role or attitude changes'.

The Second Dimension: Orders of Change: A Change Within the Rules or a Change in the Rules?

When we have been working with innovatory practitioners and managers to develop practice and service delivery in social services agencies, and considering the reforms introduced in the Community Care and Children Acts in the UK, three issues have emerged:

1. *changes in attitudes are difficult to implement;*
2. *difficulty of translating 'bottom-up' initiatives into 'top-down' policy';*
3. *the need to distinguish between different orders of change.*

1. Changes in attitudes. In the UK many of the reforms suggested in the policy statements that underpin our present system, for example *Caring for People* (DoH, 1989) and are enshrined in Acts such as the 1989 Children Act and included in the subsequent guidance documents, call for major changes in *attitude* and have other characteristics which the above research findings suggest will make their adoption slow and difficult. In industry and commerce the common call for managers to 'empower' staff demands a similar change in management attitudes. In the US the development of community based practice approaches to human services also requires a shift in attitudes towards 'partnerships' between professionals and others, and a redefining of the role of the professional (Adams and Nelson, 1995). We will discuss issues to do with partnerships and 'empowerment' in more detail below, arguing that severe problems can be caused if these innovations are approached as if they were incremental changes when they actually involve radical change in the nature of relationships between service users, practitioners and managers. This is not said as a criticism of such reforms but to draw attention to the nature of the tasks involved in managing such changes. We will see that *reforming policy without reforming the way that it is implemented can lead to many problems and unintended consequences.*

The experience of the Community Social Work Exchange in the UK (Hearn, 1991) is of particular relevance to these changes because the nature of many of the reforms were anticipated by the Barclay (1982) report with its stress on attitudinal change, an enabling and brokerage role for social workers and social services, and partnership between professionals in the statutory, voluntary and private sectors and members of the public.

2. Difficulty of translating 'bottom-up' initiatives into 'top-down' policy'. In our experience in the UK much of the relevant innovation taking place in social services and social work departments through the 1980s was 'bottom up', that is initiated and applied by relatively low status workers. We have already quoted the Griffiths report's intention *'to support the initiatives, the innovation and the commitment at local level and allow them to flourish'.* However, this process is not without its problems. It has been pointed out that:

'There are particular issues that arise when a 'bottom up' initiative is adopted by senior management and then applied to others as a 'top-down' change in policy. In practice, such

simple punctuations of events are almost always over simplifications of what is involved.'

(Tuson, 1984)

The mapping of all the players introduced in the last chapter should have made it clear that key positions are held by people at all levels in an organisation and that often crucial people, and resources, will be outside of the formal organisation's control. In our experience the significance of the distinction between 'bottom up' and 'top down' initiatives tends to evaporate in the process of carrying out this kind of systemic analysis. The significance of formal roles is diluted when you name names in identifying who sees what as a problem and who backs alternative solutions. The value of the formal organisation chart also dissolves when you recognise who actually controls the vital resources that are tied up, as most of them are, in individuals' active co-operation, effort and thought.

But those managing change and introducing new practices will need to analyse their innovations further if they are to avoid perpetuating some of the problems identified in the discussion of the common fallacies for the diffusion of innovations. This leads to our third issue.

3. The need to distinguish between different orders change. Neither Everett Rogers, nor, following him, Barbara Stocking, make a distinction between different orders of change. It is central to the MCTI approach that we recognise the complications introduced to the process of managing change and developing innovations by these differences. We found that the analysis of the impact of change on the relationships between key people involved in the innovation has proved to be one of the most important dimensions of our work on managing change and innovation. As we will see, it is of particular relevance to major issues such as the devolution of resource management, decentralising decision making, working in partnership with service users, 'empowerment' issues and collaboration between different professionals and agencies.

We have noted that management writers and innovation researchers have frequently made a distinction between different orders of change. Nord and Tucker (1987) talk about the introduction of 'routine' and 'radical' innovations, Beckhard and Pritchard (1992) distinguish between 'incremental' and 'fundamental' change, Angle and Van de Ven (1989) refer to 'incremental' versus 'radical' innovations. Each has their own shade of meaning in these distinctions and the suggested implications for the management of change. For example, Angle and Van de Ven suggest that organisations that value and reward individualism may have advantages in producing radical innovations, while those with 'collectivist systems' may be more fertile ground for incremental innovation. For Beckhard and Pritchard (1992) fundamental change is their main focus, as reflected in the title of their book *Changing the Essence*.

Kuhn's classic work *The Structure of Scientific Revolutions* (1970) also describes a similar distinction. His central thesis is that science progresses by two kinds of inquiry, by two orders of discovery. He describes 'normal' science as 'puzzle-solving'. He argues that, to be classified as a puzzle, a problem must not only be characterised by having an assured solution; there must:

> '...also be rules that limit both the nature of acceptable solutions and the steps by which they are obtained. To solve a jigsaw puzzle is not, for example, merely 'to make a picture'. Either a child or a contemporary artist could do that by scattering selected pieces, as abstract shapes, upon some neutral ground... nevertheless, such a picture would not be a solution. To achieve that all the pieces must be used, the plain sides must be turned down, and they must be interlocked without forcing until no holes remain.'
>
> (Kuhn, 1970 p.38)

Thus normal science works within the rules of a 'paradigm', within the basic laws and the conventions of a particular model, such as Newtonian physics.

The second order of discovery comes about when observations that cannot be explained within the paradigm, the rules and conventions of the scientific community, lead to the development of a new paradigm. Examples include the changes in theoretical physics stimulated by Einstein's theory of relativity, and Copernicus advancing the theory that the Earth revolves around the Sun. In doing so Copernicus was not only challenging conventional theological and scientific wisdom: he was also beginning to challenge the belief that humans are at the centre of the universe. These 'paradigm shifts' change the basic assumptions upon which subsequent knowledge is built, until the next major discontinuous shift in thinking.

These distinctions have a central place in the MCTI model for the management of innovation. As we have indicated in the discussion of common innovation fallacies *major problems in the ways that change is managed can come from confusing the order of change involved in any particular new idea, or combination of innovations.* A useful analysis of the distinction between different orders of change, and one that uses terms less loaded with the positive or negative connotations often associated with words like 'radical' or 'fundamental', is to be found in the field of short term psychotherapy and family therapy.

Most writers on the management of change make a distinction between different levels of change: radical or routine; revolutionary or evolutionary; fundamental or incremental. A useful way of understanding such changes is to see them as 'first order' and 'second order' change in the relationships between people (Watzlawick and others, 1967).

A first order change is a change **within** *the rules of a given system:* **within** *the existing pattern of relationships between people even where tasks change significantly. First order change takes place without change in the existing role relationships between people.*

A change in procedures, introducing training in multi-culturalism, shifting resources around within existing programmes, moving offices: those could all fall under the description of a first order change if the existing pattern of relationships between the people involved remains in place. In first order changes, the task, and how it is done, may change in major ways, but the way that people relate to each other does not. The impact of giving a word processor to a secretary is often of this order in the relationship between secretary and manager. Work can be done in a different way but the relationship between these two people stays the same. *Managers introducing first order change can do so by altering what they say should be done and do not have to change what they do themselves.*

Second order change occurs when there is a change in the nature of the relationship between people: a change in the rules, a change in the nature of the system; *when rules and the boundaries of a system of relationships change in an unprecedented way, when patterns of relationship are altered. The roles of each party in the relationship changes.*

To promote workers' discretion and judgement in lieu of prescribed procedure, to redress institutional racism, to change the process for allocating resources, to devolve decision making - all will involve second order changes in both attitudes and behaviour within significant relationships. In relationships undergoing second order changes the task and/ or methods change and so does the nature of the relationship between people. If a manager starts using a lap-top computer, it is likely not only to change the way that work gets done: it also radically affects the relationship between secretary and manager. *Managers initiating second order change have to alter what they do when they are an integral part of the relationships being affected by change.*

Different action has to be taken to manage these different orders of change. To introduce first order changes the manager may carry on behaving in the same way while changing what she expects to be done by others. To introduce a second order change in the relationships they participate in, a manager will have to change her own attitudes and behaviour. Where it is necessary for others to change their relationship with each other, change managers have to work toward *all* parties to the relationship changing their behaviour.

Introducing second order changes as if they were first order leads to great confusion and often hostility or paralysis. Consider what happens when a manager, who typically relates to staff by issuing instructions, wants to get staff to make decisions themselves and does this by continuing to tell them what to do.

This kind of situation is familiar to many parents and children. The time comes when the parents say that they are going to give their child a weekly, fixed amount of pocket money and that from now on the child can decide how to spend it. On the first Saturday the child spends it all on sweets and immediately the parents remonstrate with them that this is a stupid way to spend it. Most parents recognise the temptation to claw back freedom given, just as many children have experienced freedom being given with one hand while being controlled by the other. Young people are just as capable of demanding to be treated like an adult and then wanting to be looked after like a child. The frustrations of adolescence are what we normally call the painful process of making the mutual adjustments required of all parties to achieve the second order changes involved in going from adult-child to adult-adult relationships. For some it will be less painful to leave the field altogether than grapple with the uncertainties and ambiguities of changing roles, particularly where one or more parties insist on maintaining an obsolete status quo. Some people never make the transition. As we have said before issues of deviance, even 'madness' or 'badness', become caught up in the struggle to move from one status quo in relationships to a new one.

Like the parent who wants to encourage their child's ability to handle responsibility, the manager devolving decisions needs to stop giving instructions. To carry on will lead to the manager ordering people to take the initiative. But, by definition, people can only take the initiative themselves. *When a manager orders people to take initiatives,* or to do so in a particular way, *he or she places staff in a 'be spontaneous'* double bind: 'I order you not to need orders'. In these situations the manager's behaviour, like the parent's, contradicts the verbal message. Both communicate two things at once. This places staff in an impossible situation: should they do what the manager says or behave in a way that fits in with the manager's behaviour? Should they be obedient, or decide what to do themselves? When this happens everyone will be upset, except those who fail to hear or notice one of the messages. Contradictory verbal messages are confusing enough, but double binds come about when actions and words contradict each other, and are particularly damaging. This kind of contradiction is a paradox: a communication that contradicts itself, such as 'ignore this sentence'. Staff will often reject one or both communications because of the contradictions in messages, even when they agree with one or even both of them. For example they will act as if they were saying: 'I want to do it, but resent being told what to do by you' or 'I will continue to be obedient and so not make independent decisions'. This last example is characterised by staff who always want to check out the decisions they think they ought to make with their manager. We come across many organisations where more authority is delegated upwards than control intentionally maintained by the top.

First order changes involve renegotiating tasks and methods. By contrast second order changes involve renegotiating tasks, methods and roles and relationships.

Introducing second order changes in relationships often means changing the way that negotiations take place so that they are carried out in a way that begins to put the new relationships into practice. A plan for devolved decision making should be arrived at jointly. A plan drawn up at the top and handed down for consultation enters into the world of paradox where the mode of communication contradicts the message.

It is vital to distinguish between first and second order change to ensure that the way that an innovation is being introduced does not undermine the innovation itself. This will be crucial for those implementing the current reforms in health and social policy, particularly where the intention is to fundamentally change the nature of the relationships between organisations and between organisations and the public and those who serve them. Can staff involve 'patients' and 'service users' as partners in decision making if their managers continue to retain the right to remake the decisions and thus effectively undo the decisions made in partnership with others?

Managing Not to Manage Change: The Fate of Some Attempts at 'Partnership' and 'Empowerment'

In our experience the issues of empowerment and partnership present particular problems for the management of change. This is because of the nature of the change involved and the impact of such changes on the way that most large social welfare bureaucracies run. It has been noted in the US that what we know of good practice in the personal social services may not fit the organisations that are typically set up to deliver them (Schorr, 1992). The discussion of issues of empowerment suggests that there may be fundamental problems in the UK also. We are not arguing that policy makers or managers do not genuinely want to implement 'empowerment' or working in greater partnership with the public they serve. We are suggesting that unintentionally their approaches to the management of change defeat their objectives. This comes about because they change what they want staff to do without making the necessary changes in their own behaviour. Often they do not realise that this is essential to enable practitioners and junior managers to change. The following example and analysis attempts to clarify a major way in which changes fail and suggests the action required to achieve change, through consistency between the proposed innovations and the approach used to introduce them.

Partnership, Empowerment and the Need for Innovation in Management

In the UK legislation in 1989 and 1991 introduced a new Children Act and National Health Service and Community Care Act respectively. Both Acts were intended to mainstream many of the innovations that had taken place during the 1980s (Griffiths, 1988). Specifically this included working in partnership with service users, supporting carers of dependent people in the community, switching resources from what had been an unintended bias towards residential care so that services could be provided for people in their own homes, and greater service user choice over services and involvement in their planning and implementation. *'Working in partnership'*, both between service users and professionals and between agencies, and the *'empowerment'* of people to enable them to have more choice and control over their own lives, were seen as key values to be applied through the reforms.

The emphasis in children's work was to work in greater partnership with parents, involving them fully in decision making wherever possible, responding to all children in the area who were 'in need', and promoting greater collaboration between all the agencies involved in services to children.

Where children were identified as needing protection the Act clarified that the child's interests should always come first and that permanence of care should be implemented wherever possible. The Children Act was also intended to bring together disparate legislation that had grown piecemeal over the years.

The UK government's National Health Service and Community Care Act was designed to 'enable people to live an independent and dignified life at home, or elsewhere within the community, for as long as they are able and wish to do so'. The key objectives included:

- promoting a mixed economy of care;
- ensuring that service providers make practical support of carers a high priority;
- making assessment and care management the cornerstone of high quality care;
- cutting the long term costs of residential care for an expanding population of dependent, elderly people.

It was recognised that to implement these policies there would need to be changes in the management of departments. Social services departments had been responsible for identifying service users' needs and for major service provision. It was thought that more efficiency could be brought into the system if these two functions were separated. Purchasing and providing were to be split, to create an internal market and to encourage the development of the independent sector. It was recognised that decisions about service provision needed to be made as close to the service user as possible to ensure that they were led by service users' needs. This was to be implemented by introducing 'care managers' responsible for resource allocation devolved from the centralised, hierarchical management typical of local authority social services departments.

The Managing Change Through Innovation programme that this book is based on was designed to address the management of all kinds of innovation. But the implementation of different facets of the Acts and the development of community based practice involving the empowerment of service users has always been a major part of the agenda brought to workshops by participants. This work has been developed alongside and complemented by colleagues' involvement with service user groups looking at service user involvement in the planning and delivery of services (Beresford and Harding, 1993; Morris, 1994) and detailed work on the skills required to empower service users throughout the processes of assessment and care management (Smale and Tuson, 1993).

We can illustrate the problems of implementing these policies by looking at two overlapping dimensions of empowerment. Throughout Managing Change Through Innovation workshops carried out in the UK and US participants have found the order of change analysis helpful in understanding the tangles they have got into in these two areas. The first is working in partnership with service users and the second is devolved resource management.

Partnership and Empowerment Analysed as Innovations

To analyse working in partnership as an innovation it is necessary to be clear what we mean by the phrase. In the UK the implementation of Community Care reforms and new legislation on child protection is making many people reconsider their attitudes towards the public they serve. Much social work theory assumes that the citizen is a 'client', 'service user', 'carer', 'patient' or 'customer'. In any of these roles the person is defined through their relationship with 'the professional' or 'service provider'. The implication is that the person has less knowledge, information, expertise or resources than the professional. *The 'citizen' is not an equal person but the object of concern and so of professional attention. Increasingly these perceptions of social workers and their 'clients' are seen as obsolete.*

To move beyond this obsolescence requires a change in attitude that recognises that the 'clients', 'carers', 'service users' or 'customers' of social work and social services are in all major ways citizens and the same sort of beings as professional workers and other members of the community. Systemic approaches stress the need to intervene in the relationships that precipitate or perpetuate social problems. Thus a family systems approach has stressed the need to shift the focus from the individual 'patient' to the relationships within which the problem behaviour is often enmeshed (Minuchin and

Fishman, 1981; Haley, 1976). This means involving other people in interventions who were not originally, or conventionally, seen as part of the problem. Changing the pattern of such relationships means working with all of these people to change their reciprocal behaviour. This means working with people labelled as having or being 'a problem' *and* the others with whom they relate. As a social systemic, or ecological, approach widens the networks of people involved, the change agent is working more and more with people who have not been identified as 'having a problem' or as 'pathological', be it 'sick', 'deviant', 'feckless' or 'delinquent'.

The individualisation of social problems has enabled professionals to see the identified individual, or family, as less able than those who do not have the problem. If, as systems theory suggests, the problem lies in the relationships between many people, are we to assume that all participants are deficient? Shifting the emphasis from the individual to the family has enabled many families to be pathologised where once only a child or a parent may have been. Applying the same analysis to wider social situations makes this more difficult to do, though the idea of the 'bad neighbourhood' is common enough. But it becomes more clearly untenable when it becomes apparent that whole systems perpetuate social problems, even the experts whose job it is to change identified clients (Elizur and Minuchin, 1991).

Different people will bring different things to the partnerships formed in these processes. They will have different kinds of authority and power, be 'expert' in different areas and be able to control different parts of a social situation, but at root they are all, or should be seen as, equal citizens. Although this theory is commonly espoused, in practice many methods of 'professional' intervention and service provision are based on assumptions that differentiate between 'professionals' and 'clients' in quite radical ways. Consider, for example, the way in which it is assumed that the professional worker can pick up new methods of work from a few days training; that is, new ways of thinking and acting in complex social situations such as the family and other relationships involved in child abuse in all its various forms. The same professionals, their trainers and educators, will typically assume that their 'clients' will need extended 'statutory work' in the form of 'treatment', 'behaviour modification', 'task centred casework', 'family therapy', 'support through a package of care' or some other kind of 'intervention' to 'reduce risks to children', or what ever their identified problem.

Much applied social science looks for factors that influence the circumstances or behaviour of those who are, or experience, 'social problems'. It examines the relation between their personal or social characteristics and the problems. Outcome research on the effectiveness of professional intervention and services is typically designed to see if workers, their methods or services have a significant impact on the 'client', their 'problems', or their 'needs'. The underlying assumption is that they should be able to influence the person or their situation in such a way that the pathological factors in their past or current lives are overcome and the 'problem' solved or managed in such a way that it does not perpetuate undesired 'symptoms' or arrangements. *The people under study are not equal people but the objects of study.*

It is typically assumed that policy makers, professionals and academics have the freedom to choose between different models of practice; between different ways of tackling social problems. But it is often assumed that the actions of 'clients', particularly their perceived inability to resolve their problems, are determined by intrapsychic and/or social forces. It is thus assumed that they cannot make the same choices and exercise the same freedom as professionals. The professionally centred view of social change and social problem solving is based on this disparity of ability and knowledge. It is not confined to those wedded to individual therapies. It is also evident, for example, in Specht's critique of psychotherapy in social work and advocacy of community development approaches. His final sentence reads: 'That is how we make healthy people' (Specht, 1990 p.356).

The 'empowerment of service users' requires a recognition of the expertise and control that they have over their situation and their behaviour. This is not to say that there are not severe limitations on what they can and cannot do. It is to recognise that their ability and capacity to control parts of their lives is often obscured by their pathological labels. Such labelling processes take over when specific behaviours in particular situations are seen as characteristic of the person: when the person who has committed an offence becomes a 'delinquent' (Becker, 1973). Reframing such perceptions cannot be done without a reciprocal revision of the authority and control that professionals and others are assumed to have in the situation. These people also have expertise and some control in the situation. But this is also limited by the actions and reactions of others.

You may or may not agree with this analysis of working in partnership and its relationship to empowerment. The primary purpose of this analysis is to look at how adoptable this kind of innovation is and the order of change involved.

Partnership as an Adoptable Innovation

A quick comparison will reveal that working in partnership as described above has adoptability characteristics working both against and in its favour (see Fig. III on page 147). For example the relative advantage of working in partnership may be evident to professionals and it should be possible to try it out. But such partnerships, and particularly the involvement of service users in service planning, are not often compatible with existing values and practices in many agencies. The processes involved are also complex, particularly the degree to which there is likely to be a disparity between espoused theory and theory in practice. Working in partnership may or may not prove to demand more financial resources, but many policy makers assume that if given control then front line workers and service users will demand infinite resources to help those in need.

Using the MCTI approach to carry out such an analysis enables us to predict that innovations in this area will be slow to diffuse. It also enables us to see where the critical points are and to plan our interventions accordingly. Planning and intervening appropriately is also the main purpose of analysing the order of change in relationships involved in the innovation.

The changes in relationship involved in working in partnership with people, as opposed to perpetuating 'professional expert-client' relationships, have been described in detail elsewhere (Smale and Tuson, 1993) and will be familiar to many social workers with a 'client-centred' background. The key issue here is that to work in partnership as described above would involve many professionals in a second order change in their relationships with the members of the public they work with.

In the management of innovations workshops this issue was addressed in as much as it guided participants in how they should manage change. We were addressing this issue directly by running workshops for professionals and service users on 'empowerment, assessment, care management and the skilled worker' (Smale et al, 1993). Video recordings of interventions and practice observed by the rest of the group were used to analyse the behaviour of the professional. The origins of this form of workshop grows out of the work of Rogers (1957) and Egan (1985). The direct participation of service users is an added dimension that enables developing professionals to get a different perspective on what they can bring to the relationship. It also constantly reminds professionals of the 'obvious' practical things that undermine service users. We find that there is a dominant tendency for the professional to take over the agenda of such interactions and that coaching over time with effective feedback is a necessary form of staff development. This approach to staff development is typical where second order changes in relations are required. Argyris and Schon (1985) have described the same problems in terms of single and double loop learning. Service users also gain much from the workshops. They gain greater insight into the assumptions and workings of the personal social services which arm them as advocates for their own services and for others they might support.

The major issue in understanding the order of change for managing innovations is the implications for how the manager should act. The crucial issue is that second order changes managed as if they were first order changes can lead at best to confusion, at worst to paralysis and conflict.

Fig. III: Partnership as an 'Adoptable' Innovation

Adoptability Criteria	Nature of Partnership in Practice
Relative advantage: Local appeal	?
Meets the perceived needs of: Service users Staff Managers Significant others	Yes / maybe ? ? ?
Compatibility: consistent with the existing values, past experiences, custom and practice	No (some exceptions)
Complexity: be simple to organise	Complex and difficult to organise
Trialability:	? If you involve service users in decision making can they then be overruled - ignored?
Observability: the degree to which results of an innovation are visible to others	Maybe ?
Identifiable enthusiasts	Maybe ?
Adaptable to suit local circumstances	Yes
Must 'add-on' and not require major role or attitude changes	Major changes in relationships between staff and public and managers and staff

Managing Changes in the Rules of Relationships: Empowerment and Devolved Resource Management

Devolved resource management is a key dimension of working in partnership with service users and in user involvement in service planning in particular, either at a micro level of the individual person's situation or at the level of service planning for the agency.

Let us assume that I am the worker and you are the service user. I interview you and assess your needs and the services we, my agency, could offer. Traditionally the way that resources are allocated and decisions made has been decided by 'the organisation' and implemented through my relationship with my manager. This might be pretty loose, where there are high degrees of professional autonomy (and little money is directly involved); or may be very tight, where there are detailed management procedures governing professional behaviour, such as in some areas of child protection practice (and where a lot of money is being spent).

There is now to be a second order change in the nature of my relationship with you. In order to 'give you greater control and choice' of the service you receive, you and I are to work out together what the best solutions are and how available resources are to be used. In the individual situation this involves sharing information with you and fully involving you in the decision making process.

This issue is taken one step further when 'direct payments' are introduced. Here the service user is given the money to spend as they choose. It is clear that this will also mean a second order change in the relationship, perhaps to the extent that there need be no relationship at all between social workers and service users.

Where you and I are working together to plan the agency's services, let us assume that you are now on the management committee of a day centre: then we will be part of a group that has decision making devolved to it from the parent organisation.

At the heart of these issues is a simple equation. If I am to work in partnership with service users, their carers and significant others in their social networks to negotiate who can and will do what to help whom, and if I am to share decisions about who should have what resources from the agency, then these decisions cannot be directed by my manager. The policy of the department and clarity about resource constraints will continue to be the manager's concern and I can be directed to work within these legitimate constraints, but the content of decision making and the people involved in the process shifts across the boundary of the agency.

The key issue is that if I am to make decisions in partnership with you, I can no longer be told what to do by my manager without her involvement constantly undermining our partnership, which is now supposed to be the centre of the decision making process. I still act as a part of the organisation, but as its representative, not as a delegate. I can only engage in decision making partnerships if I take responsibility and stop referring decisions to my manager. I can only engage in such partnerships if I am free to do so, and only then can I share the decision with you. You will also have to take some responsibility for the decisions that we make and not be dependent upon me, or my manager, to make them on your behalf. If my manager continues to manage by ordering me to act in this way she will be ordering me to take initiatives on my own. As we have seen, to be ordered to take initiatives is a classic example of the 'be spontaneous' double bind.

If the rules of the relationship between me and my manager implicitly or explicitly require me to accept her orders it will require a second order change in our relationships if I am to make a second order change in my relationship with you. In short *to empower service users, managers and policy makers need to empower their staff*.

Where empowerment is an innovatory form of practice it will require an equally innovatory approach to management. Managers, policy makers and others who have typically directed their staff but who want to promote the empowerment of those who use their agency's services have to be prepared to start by changing their own behaviour: to practice their own policy.

To make such changes all have to change their behaviour. In our experience many want and mean to do so but keep regressing to the old norms. Such changes in behaviour, such changes in relationships also require coaching over time. It is common to come across the confusion caused by second order changes being managed as if they did not involve changes in the relationship. We come across few managers who would make this kind of detailed analysis, and few who renegotiate as opposed to restate what new roles should be. Staff usually experience this as the mangers not wanting to give up power and control. We suspect that many service users share this view. However, our impression is that many managers perpetuate the status quo unintentionally because they do not recognise what is involved in managing such changes and they do not have the behaviour repertoire to behave differently. Similarly many workers bemoan the lack of autonomy while continuing to delegate decision making upwards. The perpetuation of such relationships is also maintained because it is often the normal way for managers and staff to relate to each other in many of our social services organisations. It is also normal for 'professionals' to treat service users as 'clients'.

Managing the Change Towards Decentralisation and Devolved Decision Making

The director of a large social services department presents his plan for reorganisation of the department. He has drawn this up with a few members of his senior management team and decided on a 'new decentralised system' with smaller divisions giving each manager more responsibility for day to day decisions than ever before. The directorate are going to take care of strategic planning, servicing the committees, winning and allocating resources. Divisional managers are to take all the operational management decisions within the department's policy guidelines. The plan has been circulated for consultation. His intentions are honourable: he will listen to feedback, he says, and modify his plan in the light of the views of staff.

He wants advice on one major problem: in the past when he has 'delegated decision making' to his staff he has found that they very quickly delegate the responsibility straight back up, and constantly come to him to make decisions. How can he make sure that in the new system his divisional managers take all the operational decisions themselves? How can he get them to use their initiative?

Here we have another classic example of the 'be spontaneous' double bind. The question, and the written words in the reorganisation paper, communicate the intention that divisional managers and others in the organisation will have more say, be more autonomous, be able to take more responsibility and initiative without reference to the directorate.

But the director's words and actions, and the existence of and subsequent behaviour of 'his' small team reorganising the department, denies them anything other than a response to his initiative. *His insistence that they should have power makes it clear that he believes that power rests with him, that it is his to give away*.

Some of his staff will take the opportunity to act more independently. They will typically be those who have been struggling to break out of the constrictions, as they see it, of the hierarchy, and were already challenging for power. They may see the injunctions as permission to be more autonomous, and they may follow them. But far from being grateful at the 'giving up of power' by the director, they could resent having the edge taken off their 'revolution'. They may feel tricked that somehow he has taken charge of their challenge for 'autonomy', 'power' or 'freedom' by putting his own label on it: decentralisation. The director may be surprised that they resent getting what they have been fighting for. He will be baffled (hence his question) that they still see him as being in control when he has told them to take control themselves. They may be surprised that he has given them formal control - *if* he is now giving it to them. They may wonder 'what can be wrong with it?' Far from feeling that they have won their struggle, they may feel that they have been conned into taking more responsibility than they should: that somehow he is still controlling them. They can only resist this new, more subtle coercion, they can only 'maintain their independence' and 'autonomy' by delegating all important decisions upwards to him, rather than complying with the new orders and taking initiatives and being independent and making decisions themselves.

If they are less overtly rebellious, but still uncertain where they stand as a result of these contradictory messages, they will test out their 'autonomy' by checking their decisions with the director, which he may see as continuing to delegate upwards.

Others in the organisation will not be struggling for power or seeking more responsibility. Their response is to see the director's behaviour as a continuation of the status quo: they will not grasp the meaning of the injunctions and how they apply to everyday decisions. They will continue to come to senior managers for decisions and clarification: to delegate their decisions upwards in compliance with the directorate's 'directing' them.

It is to be hoped that there will be managers in the organisation who are acting autonomously and making their own decisions within the limits of their delegated responsibility. They may have technically been doing this 'despite' the current organisation. With a bit of luck they will carry on doing so consistent with the new policy, or they may even do so more confidently knowing they have the director's backing (assuming that backing does not creep into fronting).

It is crucial to recognise that there is an important distinction between changing the way some people do their work, and a change in the 'rules' that govern the assumptions upon which the work is based and the way people relate to each other. *Senior managers have to change their actions to bring about this kind of change when their own behaviour is an integral part of the way that 'the organisation' works. It is not enough to advocate that others should do things differently when they are part of the 'pattern of relationships' that needs to change. Managers need to ask themselves when advocating such change in others: how am I going to be acting differently?*

First and Second Order Change and 'More of the Same'

Throughout Watzlawick and his colleagues' work they point out the tendency for people in a wide variety of situations to apply *more of the same solution* to the problems that they confront, no matter that their solution has failed repeatedly in the past (Watzlawick and others, 1974).

They point out that the 'more of the same' formula will always fail, 'sooner or later - usually later' (p. 166), for two reasons: the first has to do with the constant changes that are taking place in the environment:

> *'No adaptation is achieved once and forever; life forms which do not adapt themselves to these changes are mercilessly exterminated in nature. In families the consequences are psychosis, divorce, murder, or suicide; in human microsystems they lead to increasingly threatening and wide-ranging disturbances.'*
>
> (Watzlawick, 1990 p.166)

The second reason is a good deal more complex and less obvious, and is inherent in systems themselves. Watzlawick points out that systems theoreticians have known for a long time that there are *qualitative* as well as material limits to the continual enlargement and growth of systems. (He describes several examples: supertankers cannot be manoeuvred over 400,000 tons; a person whose temperature can rise from 37°C to 40°C is sick, but another three degrees does not mean that they are twice as sick but dead, and so on.)

He goes on to point out that the great difficulty with problems caused by the failure of 'more of the same' solutions inherent in the system is their unpredictability.

All social systems need to be able to change their rules as well as to make day to day modifications, small or large, in their operations. But second order changes are often much more difficult to achieve. One reason is that they are not recognised as of a different order and so change is managed within the old rules, even though new rules are being proposed. The example of the decentralising director has illustrated this approach. Further discussion of Watzlawick's work will take up these issues and throw a different light on 'resistance' to change from that discussed in 'the fallacies' or in the work of Marris (1974). Further discussion of the work of Schon and Argyris will give us some indications as to the kinds of approaches to change required to actually make a difference. This also will build on the discussion of the 'explain and expect change' fallacy.

Giving an example of the dangers of human systems applying 'more of the same' to the resolution of their problems,

Watzlawick refers to clinical experience of a contrast between effective families and those with certain overt problems:

> '...families which can deal fairly well with life's problems appear to have an innate ability to make the necessary adjustments to changes in the internal and external conditions. In the so called pathological family this ability to create new rules of behaviour from within seems to be missing. Thus the system keeps repeating a (mostly very limited) repertoire of behavioural patterns and reacts to the increasing intensity of their problem with the catastrophic formula 'more of the same'. It cannot find a solution, nor does it come to the conclusion that the solution lies outside the available behaviour modes. In communications theory this is called a **game without end**, since on the one hand the behaviour of the system is governed by rules but on the other there are no rules for changing these rules (meta rules).'
>
> (Watzlawick, 1990 p.169)

We can see such patterns being played out in families where the parents refuse to accept the growing independence of their children. They insist on rules being obeyed that the children think are 'out of date' and oppressive. When the children fail to obey the rules are tightened or applied more severely, which provokes more rebellion, itself provoking more strictness which in turn provokes more disobedience.

In organisations we can see similar patterns as staff are seen to be failing to follow procedures which leads to 'a tightening up' on procedures, which in turn leads to greater lack of compliance, which is likely to lead to more mechanisms being introduced to force adherence to procedures.

Watzlawick (1990) goes on to argue:

> 'The functioning of a system depends on whether it can meet requirements of requisite variety. This means that its complexity must be at least as great as that of its environment, especially when new developments are such that they cannot be predicted and handled on the basis of prior experience. This does not deny the importance of experience for decision making and planning, but it points to the potential danger in a strategy based mainly on experience. In this all too restricted

view of reality there is no room for unprecedented events. The consequences can be abrupt, as in the example of the Arab oil embargo. More likely, they can remain latent for a deceptively long time, as in the almost imperceptible beginning of the now catastrophic dying of the forests.'

(Watzlawick, 1990 p.168-9)

The implications of these ideas for problems such as child abuse are far reaching. In as much as these, and many forms of family breakdown, are caused by such factors they are to all intents and purposes unpredictable, and so in any conventional sense not preventable. Strategies for lowering the incidence of child abuse may then lie outside of the factors that may be said to lead to them; that is, prevention is not simply a product of reducing the 'causal factors' but of moving the family system into the kind of relationships that do not involve abuse between parents and children. Would that we knew a simple formula for arriving at such new patterns of relationship.

We will return to these issues in chapter nine, describing how they can be further understood in terms of the underlying self-fulfilling prophecies that help to maintain such patterns of relationships and the steps that a change agent might make to break the cycle and encourage problem solving at the rule changing level.

From Family Communication Theory to Learning in Action and the Reflective Practitioner

We can see that Watzlawick's comments on families also apply to many organisations. Many management writers (Peters and Waterman, 1982; Moss Kanter, 1985, 1989, 1991; Senge, 1990; Beckhard and Pritchard, 1992) have stressed that organisations have to keep innovating to stay in touch with their ever changing circumstances and markets. The idea of 'the learning organisation' enshrines this approach (Senge, 1990): the organisation is metaphorically seen as an organism that is able to learn from the environment within which it works and constantly adapt to, and influence changes in, its circumstances.

Watzlawick and his colleagues arrived at their insights into first and second order change through studying human communication in social systems and, specifically, families. Their analysis has many echoes in another field of study - the work of Argyris and Schon on change in organisations, the education of professionals, and specifically change agents in a variety of professional fields.

In their work Argyris' (1982) and Schon's (1983, 1987) distinction between first and second order change surfaces in their differentiation between single and double loop learning. Argyris (1982 p. xi-xii) states:

'Individuals or organisations who achieve their intentions or correct an error without re-examining their underlying values may be said to be single loop learning. They are acting like a thermostat that corrects error (the room is too hot or cold) without questioning its programme (why am I set at 68 degrees?). If the thermostat did question its setting or why it should be measuring heat at all, that would require re-examining the underlying programme. This is called double loop learning.'

He goes on to point out that:

'...we strive to organise our individual and organisational lives by decomposing them into single loop problems because these are easier to solve and monitor.'

However he suggests that as we get better at solving these problems then so we get more frightened and threatened by questioning of or challenges to the underlying principles of the routine. Thus successful adaptation in the short term may make the resolution of more fundamental problems harder and so store up serious problems for the future.

Double loop learning is that learning which enables people, through reflection, to review the 'rules' of their behaviour, and so enables second order changes to take place. Schon (1987) and Argyris (1982) identify two contrasting characteristic models of theory in action based on different sets of values.

Model I. In this model the values (or governing variables), strategies and assumptions include:

'Achieve the objective as I see it', 'Strive to win and avoid losing', 'Avoid negative feelings', and 'Be rational'. Its strategies include unilateral control of the task environment and unilateral protection of self and others.'

(Schon, 1987 p.256)

One MCTI workshop participant called this 'gladiator-run management'. He reflected that his previous 'goal-directed' approach to managing and changing practice, was metaphorically to pick up the ball and get to the other end of the gladiator-run (the game from the TV show Gladiators) by pushing, shoving and otherwise knocking down anybody who got in his way and dumping the ball down at the other end. By achieving the goal, he was thereby winning, and the feelings of all those who had been knocked over in the process (those who were the losers in any change initiative) were immaterial.

Model II. By contrast Model II values and variables include:

'...valid information, internal commitment, and free and informed choice. Model II aims at creating a behavioural world in which people can exchange valid information, even about difficult and sensitive matters, subject private dilemmas to shared inquiry, and make public tests of negative attributions that Model I keeps private and undiscussible.'

(Schon, 1987 p.256)

Model II behaviour is characterised by the reflection involved in double loop learning and an organisation that is characterised by Model II theory would be open to second order change. Those who operate only Model I theory may make first order changes easily but find themselves locked into 'more of the same' instead of the reflection required by Model II theory and second order changes.

Schon and Argyris have shown that there is a natural tendency to try to make all changes follow the single loop pattern when in fact a double loop sequence is required, to operate Model I rather than Model II theories in action. We have seen that Watzlawick has also said that there is a tendency to treat all change with more of the same solutions: to treat all problems as if they were first order changes, that is changes within the existing frame of reference, observing the rules of the status quo.

Argyris suggests that organisations inhibit double loop learning by restricting information so as to control the organisation. Control is a central part of their analysis. They see individuals operating Model I theories in use doing so primarily as an attempt, albeit self defeating, to set and control the agenda of the relationships that they have with others.

Argyris focuses on the behaviour of individuals in his analysis because organisations do not reflect on their actions: individuals do it on their behalf. Like other management writers such as Beckhard and Pritchard (1992), he has tended to assume that all worthwhile change is second order change. He says:

'Intervention has always meant to me the activity of helping individuals, groups, and organisations solve problems, especially those that require double loop learning. I have focused on double loop issues because I believe that social science should question the status quo and offer people alternatives that have been rare or not available but that are highly valued.'

Our view is not that one level of change is more worthwhile than the other, but that it is important to recognise the impact of change on the specific relationships involved to identify the nature of the learning required to implement the proposed innovation. We also need to recognise that an innovation may require a first order change in some relationships and a second order change in others.

Change is never ending: it is not that one status quo is simply replaced with another. This has significant implications for some areas of management orthodoxy - such as management by objectives, which assumes that there is a state of being that can be reached, an objective, that will not be obsolete by the time we get there. All tomorrows have their tomorrow.

Argyris says:

'I have always seen interventions... as experiments. Our interventions could be derived from a theory and then tested in practice...the craft of intervention, therefore, means a

coexisting activity of helping and producing generalizable knowledge.'

(Argyris, 1982)

Schon (1987) and Argyris (1982) base their analysis of single and double loop learning and Models I and II of organisational behaviour on a distinction between 'espoused theory' and 'theory in action'.

Espoused theories are used to explain or justify our behaviour (Schon, 1987 p.255). The example given by Schon is of the managers who often espouse openness and freedom of expression, especially about negative information, as in 'My door is always open' or 'I want no 'yes men' around here: managers in this company are expected to say what they think'. But at the same time they resent criticism and expect staff to follow their lead.

Theories in use are those implicit in patterns of spontaneous behaviour with others:

> *'Like other kinds of knowing-in-action, they are usually tacit. Often we are unable to describe them, and we are surprised to discover, when we do construct them by reflecting on the directly observable data of our actual interpersonal practice, that they are incongruent with the theories of action we espouse. For example a manager who espouses openness may nevertheless systematically withhold or soften the expression of any information he or she thinks other people are likely to treat as negative.'*

(Schon, 1987 p.255-6)

Here we have another way of explaining the behaviour of the 'decentralising' director. His 'espoused theory' is to support decentralisation and his 'theory in action' is to carry on with a centralised system. This may be simple hypocrisy and if dishonest intent is at the heart of such a manager's motivation then staff will react accordingly. However, it is not necessary to assume that the director's intentions are not sincere. He may simply fail to realise that *he* has to behave differently to implement such a change in the behaviour of his staff, for it is the nature of the relationship between him and his staff that needs to change.

However, staff who want the proposed changes may help implement them by assuming that he does indeed intend to change the pattern of decision making (we will return to the importance of behaving 'as if' what you want 'is' what is happening in chapter nine). It is clear that people may not do what they intend to do for many reasons other than lack of true motivation. We should leave aside all those situations where it is beyond the control of any one person to influence the implementation of their good intentions and focus on those circumstances where they could implement, or at least contribute towards implementation, but fail to do so because they behave inappropriately themselves. A manager who implicitly believes all changes are incremental may assume that somehow you can add decentralised decision making to an existing command and control system. It seems that many managers assume that their identity as a manager means behaving in a certain way that requires him or her to continue to be seen to be leading, even though what they intend to lead into is a different form of leadership. A clue to such behaviour is the manager who asks 'what should a manager do in this situation' not 'what do I have to do to solve this problem?' We might call this *role played management.* A manager may not know how to behave in a different way, or not believe it to be possible or appropriate. Until they are able to innovate with their own behaviour some forms of change will not be possible for such managers.

Resistance as Feedback

Middle management typically have the task of translating senior management policy into operational practice and as such are routinely involved in organisational maintenance. In systems language, this means they have to operate as the homeostatic mechanism for the system; they carry out functions similar to that of a thermostat in a heating system. It is their job to take action to correct outputs when they vary too much from the organisation norms. As such it is often implicitly their job to resist innovation if that innovation is going to threaten the rules that they are there to maintain. Rarely is the game made so explicit. It is a mistake to assume that people's main purpose is to achieve the organisation's task. This is not just a comment on the feckless worker or the cynical manager. How many senior executives, especially in these days of generic general management, are primarily interested in the production of the organisation's product? How many management qualifications qualify a person in the production of the organisation's products or the delivery of its services? Who at the top of the organisation is driven to solve the problem of innovating, reinventing the solutions to the problems presented by the achievements of the organisation's mission? If questions such as these do not lead to certain key people being identified, then the failure of the organisation is likely to have more to do with this than a lack of 'management expertise'. Henry Ford, like many industrialists of his era, had a profound understanding of the technicalities of his industry and managed it in a way that was consistent with the changes in technology he introduced. Like Henry Ford's cars that form of management is obsolete today because the technical means of production, the market, the product and the labour force have all changed.

Many orthodox views of the management of change focus on 'overcoming resistance to change'. We have already indicated that we have moved further and further away from this view in developing this approach. The implications of the research and the analysis presented here is that *it is unsafe to assume that much of the resistance to an innovation is a product of inherent resistance to the innovation itself or the very idea of change. Nor can it be assumed that it is mainly located in the conservative nature of people or in the vested interests of reactionary individuals. It is probably safer to assume that resistance is feedback towards those introducing an innovation, indicating that they are not managing the process well and that they need to listen more to others and change their own thinking and behaviour;* to become more innovative in their innovation management. We have already suggested that so called 'resisters' may be opposed to the particular change for their own good reasons. Now we can see that the innovation may have many of the characteristics of a difficult to adopt innovation, or that the orders of change are seriously, if unintentionally, confused by those managing change.

In our experience this confusion can be clarified by identifying and distinguishing between those relationships subject to first or second order change. This often illustrates that much so called 'resistance' is a reaction to confusion over the nature of change required in relationships between key people.

The analysis of coaching people into Model II, or into second order changes, illustrates the extent of the processes involved in managing the introduction and the reinvention of such innovations. Attempting to short-cut or bypass these processes poses significant dangers.

We are aware that the approach to managing change being described here is becoming increasingly complex and by this stage you, the reader, are again likely to be thinking 'Is all this necessary?' Unfortunately, the answer is 'yes'. Kanter has said in the final book of what she described as her trilogy on effecting change:

> 'I also learned that there were no easy answers. Indeed, I conceive of the task of 'managing change' - a task that we all perform in our personal lives as well as our business lives - as a series of perennial balancing acts. We must juggle contradictions, we must make trade-offs between contradicting goals, and we must steer a course that does not go too far in any one direction lest events require an about face. We are perched on a pendulum that is swinging back and forth, faster and faster.'

> (Kanter, 1989 p.12-13)

We will challenge this metaphor of managing change as being about balancing or juggling in the next chapter, but first let us look at the third dimension of analysing the nature of the innovation

Innovation and Time: The Third Dimension of Analysing the Innovation

We have focused on the analysis of two dimensions of the innovation: first, how it matches up to the characteristics identified by research as related to the speed and ease of adoption; and, secondly, whether the change requires a first or second order change in key relationships and some of the consequences of this distinction. The third significant area is the stage the innovation has reached in the development-diffusion process. This is significant because the indications are that different actions are required at each stage and that different people will be involved in and crucial to the progress of the innovation's development and application.

This analysis will bring together two streams of research: the Minnesota Management of Innovations studies (Van de Ven, Angle and Poole, 1989) and the work of Everett Rogers, specifically his model for the diffusion of innovations (1983).

The Minnesota research programme examined the development stages of innovations within a variety of different organisations, from large commercial and industrial companies to new firms and public service organisations. They focused on the 'Initiation', the 'Development' and the 'Implementation/Termination' periods of an innovation. In the discussion of this final period, issues are considered that contribute to the dissemination of innovations, and so overlap with the work of Rogers and his colleagues. Rogers' review of research focuses on 'the diffusion of innovation': that is, the phases an innovation goes through as it spreads through a community.

Fig. IV: An Overview of 'The Innovation Journey' (from Angle and Van de Ven, 1989 p.666)

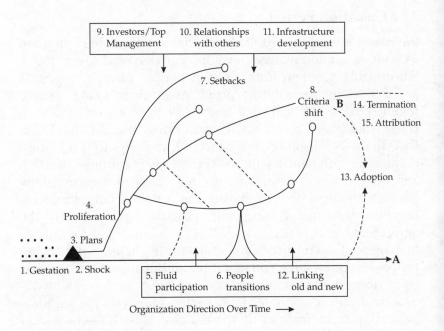

Organization Direction Over Time ⟶

We have seen that this process can be illustrated by drawing an S-shaped curve (Fig. II, chapter four) showing the relationship between time and the numbers of people adopting the innovation. In this way Rogers draws on a wide body of research to identify the significant people involved at different stages of an innovation's distribution and further development.

Angle and Van de Ven illustrate the key processes or junctures commonly found in the MIRP studies of innovation. The description of the diagram (Fig. IV) is as follows:

'Imagine on-going operations of an organisation proceeding in the general direction of point A. An innovation is launched that proceeds in the new direction of point B. The overall innovation process is partitioned into three temporal periods: (1) an initiation period, in which events occur that set the stage for launching efforts to develop an innovation; (2) a developmental period, in which concentrated efforts are undertaken to transform the innovative idea into a concrete reality; and (3) an implementation or termination period, in which the innovation either is adopted and institutionalised as an on-going programme, product, or business, or is terminated and abandoned.'

The Gestation Period

We have found this phase to be crucial for fuller dissemination as well as for innovative development per se (Brown, 1996). During this problem identification period, change managers are active in identifying problems and bringing people together. It is critical that they collaborate and gather a consensual view about what constitutes 'the problem' and that there is absolute avoidance of rushing to premature closure and premature solution formation. Solutionist thinkers and first action rug-pullers do not succeed because they haven't obtained the consensus for action. Many problems remain 'dormant' during this gestation phase until the agreement to act is negotiated. It will be important for change managers to consult and collaborate *before* producing proposals. Once some collaboration and proposal creation has been done, permission and consent have to be obtained - usually from opinion leaders, senior managers or minders (several people may fulfil these roles). Local research and reinvention of other solutions elsewhere will be part of the process of highlighting that there is a *local* problem.

When the stage of consent point in time has been reached, the initiation period is reached. It can take quite some time to reach this period, and many managers will be tempted or feel they have to press on regardless.

Angle and Van de Ven stress that the significant elements involved in the development of an innovation vary from innovation to innovation. But they claim that certain generalisations can be made that apply to many innovations during the development phases. These are summarised under each heading.

The Initiation Period

Most of the innovations tracked by the MIRP studies were not initiated in a short space of time. They had long gestation periods, often lasting several years, during which coincidental events occurred that 'set the stage' for the introduction of the innovation. Darwin's years of considering the origin of the species seem typical of the process, even though major insights may come in a flash like the falling of Newton's apple or Archemedes experience in the bath[1]. In pursuing Louis Pasteur's adage 'chance favours the prepared mind' John Brown (1996) highlights how collaboration during the gestation period increases the opportunities to respond to windows of opportunity when they arise.

The initiation period requires time for interested staff to come together to sort out ideas and turn them into new approaches to practice. The implementation of policy changes from the top also require such time if staff are to work out how change is going to be implemented by them. This is the time required to engage with staff to begin the work that we have described here as level one activity.

There is no natural end to this activity. You will always be returning to the basic issues of who sees what as a problem: reviewing the status quo to see if it solves today's problems in the best possible way and evaluating innovations to see if they are better solutions. But there are stages in the cycle that mean that the activity is less intensive.

---

[1] Managers may like to note that like many major solutions to persistent problems none of these ideas came from rushing about, but from lying down and thinking!

We need to recognise that such activities are the natural process of running an effective organisation and that they will take management and staff time. We also need to recognise that major changes will require transition management - that there will often be a situation where we have to run two systems side by side as we develop one and phase out the other. This will depend upon the nature of the activity. Decimalisation of the coinage was something that could be introduced gradually as the new coins replaced the old. But some innovations cannot be run in parallel: a production line typically has to be dismantled and retooled to produce a new model. In the personal social services it is not common for the resources to be supplied to develop the new at the same time as we produce the old. Rather innovation and change are carried out at the expense of the current practice. This is seen most explicitly in the cost of reorganisation, as we have described in chapter two. In industry research and development costs are seen as a necessary overhead. Countries such as the US, Germany and Japan and the so called 'tiger' economies of South East Asia who invested in these areas have become the leading industrial nations. Much of the management literature on the management of change and the promoting of innovation is directed at helping companies to innovate to sustain their competitive advantage (White, Hedgson and Grainer, 1996; Kanter, 1989; Waters and Peterman, 1992).

The development costs of an innovation and the difficulty of implementation can be understood through analysis using the Innovation Trinity. The hidden costs of major transitions then fall on resources which should be used to maintain an effective service. This is one of the most damaging unintended consequences of change. In the name of improving services we cut them to pay for the transition, the way that we close off lanes on motorways to make them wider. When these processes happen - and are not planned and openly accounted for - a benign critic might assume that managers do not know what they are doing, while others will assume that all policy makers and senior managers are interested in is cutting services.

However it is the case that crises, or 'shocks', trigger concentrated efforts to progress an innovation. (Darwin published when it became apparent that a rival was near to producing a similar theory.) These shocks may come from internal or external sources to the organisation. Often they are caused by people reaching a threshold of dissatisfaction with existing conditions so that they are prepared for the problem to get even worse when promised longer term improvement. Innovation is the action taken to resolve the dissatisfaction. These findings have much in common with explanations of change to be found in catastrophe theory (Thom, 1975; Woodcock and Davis, 1980), the underlying theory of crisis intervention, and the evolution of new paradigms in the development of scientific theories (Kuhn, 1970). In all these theories there is the combination of the right circumstances for a change to take place and the coming together, or collision, of previously unconnected ideas or entities.

Watzlawick (1990) has pointed out that modern biology teaches us that the decisive element that can start a whole train of new, complex developments may be a chance event of the kind which comes about at the fortuitous intersection of two independent causal chains. But once this event has occurred, the process set in motion by it is usually of an enormously complex, rule-governed nature. He refers to the French biologist Jacques Monod's work on *Chance and Necessity*, 'the two great interdependent principles of evolution' (Monod, 1972).

These themes will resurface when we review the significance of networks in the diffusion of innovations.

Angle and Van de Ven observe that those pushing for an innovation submit proposals to people who are the gatekeepers of resources, normally senior managers, to obtain the resources required to develop an innovation. They point out that often these plans are 'sales vehicles' rather than the presentation of realistic estimations of the capabilities and likely hurdles ahead as the innovation develops.

We should add that this is almost inevitable. As mentioned, there are many illustrations from the history of innovations of the unpredictable way in which they develop. We found a constantly recurring theme in the literature to be the chance nature of the innovation process, the leaps of imagination and the significance of two or more disparate ideas or areas of study coming together to produce an unanticipated synthesis (Domoney, 1992). Burke has produced several examples from the history of navigation and of naval warfare (Burke, 1978).

The Developmental Period

To bring about changes in practice there can be no substitute for persistent effort over time.

This is true for changing either management behaviour or the actions of staff on the front line. It typically took at least four years for the motor car industry to develop a new model, from market testing on to concept design through prototype building and many other development phases, to tooling up the lines and finally producing and selling the new model. This period has been reduced considerably but not without putting extensive effort into collaboration at the gestation-design stages (Clarke and Fujimoto, 1991). Many commercial organisations spend huge sums on the development phases of research and development. All too often in public services it is assumed that research can be disseminated in a raw form and turned into new practices by front line managers and staff. It is as if we believed that all you need to do is present the latest ideas in car design to the shop floor management and workers and let them get on with developing and building the new cars. Consider the following description of the development work required to move from research findings and theory to practice:

> '...designs which seem logical on a desk travelling at nought miles per hour don't necessarily work on motorways. Computers weren't enough to crunch the problem. We knew the answer would depend as much on intuition as dedication. So we swapped our designers' thinking caps for crash helmets. (It's remarkable what getting behind the wheel of a Ferrari does for your design priorities.) In a single year we clocked up an incredible one hundred and forty two million miles of testing. (That's more miles than there is between us and the sun.)'

> (Michelin tyre advert, 1987)

Who does this kind of development work in the personal social services? Who recognises the need? Who provides the resources? Is 'road holding' that much more important than the problems we confront?

The processes involved in the development phase of innovations are rarely straightforward. Typically, once a developmental process has begun, the original innovation quickly proliferates into several ideas. This makes the path of the innovatory process complex to manage. Managers should anticipate difficulties in maintaining the continuity of organisational learning from the development of new practices. The MIRP researchers found that often it was difficult to maintain the continuity of, and to maximise the organisational learning from, the development of an innovation. The major factor was the normal turnover in staff that takes place as an innovation takes shape. Moreover, technically competent staff are often working at the edge of their capacity because the nature of the innovation process means that they have little or no experience of the work at hand. This situation, imply Angle and Van de Ven, increases instability, but Kanter (1991) has pointed out that often people work best under such conditions. Our own experience of working with innovatory practitioners through Practice and Development Exchange endorses Kanter's view. For example we had no experience of discussions of 'stress and burnout' during the activities of the exchanges, despite the fact that we were working with practitioners who worked with high risk clients and frequently for longer hours than they were expected to.

The path of the early stages of an innovation is rarely straightforward. Mistakes, setbacks and changes in circumstances in the environment cause revisions in the best laid plans. The MIRP studies also found that the criteria used to evaluate innovations often shifted over time, as did the attitudes and priorities of the senior managers and policy makers sponsoring change.

Implementation/Termination Period

We have already suggested that a crucial dimension of managing change is to distinguish between what stays the same and what needs to change. The MIRP studies found that throughout the developmental period 'home grown' innovations are usually implemented by 'linking and integrating the 'new' with the 'old,' as opposed to substituting, transforming, or replacing the old with the new.

Some of these findings come from industry and commerce where the innovations have a technological component, and we should exercise some caution in translating these findings directly to human service activities such as health, social work and social services. Bulmer (1986) has argued that the nature of social scientific research is such that in the field of social policy, and so presumably practice, there cannot be a direct relationship between new research evidence and practice such as that which exists between the physical sciences and engineering. He suggests that social science can only influence change through a process of 'enlightenment' rather than direct prescription. However, this may not be due to the nature of social science but because, as we saw above when discussing the dissemination of research results and the Michelin tyre advert, there is almost a complete lack of development work of the kind routinely carried out in product development in engineering and related fields.

The MIRP studies emphasise the crucial role played by top management and the need for them to be committed to the development of an innovation. Obviously if resources on the scale involved in the Michelin example quoted above are involved, it is impossible to develop the product without their support. In social services the support of managers, especially when they are gatekeepers of resources, has also been shown to be important for the development of some innovations (Crosbie and Vickery, 1989). But many innovations, and probably most practice developments, also take place 'despite the organisation' (Smale and Tuson, 1988). Peters and Waterman (1982) reflect on the same processes in the commercial and industrial world and emphasise the need for managers to take this into account and to give their staff room to 'bootleg', that is to take time out to develop ideas for new products alongside the performance of their normal tasks. The management literature increasingly highlights the success of the companies, such as 3M, who encourage this kind of activity (Mitchell, 1991).

We have already referred above to the characteristics that influence the rate at which an innovation diffuses through a social system. The MIRP studies endorse these findings, emphasising that where innovations have been developed outside the organisation successful adoption depends upon the innovation being modified to fit the local situation (Angle and Van de Ven, 1989).

Throughout the MIRP studies there are examples of the irrational elements that influence the process an innovation goes through, supporting the critique of the innovation myths presented in chapter two. These surface again at the final stages of the formation of the innovation. Managers and other significant people attribute success or failure to many factors which conflict with the researchers' observations. However, *it is these attributions, rather than the 'facts', which influence future action within the organisation and the careers of innovation participants.*

Marcus and Weber (1989) make a very important general deduction from their findings on the management of externally imposed innovations:

> 'Be forewarned of the possible consequences of passive acceptance of external dictates by those who strictly follow the letter of the law; they may be doing so in bad faith and may not achieve the results intended.'
>
> (quoted in Angle and Van de Ven, 1989 p.686)

Angle and Van de Ven (1989) refer to this reaction as the *'Not Invented Here' (NIH) syndrome*, pointing out that it is well known in all sorts of organisations. It applies particularly to those adopting agencies or organisations that have not developed any sense of commitment to an innovation and so behave 'bureau-pathically' and simply do what the letter of the law requires.

Summary

To consider the stage that the innovation is at, and so the further development activity required, change managers will need to consider the following questions:

At what stage is the innovation in its own development:

- *Gestation: Who needs to be brought together to begin to discuss problems and to consider solutions and proposals?*

- *Initiation: What activities need to be undertaken to turn good ideas into practical proposals for implementation?*
- *Development: What action needs to be undertaken to adapt innovations to the particular circumstances pertaining in specific adoption sites?*

Finally *Implementation*, the process of developing an innovation or major changes involving a series of innovations, can be planned using the companion work book to this volume, *Mapping Change and Innovation*.

CHAPTER SEVEN

Understanding The Context of Change

Introduction

The context within which you are working is the third part of the Innovation Trinity. You will recall that we have used the word 'trinity' to describe the relationships between the three ways of analysing the innovation because when explored, they all merge into one. The adoptability criteria involve the perceptions and current attitudes, skills and beliefs of the people concerned, just as the impact of the innovation is on the relationship between these same people. So the context is mainly composed of what other people are doing. The separation of these dimensions is not meant to imply that they should or can be split from each other. The distinctions have only been made to help you explore the different facets of the complex situation you are in, and so target your energy and interventions. Understanding the context is the wide angle view of the situation, the relationship between your concerns and actions and all of the other things that are going on around you.

When we first started our work on managing change, and in the first working edition of this book, we accepted the conventional wisdom that the organisational context of change was a crucial factor. Much of the management literature is aimed at managers who want their organisation to achieve or maintain a competitive advantage by being a fertile environment for innovation. Indeed some of the leading writers in the field were motivated by a recognition that large, once leading multi-national corporations were losing their 'competitive edge' to companies from, first, Japan and then the other so called Asian 'tiger' economies (Moss Kanter, 1989).

However, as our work has progressed we no longer see the organisation as the key dimension of the innovator's context. The employing organisation is of course important, but increasingly we have come to see that relationships across organisational boundaries are of crucial significance. It may be that the image that we have of the bounded organisation is becoming obsolete (Kimberly, 1988). Certainly the relationship between the people of the organisation and those outside of it, whether they be customers, financiers, policy makers, service users, or other key innovators, are a more productive focus of attention for the change agent than intra-organisation relationships. Initially we suspected that this might be a bias in our work since we had tended to work mainly with innovative practitioners who acted with a fairly high degree of autonomy and, as we highlighted in the opening chapter, often saw their own organisation as at best indifferent and sometimes hostile to the kinds of practice initiatives that they were introducing. But the literature on the diffusion of innovations supported our experience that the networks of key people were often of greater significance then formal work relationships. Hence in this chapter we invite you to look within and also beyond your organisation's boundaries as you attempt to *understand the context of change so that you can make use of compatible forces and avoid unnecessary conflict.*

There are at least three dimensions of your environment that need to be considered, including:

- *the organisation within which the innovations are to be located;*
- *the relationship between significant people within and without the organisation;*
- *the direction of other changes.*

The Organisation as a Part of the Context of Innovation

This subject can be addressed from at least two perspectives. First, that of the senior or middle manager who wants to develop and maintain a creative environment. This environment will enable staff to be constantly innovative and open to adopting the innovations of others. The major questions confronting such a manager are to do with how to establish appropriate attitudes, collaborative relationships between staff and partnerships between staff and service users or customers. In short, the task is to change the organisation towards the right kind of organisational culture. Many contemporary management texts address these issues (Peters and Waterman, 1982; Peters, 1987; Kanter, 1985; Beckhard and Pritchard, 1992; Senge, 1990). It should be underlined that the MCTI approach is relevant to the implementation of these philosophies. Each of these approaches invites managers 'to change the culture of the organisation', which requires the introduction of a set of second order innovations: that is changes in the nature of the relationships between certain people.

Although we begin our discussion with the characteristics of organisations open to innovation, it is the second perspective, that of the change agent, either manager or practitioner, focusing on progressing a particular innovation and needing to understand the context within which the required action has to take place, that is the primary focus of this chapter. The questions that the innovation manager has to address focus on what elements in the organisation help or hinder the progress of the innovation. To introduce this discussion we will briefly review major findings on the organisational characteristics that facilitate change so that the innovation manager can identify the tasks that need to be done within their own organisation: what the innovation has going for it and against it. We will then review strategies for 'changing the culture of the organisation'; and suggest that for the innovation manager this is only one starting point, only one collection of potentially significant relationships.

Characteristics of Organisations Receptive to Innovation

Research on the diffusion of innovations indicates that many of the characteristics of innovative organisations are those of innovative individuals. However there are certain organisational characteristics that need to be stressed such as 'system openness leading to innovation', while 'formalisation tends to prevent it' (Rogers, 1983).

A more comprehensive picture comes from research into successful commercial organisations in the US. Kanter (1985) discovered that successful international companies able to sustain a high degree of innovativeness, and so their competitive edge, differed markedly from their less competitive rivals who stifled innovation and change and so lost their relevance to the marketplace. Her work substantially confirms the findings of a growing body of research and management literature in this field (Peters and Waterman, 1982; Foster, 1986; Peters, 1987; Kanter, 1989). She characterised successful companies as *integrative*, and those who were less successful as *segmentalised.*

Integrative organisations tend to:

- display a willingness to move beyond received wisdom;
- combine ideas from unconnected sources;
- embrace change as an opportunity to test limits;
- see problems as wholes - part of greater wholes;
- consider the wider implications of actions;
- operate at the edge of their competence, focusing resources on what they do not yet know rather than controlling the status quo;
- judge performance by visions of the future, not by past performance;
- work to reduce conflict between organisational units;
- create mechanisms for exchange of information and new ideas across organisational boundaries;
- ensure that multiple perspectives will be taken into account in decisions;
- provide coherence and direction to the whole organisation;
- have a team-oriented co-operative environment.

By contrast *segmentalised organisations* tend to:

- compartmentalise actions, events and problems, keeping each piece isolated from each other;
- approach problems as narrowly as possible, independently of their connections to other problems and the overall context;
- assume that problems can be solved when carved into pieces and assigned to specialists who work in isolation;
- have a large number of compartments walled off from each other;
- separate department from department, level above from level below, field sites from head office, labour from management;
- have minimum exchanges across these boundaries;

- often consign innovation to specialist research and development departments;
- allocate resources to specific activities leaving little slack;
- have each unit and the whole combine to protect the status quo from change.

In her later work Kanter (1989) points out that many traditional large, hierarchical corporations are not innovative or responsive enough; they become set in their ways, riddled with pecking-order politics, and closed to new ideas or outside influences. But the pure entrepreneurial firm - the fast-growing start-up - is not the answer either; it is not always disciplined or co-operative enough to move from heady, spend-anything invention to cost-effective production, and it can become closed in its own way, too confident and too dependent on the magic of individual stars. The key issue then, which is supported by the diffusion of innovations literature and our experience, is the ability of the organisation to be open to using information across its own boundaries, and within itself.

Increasingly management writers contrast effective 'entrepreneurial' organisations with large-scale bureaucracy and hierarchy. The new corporate ideal involves a smaller fixed core of managers, but a large set of partner-like ties between staff. There is less 'inside' that is sacred, permanent, untouchable or unchangeable, whether people, departments, business units, or practices - but more 'outside' that is respected, representing opportunities for deal-making or leverage via alliances with people in other organisations and, particularly, customers (Kanter, 1989).

According to this analysis, the major concern of bureaucracy is to administer a known routine uniformly, guided by past experiences; whereas the major concern of an entrepreneurial organisation is to exploit opportunity wherever it occurs and however it can be done, regardless of what the organisation has done in the past. It is argued that as more staff are empowered within the organisation they can initiate activities that create work for still others; the range of activities is continually expanding. It becomes difficult to set limits, difficult to determine how much work is 'enough' (Kanter, 1989).

This contemporary view of management is fairly representative of current trends. Modern theorists and researchers consistently emphasise flexibility, synergy between organisational activities, collaboration rather than internal competition and, above all, sensitivity and responsiveness to the needs of people using the organisation's goods and services (Kanter, 1985; 1991; Peters, 1987). But we should be cautious. These writers are targeting their books at senior managers and perhaps take an orthodox position on leadership and the role of the senior manager as director of change and the organisation's culture. More 'academic' writers are far less clear that leadership characteristics that produce specific results can be isolated from many other factors in the situation (Smith and Peterson, 1988; Van de Ven, Angle and Poole, 1989). It should also be remembered that senior managers have the responsibility for maintaining the organisation, and often their own position within it: functions that are not always identical to achieving the organisation's task.

Problems with the Organisational Analysis: What Do You Do?

A basic problem with the analysis of the organisation contained in the literature referred to above can be exposed by a simple question: what are you supposed to do with the information? If you are in a senior management position then you can work towards your organisation being the kind of organisation that will support initiatives and be a breeding ground for innovation. If you are in the middle or at the front line of such an organisation then you can make sure that you work towards integration and against segmentalisation. But beware of the learned helplessness that can be precipitated by global programmes of reform that set out to change the nature of the organisation: to change its 'culture'.

Schaffer and Thompson (1992) have criticised such corporate change programmes. They argue that managers adopting programmes such as 'Total Quality Management' are likely to spend vast resources on such strategies only to watch cynicism grow amongst the staff and to eventually discard many potentially useful improvements. Scott Adams (1996), in his brilliant 'Dilbert' cartoons depicting the absurdities of corporate life and in his best selling 'management book' *The*

Dilbert Principle, clearly illustrates this cynicism. As the book's cover proclaims:

> 'In a world of Total Quality Management, re-engineering and empowered secretaries, Dilbert has become the poster boy of corporate America. Millions of office dwellers tack Scott Adam's comic strip to their walls when murdering the boss is not an acceptable option.'

These views endorse those introduced in chapter one, that many of the ways in which innovations have been introduced have actually inoculated organisations against good ideas and improved ways of working.

The key issue here is that *managers and practitioners wanting to manage change well should tackle specific tasks and realisable concrete goals and be constantly aware that different innovations have to be managed differently.*

Many readers who have attended conferences on the 'learning organisation', or read some of the management texts prescribing cultural change, may well have been convinced by the strength of the arguments and indeed some of the evidence of their validity. But that still leaves the question: what to do about it? Remember our approach is to take large scale changes and identify within them specific innovations. You might see as part of the overall strategy of moving an organisation into a 'learning organisation' that it will involve units collaborating more effectively with others doing similar work by setting up joint task teams for particular projects. You may also see that front line units working with the public need to be far more open to hearing the user's voice in planning and delivering services, just as parallel changes need to take place at the policy making level. Each of these innovations can be planned using this approach and will have to be managed differently. The innovations can only be implemented if different relationship change appropriately, and the impact on different people will vary considerably.

Managing and planning change involves differentiating between the complex, interrelated elements concerned, and making connections between people and the different changes taking place.

It is necessary to identify specific innovations within large scale changes in policy so that particular action can be planned to maximise the chances of each new dimension of practice being implemented. The growing interest management writers have shown in 'the culture' of the organisation has colluded with beliefs that the management of change is inevitably accompanied by the wholesale restructuring of organisations. This perpetuates the problems referred to in chapter one as the 'restructuring fallacy'. *But it is also essential to make connections between those things that support your innovation, and to avoid those things that might block progress.*

Another potential flaw in the exclusively organisational approach to fostering innovations is that the development and spread of new ideas, practices and technology are almost always dependent upon people outside the organisation. Thus the Peters and Waterman analysis of successful companies (1982) invites us to believe that if all companies adopted the characteristics of successful companies, then all would be successful. This seems to overlook that fact that they are often successful at the expense of each other and the assumption that the competitive advantage is due to the innovatory characteristics of the successful cannot be deduced from looking at what is going on within the organisation alone. The success in the marketplace can only be identified by looking at the complex relationships between the companies' products and all the other market and economic forces at play. Perhaps this helps to explain why so many of the Peters and Waterman companies have slipped in the success league tables without obviously giving up what Peters and Waterman identified as their winning strategies. The diffusion of innovations literature places far more weight on the relationships between people throughout social networks or 'markets', than those between people within the particular units, or firms, that make up those networks.

In summary then we can see that *'integrative organisations' and 'learning organisations' have one crucial dimension in common: they are open to communication between people who can learn from others engaged in similar tasks.* Our experience suggests that this is indeed crucial. Indeed we would go further and suggest that interpersonal networks are all important, both within and between organisations and with other people in the environment. *The existence of, and the flow of, information around these networks makes changing practice possible. Where they do not exist, or where information flow is poor, it is impossible to change practice without spontaneous change from within the individual practitioner.*

Being able to access the key players identified through mapping the people as described in chapter four is all important. Your organisation and the way it operates can make it very difficult to do this both internally and across your organisation's boundaries. We suspect that no organisational form can make its staff innovate but that some are much better than others at getting in the way - and these will have to be modified if staff are to change practice in ways that keep pace with the changing world. This is not a suggestion that all organisations should be run this way. Where you have uniform products that require consistent behaviour amongst the workforce, like MacDonalds hamburgers, the opposite will be true.

'The organisation' then is not synonymous with the social context within which an innovation develops, and even less so as it spreads throughout the social system. It is too limited a concept for the following reasons:

- innovation within the organisation is often dependent upon ideas and other contributions from outside the organisation;
- the diffusion of innovations is dependent upon the relationships between people across organisational boundaries, the professional and social networks of significant staff.

Finally we should note that the study of innovations within organisations has led scholars to question the nature of organisational theory (Kimberly, 1988). Organisational theory itself is in flux, leading contemporary sociologists to describe and deconstruct the many different models or metaphors that have been used to explain the essence of organisation (Morgan, 1986).

From 'The Organisation' to 'Networks': The Relationship Between Significant People Within and Without The Organisation

Our experience of working with innovatory practitioners and managers has been in line with Everett Rogers' research on the diffusion of innovations, in finding social networks the major medium for innovation development and practice change. The spread of different innovations is best dealt with through different kinds of networks, and the networks available to the innovator will be a crucial dimension of the context for change. Rogers found that:

> '...it is useful to distinguish between centralised and decentralised diffusion systems. In a centralised diffusion system, decisions about such matters as when to begin diffusing an innovation, who should evaluate it, and through what channels it will be diffused, are made by a small number of officials and/or technical experts at the head of a change agency. In a decentralised diffusion system, such decisions are more widely shared by the clients and potential adopters; here, horizontal networks among the clients are the main mechanisms through which innovations spread. In fact, in extremely decentralised diffusion systems there may not be a change agency; potential adopters are solely responsible for the self management of the diffusion of innovations. New ideas may grow out of the practical experience of certain individuals in the client system, rather than coming from formal Research and Development activities. Originally, it was assumed that relatively centralised diffusion systems like the agricultural extension service were an essential ingredient in the diffusion process, but in recent years several decentralised diffusion systems have been investigated and evaluated, and found to represent an appropriate alternative to centralised diffusion under certain conditions.'
>
> (Rogers, 1983 p.7)

The PADE work on the development of community social work consciously used a strategy of innovation diffusion through 'decentralised diffusion networks' (Hearn, 1991; Crosbie and others, 1989). This was chosen because we believed that we should practice what we preached and match the mode of development with the message being communicated. It was recognised that a centralised 'authority' disseminating a decentralised approach to social work practice based on partnership with people in the community would be a second order change introduced as if it were a first order change. We always attempted to support the independent activities of innovators through independent PADE exchange networks and to remain aware of the paradoxes that could be produced by our actions as a central development agency (essentially the position of the National Institute for Social Work within the UK). This strategy would not be appropriate if the message to be communicated was an 'expert system' rather than one founded on a belief in partnerships between people, decentralisation, devolved resource management and empowering members of the public by giving them more choice over the services they engage with. Similar paradoxes present themselves to other centralised bodies introducing national, state or local authority policies.

The development of the Association of Family Therapy (AFT) in the 1970s provided an example for the strategy adopted in the early days of PADE (although AFT was not a consciously planned diffusion process). In the late 1960s and early 1970s there was a rapid expansion of interest in family therapy as a more effective response to child care and mental health problems. Ideas about the family based on the work of theorists like R.D. Laing (1966, 1969) had been popular with many social work students. Now the work of leading practitioners such as Ackerman (1958), Bowen (1976), Haley (1987), Minuchin (1974) and Satir (1964) expounded a 'family systems' approach to helping people, particularly children, with a range of problems. The aim was to try to change family functioning to release 'scapegoats' and other 'identified clients' from their pathological behaviour. Histories of the development of family therapy have been written (see Bentovim and others, 1982 and Guerin, 1976). (This discussion is deliberately subjective. Its purpose is not to analyse how family therapy spread, but how the process of PADE was influenced by the way people became involved and sustained their interest, despite the opposition of some members of their agencies.)

Some people interested in family therapy attended a few conferences and workshops and began to try out ideas in their own practice. There was an overlap between family therapy ideas and techniques and methods familiar to some group work practitioners. However, much was also new and presented difficulties to most agency workers. Video recording of interviews and one-way screens for 'live supervision' were rare. The resources were not readily available in increasingly cost-conscious agencies.

Here then was an innovation in social work practice that had considerable promise but required a development of knowledge and expertise which stretched, or went well beyond, available training and other resources. To practise in this way also often meant changing the way referrals were handled and the working relationship between colleagues. The practice often challenged the orthodox supervision processes and undermined the professional competence of the supervisor. In short it had many of the features of any innovation, in having organisational ramifications as to how such practice could be carried out, as well as precipitating more personal staff development issues.

Small groups, typically based on a geographic region, began to meet to share ideas and support and supervise each other's work. Training events were initiated by these groups. But a major function was the reciprocal benefit gained by participants attempting to change practice within their agencies. The ideas and support gained from cross-agency contact seemed particularly important to sustaining the innovatory drive of participants.

The further development of these groups into a national organisation and family therapy's subsequent 'professionalisation' and 'institutionalisation' is another story. And one that maybe coincides with the tailing off in the spread of family therapy as a developing form of practice. The formalisation of networks can obstruct people wanting to learn about new ideas. In the early days membership of AFT was open to anybody interested. Accredited family therapy courses exclude those without the resources to join or those not selected. The lessons for PADE lay in providing anecdotal evidence of a way of spreading new ideas for practice and supporting those adopting the innovations.

Against the background of these developments we have become increasingly aware that the *central characteristic of effective agents of change is their ability to maintain a marginal position between two or more systems or organisations.* We have already attempted to make this clear by introducing the term 'transactor' to describe change agents introducing a particular innovation. It is stressed that the core activity of those managing innovations is to engage in *transactions* with people, often in different parts of an organisation and across organisational boundaries and often with different perceptions of problems and their solutions and with conflicting interests. We will return to these issues in Part Four of this book.

Increasingly organisational and management theorists are not looking to the internal organisation alone but to the ability of 'the organisation' to be open to stimuli and feedback from outside. The theory of the 'learning organisation' is a major example of this move (Beckhard and Pritchard, 1992; Argyris and Schon, 1978). Rogers' model for the diffusion of innovations leads us to see relationships across organisational boundaries as of *greater* significance than those within. New forms of practice and service delivery are task-focused initiatives. Change agents, innovatory managers developing new forms of practice, should focus their attention on the relationships that promote the innovation rather than perpetuate constant restructuring and organisational redesign, or, as we called it in chapter two, the *'Reorganisation Above Task Syndrome', or RATS in the system.*

Managers wishing to encourage new forms of practice need to allow and encourage wider network relationships, and allocate 'time to explore'. This will mean 'library time' and time spent 'scouting' elsewhere. Brown (1996) estimates that this can mean allowing front line practitioners up to 10% of their working week given over to 'exploration and research' - either reading state of the art research, or making new contacts, or building up a wider network of people willing to give 'free advice'. Innovatory managers themselves will need 20%-25% of their working week similarly given over to working on the network relationships and transactions that support or encourage the 'permission to alter practice' process. We should note that the call to develop 'evidence based practice' in health and social services and other fields will require such space. The intention in evidence or research based practice is that research on effectiveness should be applied in service development: a particular form of practice innovation.

The discussion of common myths about innovation in chapter two and the analysis of the nature of change introduced an 'interactionist perspective'. This analysis illustrated some of the problems generated when the internal dynamics of one party to an interaction is the only focus of attention in attempting to understand the behaviour that takes place when two or more parties are together. It has been pointed out that such an analysis is like trying to understand the performance of a hockey team by focusing on the social history and psychology of individual players and never seeing the whole team play (Laing, 1969). In practice, such analysis is commonplace: the sports pages of any newspaper will typically analyse the performance of an ailing team or sports personality without reference to the skills and tactics of the opposition. In many situations we seem more capable of doing this than struggling with the complexity of understanding the contribution of all parties to social interactions.

In the UK current social policy stresses the need for public services to work in partnership with each other, with other organisations involved in social problems and to become more responsive to the needs of service users. Service users are gradually being more involved in the planning of services through the participation of users' groups in community care and other forms of social care planning. There is a broad consensus supporting these policies. They require people to recognise that the key relationship is between the requirements of the people outside the organisation and the actions of those within. This means shifting the focus away from attention on any particular form of internal relationship. Organisations should then follow and fit into the pattern of relationships required by all key stakeholders, including service users and the significant people in their social networks (Smale and others, 1991, 1992). Reorganisations of social services that have taken place prior to forming effective partnerships with others and the greater involvement of service users in the planning of services will probably be doomed to early obsolescence. This is not to suggest that partnerships can be formed through reorganisation. It is a prediction that the development of good effective partnerships will have consequences for each person, the way that marriage changes the behaviour patterns of each person. We can probably all think of examples of marriages where a determined commitment to maintain a single lifestyle leads to divorce.

The Direction of Other Changes: Going with the Flow

Practitioners and managers introducing innovation need to look at the other changes in the environment to see 'which way the wind is blowing'. The transactor will be looking for the compatibility of the innovation with already-accepted changes, to be able to link the innovations to movements that are already going in the same direction. Just as the innovations manager will be identifying the main actors to seek allies, so she will be looking at what else is changing and will seek support from the nature of compatible movements. Management writers stress the need to promote synergy within organisations: that is the parallel development of compatible elements that provide benefits above and beyond what units can do separately (for example Kanter, 1989 p.36).

Understanding the context within which you are trying to bring about change begins by understanding which way the wind is blowing and what is blowing in the wind. What other changes are already taking place in the organisation and the communities and markets it serves? What changes in policy have, or are likely to take place? What are the changing needs of service users and customers and how do they perceive their future needs? We need to understand these forces if we are to use them to help get to where we want to go.

We have stressed that *the MCTI approach to managing innovations does not focus on 'overcoming resistance' to change but invites you to seek out, and work with those people and movements that are moving in the same direction*. It is always better to adopt a judo approach to confrontation with those who want practice to develop in a different way, rather than to try to meet force with force.

The motivation behind other changes and the force of organisational authority will be important, just as the strength of the wind is important to sailors. Variable and gusty winds require constant responses from the sailor, just as change agents need to be agile in their management of change to make best use of changes in the context they work in.

Juggling Metaphors and the 'Juggling Metaphor'

A recurring metaphor that has been used to describe the process of managing change is to liken the manager or change agent struggling with all the different factors to a juggler who has to keep all the balls in the air. Because the manager works in a changing environment, complexity has been added to the metaphor by suggesting that the manager has to juggle standing on a moving platform (Kanter, 1989; Lorenz, 1992; Office of Public Management, 1992).

Movement in the platform is introduced to the metaphor to add a level of complexity which illustrates that the precarious exercise is even more difficult than on first sight. This is a good example of how a global approach to change which emphasises the difficulties can mislead. It is not helpful to try to live up to the picture of the metaphor and try to keep control of all aspects of the problem all the time. The trick is to distinguish between what changes and what stays the same, to be specific about the innovation and to understand the environment within which it is taking place. Managers cannot control everything all the time; they can, however, nudge events in the direction they want them to go if they intervene successfully. The benefit of differentiating between the different elements involved in global change can be illustrated by returning to the juggling metaphor.

In practice 'changes in the environment', just like juggling while moving, can make the task easier. Putting the juggler on a moving platform does not change his relationship to the balls; it does not make juggling more difficult. True, he may have to take some air resistance into account but the balls will move through the environment at the same speed as the juggler. If the platform was moving at the same speed and in the same direction as a prevailing wind, it would make juggling much easier. If the wind was very strong, it may be that the only way a juggler could perform on that day is to be placed on such a moving platform.

However, other more innovation friendly metaphors are available, which emphasise that *the management of innovation is not like 'juggling'*. We have referred above to sailing; others have referred to white-water canoeing (White, Hodgson and Crainer, 1997), chutes and ladders (Utterback, 1996) or a game of chance (Brown, 1996). These all emphasise that the skill lies not in attempting to get and retain control by 'wrestling and overcoming' but in influencing events by recognising and learning about how to 'ride the system's forces' - the 'water pools', the 'winds' - by identifying which 'rolls of the dice' will be helpful.

We have stressed that it is useful to break down global notions of 'change' into separate innovations, to differentiate between different kinds of innovation within a package of reforms and to look at what does and what does not change. Systems theory, as referred to in the discussion of first and second order change, draws attention to the way in which reciprocal patterns of behaviour can become stuck, perpetuating the status quo and making change difficult. An analysis of these patterns can lead to interventions designed to change the rules and to release participants so that they can move on to new behaviour. But it does not always help to draw attention to the possibility that any change will have infinite repercussions and so change everything. Such pictures can induce paralysis in the most ambitious change agent. As we see with the juggler metaphor, the relationship between the elements, their movement relative to each other, is crucial. Again we see the need to differentiate between the elements in a 'sea of change'.

'What Changes - What Stays the Same' Revisited

It has become conventional wisdom to recognise that change is an inevitable fact of organisational life, that all things are changing all the time. In practice, this does not help and can even cause great, avoidable anxiety and confusion. At worst - and it frequently happens - essential services are unnecessarily disrupted, even destroyed, as change is bulldozed through, with complete insensitivity to what needs to be retained. This is far more likely when change managers focus on their innovation at the expense of all else.

As we described in chapter two, we have found it helpful to recognise that things change at different rates, that relative to some rapidly changing dimensions of work and life, other things stay the same. It should also be noted that many change strategies - wholesale restructuring, for example - often change things that, far from needing to change, actually need to be sustained. It is common to find pockets of innovatory work, which have pioneered new practice, being destroyed when the new practice becomes general policy and implementation is attempted through restructuring the organisation: many lawns are sacrificed for new grass.

Time is the key issue. It is true that all is flux and that everything is changing. But just as it is often useful to envisage the earth as flat even though it is actually round, so it is helpful to recognise that some things stay the same relative to others changing, even though everything is constantly changing. This 'illusion' of stability may be necessary for our sanity; it certainly helps to understand the relative relationships between the various changes that are taking place when intervening to introduce an innovation. *All things change but some things are more stable than others.*

The often quoted example of butterflies beating their wings in one part of the world leading to hurricanes in another is an illuminating illustration of the systems or ecological model (or is it a metaphor?). But it is actually a statement of faith in the latest epistemology and may not be helpful if managers are overcome by the enormity of the task, if they feel that initiating an innovation will mean they have to manage changing everything. We saw in chapter two that it is important not to give up more than needs to be changed: to differentiate between what changes and what stays the same.

The relationship between persistence and change is of the utmost importance in the management of the process. Changing more than needs to be changed multiplies loss and the probability of unintended consequences.

Finally, it is important to recognise that innovation, like crisis, highlights the flaws in the organisation's structures and management in the way that antifreeze finds leaks in a water cooling system.

Problems arise such as confusion over who makes what decisions and unclear lines of accountability. A major issue confronting the innovation manager is what to do about these flaws, whether to engage in remedial activity to change the organisation, or find a way round the flaws to progress the innovation despite the organisation. Confronted with this dilemma the innovation manager will have to decide on what course to take. The scope of their responsibility will be a crucial factor in the decision. Many of the successfully innovatory practitioners and managers that we have worked with over the years have adopted the latter approach and introduced new ways of working despite their own organisation. Others have got stuck in the quagmire of their organisation's pathology.

This chapter has focused on the third dimension of the Innovation Trinity: the context within which change takes place. It completes Part Two of the book. In this we have drawn attention to some significant dimensions that need to be considered in the process of developing, transferring and adopting innovations: the need to analyse the nature of the innovation; to identify the significant people involved; and to consider important dimensions of the context within which innovation is taking place, including the nature or culture of the host organisation. Part Three of the book will focus on the different types of development activities that need to be adopted to produce change from the perspective of the policy maker or senior manager wanting to diffuse an innovation throughout a whole organisation or system

PART THREE

Negotiation, Staff and System Develelopment: The Policy Perspective

In Part One we discussed the need for a new approach to managing change and innovations and in Part Two we described how the Innovation Trinity can be used to help change agents to plan the action they need to take to manage change effectively. Up to now the 'change agent' in our mind has been the individual manager, practitioner, or innovatory team wanting to change their practice and that of their colleagues. The approach has proved to be useful to practitioners and managers at all levels of the organisation, from individual practitioners wanting to change the practice methods they use, to teams adopting a new orientation for their work, and to middle and senior managers introducing significant changes in the practice of their organisations.

Now, in Part Three of the book there is a change of gear in as much as the major vantage point of the reader is assumed to be someone who is wanting to introduce change throughout the system or organisation that they are working with. This could be a team within an organisation wanting to disseminate their practice to others. It is more likely that the strategies and tactics outlined in this section are most useful for mainstreaming innovations: when new practice and the changes in management become the new policy of the organisation or service involved. It is clear that, at the detailed level of the individual team, many of the processes described in Parts One and Two of the book will need to be used. Even where uniform practice across a whole system is to be introduced their will be a degree of reinvention. MacDonalds hamburgers are the same throughout the world and their restaurants have the same tiles and fittings. But each building has its idiosyncrasies and in each country the supplies of meat and raw materials present local problems that need to be solved again and again.

Individual change agents and staff can use chapter eight to see how they might change and develop their knowledge and skills within their teams. Policy makers and senior managers can use it to plan the staff and organisation development activities that are required to introduce significant changes in practice: to translate new policy into new practice.

The reader will recognise orthodox approaches to training within the repertoire of activities described; but you will also see that far less common approaches to staff development are required for some innovations to develop into new mainstream practice.

CHAPTER EIGHT

Changing Practice: Individuals, Teams, Organisations And Service Systems

Introduction

The effective management of change, particularly the introduction of new approaches to practice and the dissemination of research and its translation into improved practice, must be based on an awareness of the *processes* new methods (that is, innovations) typically go through as they spread. Preceding chapters have described how the nature of the innovation and the people involved will make a significant difference to the rate of diffusion. We have also seen how different activities need to take place at each stage as different people become involved in a new approach to practice. Stress has also been placed on the need to use and take account of various factors in the social context in which the innovatory action is taking place. Many of the activities we have described take place all through the innovations curve introduced in chapter three, but many innovators managing change will probably have seen themselves at the bottom end of the curve as far as their organisation is concerned. Now we move on and address the issues involved in mainstreaming the innovation, that is planning its adoption throughout the system we are concerned with.

Let us assume that a new policy has been defined, and that new forms of practice have been identified that policy makers want to diffuse throughout the system. At a national level this might have been done by issuing discussion documents, public debate, white papers, legislation and other formal policy mechanisms. However, often a less formal set of debates and more obscure processes take place to define the innovations that national development organisations attempt to spread. At the local level of the voluntary, independent organisation, or the local team or service unit the process may be even more idiosyncratic and diffuse. Our focus here is on: how can staff be developed to implement new forms of practice and service delivery; how can a new prescription for practice be disseminated throughout the organisations within the personal social services? We present here steps in the development of an approach that identifies the different activities that need to be undertaken at the different stages so that more and more people in the system will be able to adopt new practice: that is, the different activities that need to be undertaken for the innovation to spread through a system.

Attempts to introduce new practices through new policy change on a national or local level are often based on the 'simple linear' approach described in Part One. It is often assumed that new ideas and research findings can be disseminated through a universal strategy that can be imposed upon an unchanging world, and despite the nature of the proposed reform. How often is it assumed that important new ideas should be disseminated by conferences that follow a 'famous speaker-small group discussion' format? It is now often acknowledged that books and journal articles are not widely read and so people have turned to the production of 'accessible-short-readable briefings' as a major complementary or alternative tactic for getting policy proposals and research findings acted upon. Such activities may make an important contribution but they are only small links in the chain of events that need to take place.

Later in this chapter a typical S-shaped diffusion curve (Fig. V on page 213) is used as a framework for outlining the different phases in the diffusion of a new form of practice. The different development activities required at each stage are then identified for the implementation of a planned approach to the management of change at a wider community or national level. Within each of these phases change managers will need to bear in mind many of the issues discussed in Parts One and Two of this book. For example it will be necessary throughout for change managers to work towards shared understandings, that is a convergence of ideas, about what needs to change and what should stay the same. The Innovation Trinity will continue to be useful for planning the detailed interventions that need to be undertaken within each new site, and also to guide realistic time scales. We have already commented on the wide difference in expectations we have about the length of time it takes to change 'client' behaviour, or to learn individual skills, compared to the overnight response we are tempted to expect to policy changes. The adoptability criteria summarised in chapter six will still apply, and the length of time that it will take for all staff to be implementing a new form of practice, that is the steepness of the innovations curves, will also depend upon the effectiveness of the communications through the system (Rogers, 1995).

Before considering a system wide strategy for changing practice we need to consider the different activities that are undertaken under the general heading of 'training'. In our experience many managers turn directly to training to change practice without due consideration of the mode of staff and organisational activity required to match the innovation and changes being introduced.

TRAINING STAFF AND ORGANISATIONAL DEVELOPMENT

Those engaged in adopting new methods of work often need to acquire new knowledge and skills. The need to identify the training implications of new policy initiatives is widely recognised. But training individuals is only one part of changing people's practice. There are important functions that have to be carried out by managers as they literally 'manage' the process of change. If new skills are not to be quickly eroded by attempts to fit them into old customs and practices the organisation has to become a conducive context for both newly qualified practitioners and old hands who have developed new methods.

The Medium and the Message

It was stressed in chapter four that the *transfer of new forms of practice is a contagious process; that change managers need to introduce 'virulent viruses' into their organisations to spread new practice.*

It is important to address the relationship between the *mode* and *content* of staff and agency development, whether initiated by agency managers or external change agents. The *way* a practice innovation is disseminated should be governed by the *nature* of the proposed new method. We have argued in previous chapters that 'transactors', that is change agents, managers and trainers, should practice what they preach. Besides the obvious reasons of integrity, there are more pragmatic reasons. It has long been recognised that 'leadership by example' is the best, if not a necessary, dimension of management. Reviews of research on skills training and the diffusion of innovations research indicate that the *most* crucial element in the spread of new methods is access to adequate 'role models': people who can *demonstrate how* a new method of practice is done. We have seen how most people adopt a new method by *copying* peers, opinion leaders or 'product champions': a *process of contagion rather than conversion*. Those setting out to introduce a new method, be they managers, trainers or some other kind of change agent, are likely to be seen as a role model for the proposed approach. Intentionally or not, those we seek to influence are far more likely to 'do what we do' rather than 'do what we say they should do' (Carkhuff, 1969, 1987; Rogers, 1983; Smale, 1983; 1985). *The absence of an adequate supply of such people is a, if not the, major reason why new approaches to practice can be so fervently advocated, but not applied in practice*. Another is the lack of opportunities for learning through 'coaching' (Argyris, 1982; Smale 1987). Larkin and Larkin (1996) have pointed out that front line supervisors are the key opinion leaders in most companies; without them advocating and modelling new company policy, front line practice is unlikely to change.

The supply of role models is not the only inhibition to the transfer of new methods: when they do exist within an organisation they are often not used. *How often do senior managers look for practitioners or managers who can do the new job and put them in a position where they can pass on to others their experience, knowledge and skill?* The Community Social Work Exchange experience indicates that it is a rare strategy (Hearn,1991), while other research indicates that the experience and knowledge of expert practitioners is rarely sought when managers are making technical policy decisions (Newburn, 1993). Inhibitions in using what, to many, would seem like an obvious approach include 'the prophet in their own country' syndrome, and the many inhibitions and assumptions that exist within large organisations about who should know and do what. A major constraint is the assumption that certain post holders are the 'right' people to have specific expertise. This is a particular problem for the development of social work practice where managers and training officers may be implicit role models despite the inevitability of the increasing obsolescence of their own practice knowledge. From our experience it seems that these problems are more acute in social services organisations in the

UK, where there is a particularly negative attitude toward technical knowledge. In the US and in many other fields professional knowledge and specialist expertise are held in higher regard, although Schon (1983, 1987) has noted a demise in the faith in professional knowledge across several areas of activity.

One reason for ignoring the expertise of staff within the organisation is a belief in the 'simple linear' approach to the dissemination of new ideas, and simple assumptions that 'training' staff is a necessary and sufficient approach to changing practice. Here the assumption is that a new method of practice or service delivery is formulated, evaluated and if proved effective then the mass of staff are introduced to the new methods through training courses, which are typically accompanied by changes in procedures and maybe job descriptions. Unfortunately this simple linear approach adds to many inoculations against new methods being mainstreamed. A major reason is that resources are usually scarce so that training is usually short and incomplete. Again we are reminded of the assumption that in the personal social services we often recognise that service users and their families are unlikely to change their habitual behaviour without intensive intervention or extensive support over time and sometimes both. Yet these same organisations often expect their staff to pick up new approaches to practice and service delivery after a couple of days training and a few pages of practice guidance. This critique also assumes that training is an appropriate approach to practice change and it is not always so. We need to ask: what is 'the problem' that training is the answer to?

'Training' or Renegotiation of Roles and Relationships?

Any discussion of the 'training implications of new policy' should first question whether 'training' is the right form of activity.

Where the introduction of an innovation means a change in the roles and relationships of staff, then these new relationships need to be negotiated.

Where the innovation changes the nature of the task and/or conditions of service, then negotiation between management and staff should also precede staff development and training.

There are areas of staff and agency development which need to be looked at in a new light if the *methods* of service delivery and staff practice and management are to be consistent with the *message* being conveyed in policy statements. This is particularly important where new policy requires changes in the relationships between staff and service users, such as those necessary to implement 'empowerment', 'service user involvement' and 'partnership'. The complex division of labour involved in integrated agency functioning requires a high degree of co-operative working between managers, and all kinds of staff, even before thinking about entering into partnership with those beyond the boundary of the agency (Smale and others, 1991).

'Training' professionals and other front line staff to work in partnership with members of the public; inter-departmental, inter-professional, inter-group and inter-personal working: these must all be practised in approaches to staff and organisation development, as well as preached in policy statements. This should involve an acceleration in the shift from short courses for homogeneous groups, to workbased workshops and development exercises for heterogeneous staff groups within an agency, and across agency and professional boundaries, particularly for those people working with the same clients or geographical community. To provide optimum learning, be sufficiently open about the negotiations involved, and demonstrate partnership, much staff and organisation development should take place in situ, using consultants/ trainers with existing worker groups.

In the UK during the 1980s, a fundamental issue which permeated the early Community Social Work Exchange debates was the Barclay report's emphasis on the need for a 'change of attitude' among those practising and managing social work and social services delivery (Barclay, 1982). This same issue is still relevant to the implementation of the spirit of the recent Acts in the UK as it is in the development of community based-decategorised practice in the US. This centres on the recognition of the often overlooked fact that the vast majority of people have their needs met by relatives, friends, neighbours or other people in the community; that the professional social services are not at the centre of community care; and that they can only be fully effective through partnerships with the public they seek to serve.

In the UK the importance of achieving changes in attitude was made even more crucial by the intentions of the NHS and Community Care and Children Acts at the beginning of the 1990s. These included:

- the fundamental emphasis on 'partnership' and 'greater choice';

- seeing social workers and other social services staff as brokers, linking those in need to resources in the community and the commercial sector, or as 'gatekeepers' of care rather than primary care givers through their 'casework' or agency service provision;

- the recognition that *service users', clients' and carers' own definitions of their needs should be at the forefront of service delivery*, and that the range of services from which *they* should choose should be expanded;

- the need to understand local and area needs and resources as perceived by all groups in the community, to engage in community care planning and 'social care planning' for all groups of service users and providers (see Smale and others, 1991).

We saw in chapter four why some of these reforms of practice present complicated change management issues in our discussion of first and second order change in the relationships between the key people concerned. Now, against that background, we should ask the question: is 'training' the right term, the right form of activity to be used to introduce such changes?

Because of the probability of changing key roles and relationships, any discussion of the 'training implications of new policy' should question whether 'training' is the right term to be applied. It is a term which often implies, amongst other things, technical expertise to be used by staff *on* ordinary people rather than working *with* them; a neutral value stance where values are being changed; and an absence of political judgements where power and authority relations are an integral issue at stake.

The request to 'train' staff to work in partnership with citizens and to collaborate with other agencies can mean attempting to get groups of workers to adopt different attitudes towards the public. It also involves a new mode of organisation and a different set of working relationships with other groups of staff as defined by senior management, a political group controlling the department, or a section of workers within an organisation. 'Training' as a way of getting subordinates or colleagues to accept 'management policy' has become a commonplace in many organisations, including social services and other social work agencies. There is a danger that this approach suffers from the problems described in chapter four: a 'second order change' is introduced as if it were a 'first order change' of instructions. This is a crucial dimension of policy changes designed to empower clients and their carers. *If workers are to empower people, politicians and senior managers have to empower them to make decisions at local level, in partnership with clients, their carers and other people in the community.*

It is probably more effective, and certainly more honest, for managers to *negotiate* changes of attitudes and policy with staff rather than set them up as 'training events'. The use of outside consultants, often called 'trainers', may be vital to this process but should not then cause the process to be called 'training'. These distinctions are also important in inter-agency working. For example 'training' nurses and social workers in each other's 'roles and functions' is put forward as a way of achieving collaboration. It will be more effective to recognise that role relationships have to be negotiated by both sides. An alternative might be to get nurses and social workers together to *negotiate* who can best do what at a local level; how they can communicate to achieve their separate and joint goals; and to 'train' them in negotiation skills. To involve service users, carers and other family members in these negotiations would be appropriate, to ensure that they receive the service from the people or professionals they want to interact with. We know that different service users want different people to help them with different aspects of their care (Sinclair and others, 1988). They are, after all, usually the final arbiters of the quality of service. It has been argued that two way negotiations between professionals should normally be replaced by three way negotiations involving those receiving services (Domoney, Smale and Warwick, 1989).

Negotiations Between People to Establish New Relationships

Managers introducing changes in policy will need to recognise whose conditions of service are affected and identify the relationships that need to change. They will then be in a position to decide who has to carry out what negotiations with whom, to get agreement for changes in working practices and changes in significant relationships. Policy makers, or development agencies planning for the dissemination of new methods of practice, will need to make distinctions of this nature if they are to avoid staff and others feeling that they have been denied their contribution to decision making. As we saw in chapter one, this may be appropriate or practical, but it will cause significant problems if staff can decide how decisions are to be implemented. Most innovations and proposed changes in policy have implications beyond the skill level of the individuals involved. A staff development strategy based entirely on individual skills can at best only be a partial solution. Experience of a variety of development activities, particularly consultancy in agencies, has highlighted the confusion that exists over these issues. The boundaries are, of course, difficult to draw in practice, but six types of event, or modes of staff and agency development, can be identified that are often loosely referred to as 'training'.

SIX MODES OF AGENCY AND STAFF DEVELOPMENT

1. Consciousness Raising Events
2. Training Courses in Specific Skills, or Aspects of Service Delivery
3. Workbased Learning Programmes
4. Team Building Workshops
5. Workshops on Interdisciplinary Working: Developing Partnerships at Local Level
6. Organisation Design.

1. Consciousness Raising Events

1.a. Conferences and forum discussions. These are best used to illustrate the major dimensions of a new approach to practice, new policy initiatives or major research findings. The major advantages of an innovation and its achievements as demonstrated by early evaluations can be communicated to a wide variety of audiences. The uninitiated or the uninvolved can be informed of what the choices are. These events complement, and introduce people to, literature about practice experience and research. *They are only the very first step in the spread of a new method, promoting knowledge about what could be done.* Diffusion of innovations research indicates that these events influence other innovators and 'early adopters' and have little impact on others (Rogers, 1983). They are important for informing 'product champions' and giving them the opportunity to compare notes. These events should be targeted on these people and the 'opinion leaders' in the area of concern.

Consciousness raising events also include exchanges between experienced innovatory practitioners and managers. There is a need for information and sharing of ideas amongst the initiated. This helps them develop the conceptual and theoretical base for new developments and the technology of new practice and approaches to management. These events are often targeted at senior managers on the assumption that they will then 'cascade' information back in their organisations. 'Product champions' and potential early adopters are more likely to want to attend such gatherings and make better use of the information, and the contacts they make.

Such targeted recruitment is easier said than done. In a major dissemination exercise undertaken for the DHSS we attempted to recruit to a series of conference events people keen to develop child care practices and policy within their agencies (Smale and Vernon, 1986). But many of those *sent* were chosen by their departments on the basis of their job descriptions, irrespective of their motivation to reform practice.

It seemed that many of the participating authorities assumed that the cascade fallacy would work, even though only one of eleven authorities followed up had made any deliberate attempt to learn from the delegates who attended the conferences. There were at least as many sceptics as open minds or sympathisers at these events. Events that could have given ammunition and support to agency change agents may well have ended in arming their opposition.

1.b. Experienced practitioner manager forums. There is a need for information and sharing of ideas amongst the initiated, not just to fuel other training activities but also to develop the conceptual and theoretical base for new developments in practice, services delivery and management. Just as conferences and forum discussions will attract 'product champions', so these exchange activities are the key arena for innovators. They will gain considerably from such activities, both in arming themselves with appropriate information and through the support of like minded peers. These activities have been crucial for initiating and expanding network activities in the Practice and Development Exchange and other NISW development activities.

If there is to be a significant change in the relationship between professionals in the personal social services and the public, the membership of many of these exchanges need to include all those forming the new *partnerships* in practice (Smale and others, 1989). Involving service users in conferences and exchange forums on community care excites surprise and consternation amongst some management and practitioner participants. Some believe that partnership is best when put into practice by others.

2. Training Events

This includes the short course and skills workshop format of a few days length, extending up to longer term training packages through the spectrum to post qualifying courses. These events can be targeted at particular areas.

2.a. Specific skills and knowledge areas. Particular staff groups frequently need to develop skills and knowledge in specific areas to implement innovation. Within the social services skill areas could include: assessment skills, assessing community needs and resources, group work and inter-group work aimed at 'client', carer and resident groups; holding meetings which involve a wide spectrum of people; neighbourhood working skills; workload management; all aspects of working with volunteers; inter-professional working; local social care planning; negotiation skills inside and outside the agency; recording work and monitoring the impact of their interventions, and so on. 'Competencies' underlying some of these areas have been identified in

Empowerment, Assessment, Care Management and the Skilled Worker (Smale, Tuson and others, 1992). Other fields will have their own areas of technical expertise and knowledge to underpin evidence based practices.

2.b. Innovatory aspects of service. Knowledge and the experience of innovators needs to be passed on to individual workers and implemented in their teams. In the social services this could include, for example, 'caring for the carers' strategies, mobilising client networks, setting up different kinds of day-centre facilities, using street wardens, joint assessment with primary health care teams for preventive action, local participation in decision making, and so on. In other fields new technologies, new equipment and new approaches to customer service will require targeted staff skill and knowledge development.

In our experience staff are hungry to hear how they might set about developing their skills and knowledge. Typically, they feel ill-equipped by their previous training and experience to get into 'high stress' areas of work and those areas that take them beyond one-to-one working with 'client'-labelled members of the community (Newburn, 1992; Sinclair and others, 1988). They are significantly less keen to examine and change the basic assumptions upon which their practice has been based and this is precisely what is often required by a significant change in attitude or role.

Short courses are rarely sufficient to tackle the issues involved in basic assumptions and attitudes. A degree of security in the workplace is required so that the new behaviour involved can be experimented with in a situation where feedback from observing colleagues can be given over time. Short courses have other shortcomings. Many course members report being 'up against terrific resistance' in their agencies. Taking individuals, or even small groups, out of their setting is like 'taking clients into care' and as such, perhaps, the antithesis of basic assumptions underpinning systemic approaches to social problems and working through partnerships with the public and between agencies. This mode of training is easily understandable and, even in these hard financial times, reasonably convenient for employing agencies, but although the impact on the individual may be enormous this may not be reflected in a change in the performance of the agency.

The role of the line manager is critical. The manager or team leader can either endorse, support and enhance any new learning, or oppose, block and otherwise extinguish any new development. Front line managers are typically the key opinion leaders in an organisation for the staff performing mainline tasks (Larkin and Larkin, 1996). Learning is a slow and longer term activity and needs a service development supervision approach for it to continue (Brown, 1996). There needs to be time for discussion, research analysis and practice (in the sense of trial and error learning) and there needs to be an infrastructure of support materials, mentors and so on. Brown (1996) identifies how this is supported by an organic growth metaphor where gardening concepts of new shoots, fertile ground, soil condition, are more meaningful; and in the same vein at least one director of social services in the UK has coined the phrase 'change is not a training event' (Lauerman, 1992).

3. Workbased Learning Programmes

There is a growing awareness of the value of workbased learning groups. These can be led by managers, staff led or involve external consultants and trainers. They can use distance learning materials and/or be based around accredited programmes within the agency as a learning centre or linked to college programmes. The key issue is that the day to day practice of staff and managers is reviewed and is the focus of new learning. This helps overcome the major problem of the application of new learning experienced in many orthodox, college based training programmes (Darvill, 1997a, 1997b). Team building and inter-disciplinary working workshops can be seen as important dimensions of such programmes.

4. Workshops on Team Building

Within this discussion we are not only referring to the 'team' as the group of staff that report to a manager or 'team leader'; or those who work within a particular geographical area. Our working definition is as follows:

A 'team' is a group of people whose combined efforts are required to complete the whole of a task.

There are many reasons why staff need to work effectively together, particularly where the tasks undertaken involve a series of people. Collaborative approaches to social services delivery and practice embrace the functions of the whole agency and partnerships with health and other professionals, other agencies and organisations, and members of the public. It has become fashionable to talk about 'virtual organisations', referring to those staff grouped together from different organisations to carry out particular jobs. The use of the term 'team', be it agency or inter-agency team, is used here to cover the same function without implying that some new, high tech entity has entered the system.

Specialisation, the division of labour to make the best collective impact, *requires a higher degree of collaborative working*, teamwork, *than generic, one-to-one practice* which can be, and often is, maintained by a 'private practice', 'treatment' approach (Smale and others, 1991). Training the individual fits such privatised practice. But it is inadequate where collaborative working is the norm and is an incomplete, if not actually obsolete, form of staff development for staff who are expected to work in partnership with others and in multidisciplinary teams. It may be necessary to look explicitly at how people are relating to each other as one part of 'team building'. But for many teams, team building will be focused on their shared tasks. Teams, however constituted, have to work together on how they are going to identify their goals and tasks, draw up priorities consistent with agency policy, divide their effort and relate to each other, so that their customers and more distant colleagues do not experience their 'help' as a chronic series of well-meaning beginnings with different people. They should also jointly monitor the impact of their efforts.

Different methods and approaches to 'training' are best carried out as part of a strategy of team development. Workload management, assessing community needs, group work and inter-group skills, are examples of areas of professional development that are often new to all of the team and are best developed within the team context. These are not just *aids* to collaborative working but an essential part of putting collaborative working into practice. For example, if we consider care or case management: *'a package of care is not a bundle of inanimate goods; it is a team of people'* (Smale, Tuson and others, 1992).

One strategy for approaching 'team building' is to train 'team leaders' in team building skills. This is best seen as a partial solution. An alternative strategy is to use consultants to work on the actual relationship between team leaders and their teams as needed. 'Consultancy' can be provided by professional peers *outside* of the immediate team or agency, be formally arranged, or operate through more informal relationships. Examples of this kind of development work can be found in the work of the Community Social Work Exchange and other PADE activities. The Consultancy Development programme piloted the use of 'expert' practitioners and managers with hands on experience in one agency giving consultancy to peers in other organisations. It was developed through a recognition that 'experts' in innovatory practice needed to develop their consultancy skills to pass on their knowledge to others. PADE and other NISW networks have been a source of informal 'consultancy' for participants (Hearn, 1991).

Another approach is to manage the team as a 'learning set' where action-learning and social-learning evaluations are approaches used to consider where the team is at in its own stage of development. The team itself (an anthropomorphic metaphor) can be perceived as the 'service innovation' that responds to a problem area, that is the team's practice is in a constant state of innovative development as 'it' attempts to improve how it 'solves' predictable social problems (Brown, 1996; Connell and others, 1995).

5. Workshops on Inter-Disciplinary Working: Developing Partnerships at Local Level

Where boundaries are drawn around a 'team' is idiosyncratic if not arbitrary, and often dependent on historical accident. Are home helps in or out of social services area teams? Are residential, day care and field work in a geographical location all part of 'a team'? The answers to these questions are dependent upon local circumstances and activities. Over recent years in many UK local authority social services departments the above staff have been divided into 'purchaser' and 'provider' divisions of the organisation. This was based on a theory of how business should be done, rather than a theory of how the shared care tasks of working with service users and their families are best carried out. There can be no clear distinction between 'team building' and 'inter-disciplinary working'. Just as team building is central to developing new approaches to community care and partnerships in practice, then so it is with inter-disciplinary working (Smale and Tuson, 1988; Smale and others, 1991; Smale, Tuson and others, 1992).

All the arguments put forward for team development similarly apply to inter-agency and inter-disciplinary working. Different staff have to negotiate who should do what with whom, based on the actual levels of skill, knowledge and resources that exist at the local level, rather than formalised distinctions or stereotyped pictures of what each other can or should contribute. A review of the development needs of staff in health and social services who adopted a community orientated approach, stressed that there are at least three parties to any effective partnership: one or more professionals, service users and their carers (Domoney, Smale and Warwick, 1989). People can be prepared by orthodox training, but it is much more likely, in our experience, that practice will be changed when development work takes place within and between agencies and which directly involves patients and service users. This should be designed to give staff the opportunity to re-examine their actual working roles and relationships and negotiate how needs can best be met by combining their existing resources with those of members of the public.

6. Organisation Design

All of the above activities could correctly be referred to as 'organisation development'. There is an important distinction between those activities that focus on developing the knowledge, skills or competency of the staff and their ability to work with each other effectively; and issues of organisational design. We are increasingly aware of the tendency of some managers to be preoccupied with systems design activities at the expense of other dimensions of management, leading to some organisations being constantly restructured, reorganised or reconfigured. Organisation design here refers to reallocating staff and redefining management accountability, expanding or reducing staff and other resources as the task changes.

Discussing *the fallacy that new ways of working have to be led by restructuring,* we drew attention to the fact that some innovations were changes in the structure of the organisation, and that changes in practice, that is innovations, will often have organisational consequences. This is particularly true where the innovation can only take place through a change in the nature of the relationships between key people: a second order change. The example of 'empowerment' or partnerships in practice discussed in chapter five is a clear example of practice change involving changing the nature of accountability in the structure of the organisation.

It is essential to see that *task led organisations, and those sensitive to, let alone working in partnership with, their public will be constantly evolving to meet constantly changing needs.* The perception that people have of organisations is crucial for understanding these processes (Morgan, 1986). The metaphor of the organisation as machine - to be taken apart and rebuilt as if it were an inanimate collection of objects - is increasingly obsolete in the management literature. But it lives on in the minds and actions of many contemporary managers and policy makers.

Other approaches, or metaphors, invite managers and policy makers to see this differently. A human systems approach, for example, will invite people to see their actions as attempting to change the patterns of reciprocal behaviour, or the 'culture' of the organisation. Morgan (1986) has described other metaphors used by people: organisations as 'machines'; 'cultures'; 'brains'; 'psychic prisons'; 'eco-systems'; 'political systems'.

At the very least, organisations are, as Morgan illustrates, pluralistic social systems. The imagery of everyone in the organisation marching to a common purpose and vision of the future with 'mission statements' is simply that - an image being used as a means of communication. Pragmatically, there are always winners, losers and vested interests that have to be taken into account in consideration of how organisations develop, adjust and change within their contexts:

> *'We have seen that the winners are often the ones that are the most experimental and flexible in matching the early forms of 'the product' with unexpected demands and opportunities,*

and that think through the development of their innovation in the most thorough and systematic way.'

(Utterback, 1996)

In chapter three we suggested that this approach to Managing Change Through Innovation in management is an approach to organisational development. It is one that suggests identifying all the innovations involved in major changes, analysing each of them using the Innovation Trinity to identify how each needs to be managed, while at the same time recognising 'the context' within which each change is taking place, and making the most of links to changes moving in the same direction. We do not wish to claim a monopoly of wisdom for this approach. A vast and ever growing literature exists on the subject (Domoney, 1992), to say nothing of management and consultancy practice wisdom.

Discussing the 'reorganisation fallacy' we stressed that restructuring the organisation, its staff groupings and lines of accountability, was a poor and potentially counterproductive way of attempting to change front line practice. However *change agents and their managers need to recognise that as practice changes so elements of the organisation will need to change and the relationships between different groups will be affected by first and second order changes in parallel with such changes in individual relationships.*

Organisations that have as their task 'change in the behaviour of the people they work with' have an added dimension of awareness to take into consideration. *Change agent organisations will need to change as they are successful in changing the problems they set out to tackle. Planned obsolescence should be the goal of any such organisation.*

Having described the major building blocks involved in renegotiating staff roles and developing their performance, we will now look at *who has to do what, with whom and when as an innovation diffuses through the system.*

SYSTEM DEVELOPMENT: PROMOTING RELATIONSHIPS REQUIRED TO DEVELOP NEW PRACTICE THROUGHOUT A SOCIAL SYSTEM

This dimension to Managing Change Through Innovation illustrates the interactions between key groups of people. It is a generalised version of the mapping process outlined in previous chapters and described in more detail in *Mapping Innovation and Change* (Smale, 1996). The emphasis is on:

- spreading new practice or innovations throughout the whole of an organisation and across organisational boundaries, rather than on the detailed picture of previous chapters where the focus is on practitioners or managers being able to change their practice and that of their immediate colleagues;

- the different phases of 'development work', which will be related to the different activities that are appropriate at each phase in the adoption of new ways of working.

To illustrate the different actions that need to be taken, we have augmented a typical Rogers diffusion curve describing the people involved at each stage as an innovation is adopted over time, identifying the developmental tasks required at each phase (Fig. V).

Fig. V: Diffusion of Innovations and Development Tasks

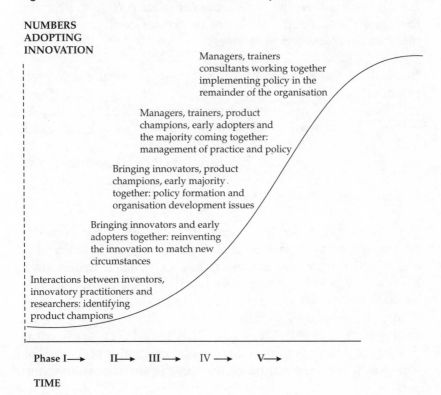

NUMBERS
ADOPTING
INNOVATION

Managers, trainers consultants working together implementing policy in the remainder of the organisation

Managers, trainers, product champions, early adopters and the majority coming together: management of practice and policy

Bringing innovators, product champions, early majority together: policy formation and organisation development issues

Bringing innovators and early adopters together: reinventing the innovation to match new circumstances

Interactions between inventors, innovatory practitioners and researchers: identifying product champions

Phase I→   II→   III→   IV→   V→

TIME

Each of these blocks corresponds to the five phases that are outlined below. You will recall that the steepness of the curve is determined by the adoptability of the innovation, and reflects the numbers adopting new methods over time.

Phase One

Interactions between the innovators. This phase concentrates on the *invention of new practices, methods and procedures to solve a problem, or to build on a conceptual breakthrough*. Such work will include finding solutions to unsolved problems; working out the practice implications of research; translating findings into practice or policy prescriptions for action.

Practitioners, researchers and other experts need to be brought together to struggle with new ideas for practice and their applications to practice or policy. This is the embryonic 'think tank' and gestation stage: *practice exchange* amongst the experts. The network of those involved in new developments is very important, as we have seen in chapter three. Thomas Kuhn (1970) in his classic work on *The Structure of Scientific Revolutions* coined the phrase the *invisible college* to describe the network of people who are in crucial contact with each other as they develop new ideas.

Innovators need support from people outside of their organisations, within which they are often isolated. These relationships are not always harmonious; indeed they may be extremely competitive. *The Double Helix*, the story of Crick and Watson's race to discover the structure of DNA, is an example of a complex mixture of the competitive and collaborative effort involved in making a major scientific breakthrough (Watson, 1970).

Innovators get a sense of identity through these complex relationships: confirmation that their efforts are worthwhile, and a relief from the isolation they experience within their own organisation. At the very early stages innovators are likely to face indifference from their immediate colleagues and managers, who may assume that they should be putting all their efforts into the status quo. This may be experienced as 'resistance', but it is important to recognise that it probably has little to do with the nature of the developing innovation, and more to do with the realities of the senior management position and the 'activity' of the innovator. This is a problem facing all organisations; for example:

> 'At the same time, managers must not neglect pleas that advocate major commitments to new initiatives. Typically top management is pilloried by two opposing, responsible forces: those that demand commitment to the old, and those that advocate for the future. Unfortunately, advocacy tends to overstate the market potential of new product lines and understate their costs. Management, then, must find the right balance between support for incremental improvement and commitments to new and unproven innovations. Understanding and managing this tension perceptively may well separate the ultimate winners from the losers.'
>
> (Utterback, 1996)

Faced with these circumstances it is not surprising that innovators tend to be cosmopolitan, organisational misfits (Rogers, 1995). Their managers may find them difficult to work with and often provocative in public. But outside of the mainstream, small numbers of such people are involved in high degrees of collaboration, linked to form 'insider groups'. Interchange between such groups can be very productive if common ground is stressed and competition kept to a minimum during the exchange of ideas and knowledge. Extremely competitive individuals are probably best left in their own corner.

The adoption of new ideas by large numbers of people will not be of primary importance during this phase. The emphasis is on getting the 'product' right. Typically, innovation is carried out in idiosyncratic circumstances, by people who possess a sense of mission and are not afraid to take risks or be controversial.

When new methods of work are being invented and reinvented, time from employers usually has to be 'borrowed' or negotiated. Peters and Waterman (1982) in their study of successful companies stress the need for the organisation to allow this kind of work if it is to keep up the flow of new products required to stay in business; significantly they refer to this essential component as 'bootlegging time'. For a few companies this is an essential component of their readiness to innovate (Mitchell, 1991; Henry and Walker, 1991). In our experience few, if any, resources are explicitly allocated or gambled by human services agencies on such endeavours, but the loose nature of space management in most organisations means that often the time is 'available' to those willing to 'take' it. However, many are unhappy that innovation is only given 'blind eye' permission, with resources being borrowed by 'working the system' rather than formally allocated. Indeed Crosbie and Vickery (1989) found that time and staff needed to be formally allocated to enable many social services area teams to have the opportunity to develop innovatory schemes that significantly extended the repertoire of services available to the public. They found that schemes that were developed without such resources remained vulnerable.

Some are able to use as much time as they want to, as long as they keep up with all their 'statutory' work. This of course increases the feeling frequently reported by innovators: 'we did it despite our organisation'. For there to be any attempt at planned change, particularly across organisational boundaries, project funding is needed to resource and co-ordinate such activities. PADE has carried out such work, notably in the Community Social Work Exchange, and the Research into Practice: Residential Work with Elderly People group (Hearn, 1991; Payne, 1989).

For an organisation or policy maker wanting deliberately to promote development at this stage the major focus should be on networking. *Phase One activities will include:*

- identifying who is doing what where;
- establishing a directory of innovators;
- carrying out literature and research reviews;
- bringing together practitioners, researchers, managers and policy makers to arrive at syntheses of practice experience and research knowledge;
- linking up innovators, maintaining support networks;
- writing up methods of work;
- research work on:
    ◇ defining the problem

◊ new methods of work

◊ outcome studies on intervention.

Phase Two

Bringing innovators and early adopters together. This phase focuses on the application of new methods and procedures to solve problems of practice within 'avant garde' agencies or groups within departments.

During this stage new methods have to be 'reinvented' to fit in with the current practice of 'early adopters' and the existing methods and procedures of organisations. Organisations open to change will make space for such work, or turn a blind eye to those engaged in it. The innovation may remain marginal to the activity of the organisation, but discussion and decisions about the mainstreaming of the method will begin. Riley (1997) illustrates how *local* data collection is a necessary beginning point. This is part of 'reinventing' the definition of the problem which helps to mobilise commitment to action.

Early adopters are normally dependent upon people outside of their organisation for information, inspiration, support and above all as a reference group - that is the peers and innovators they identify with and with whom they share a vision of how the job should be done.

The activities of Phase One will need to be continued with an expansion of the networks of those involved to include more early adopters. For an organisation or policy maker wanting to deliberately promote development at this stage, *Phase Two, activities include:*

* *Information targeted on 'those who will listen':* dissemination on a wide scale at this stage may still be a waste of time. Many people involved in attempts at mass dissemination may not be particularly interested in adopting the new methods: they will be quick to point out all the difficulties, and there is often much 'personal and organisational resistance' to an idea. The very enthusiasm and uniqueness of the innovators and their circumstances will often fuel as much so called 'resistance' as they overcome. Typically, widespread dissemination at this stage

through large conferences and so on does not give enough time for the necessary detailed working through of all the problems of adoption. *Many may be inoculated against an innovation by such procedures.*

- *Initiation, extension, and maintenance of support-diffusion networks* enabling innovators to meet with each other and with potential early adopters.

- Research findings and practice descriptions have a major role to play for a minority of practitioners and managers. These are the 'cosmopolitan early adopters' who are susceptible to conversion by such information, and the product champions who need such information to negotiate with 'gatekeepers', 'opinion leaders' and other policy makers.

- Expanding 'who is doing what where' directories and dissemination to potential early adopters.

- Team building and organisational development in avant garde agencies.

- Introducing new methods into basic professional education.

- Preparation of material for widespread dissemination through writing for a general market and specific training courses and training materials.

- Promotion of the 'training' and consultancy skills of expert practitioners.

- Training courses for product champions, trainers and managers.

- Reinvention of methods for different circumstances.

- Consciousness raising events such as conferences, and articles in the trade press. These are a first step in drawing attention to the need for change and signposting future directions.

Phase Three

Bringing together the innovators, those ready to change, sympathetic management: 'product champions', the 'early majority' and 'management'. This is the phase often referred to as *'mainstreaming'* new methods of practice and procedures to solve problems. Within an organisation this stage is most obvious when the innovatory work of a unit or of the most entrepreneurial members of staff is adopted by senior management as 'policy' for the whole agency. On a national scale this stage is reached when 'social policy' initiatives implement new approaches which have been tested by innovatory organisations, demonstration projects devised from political and professional theory, or some combination of these influences. The Griffiths report is an example of a recommendation for the adoption of innovations on a wide scale and an attempt to establish the machinery to implement the recommendations of the Barclay report (Griffiths, 1988 p. vii). But many innovations will spread without this explicit policy input, and on the other hand policy reforms often lead to little change in practice, as we saw above with the diffusion of family therapy. However, Schorr (1992) has highlighted the failure of effective programmes to be sustained let alone replicated in the US.

A common strategy for introducing change on a large scale within or across organisational boundaries is to embark on a programme of training and organisational change, identified in previous chapters as part of the 'simple linear' approach to diffusion. As we saw above conventional wisdom assumes that practitioners will need to be trained in the new methods of work, that services will need to be reorganised and that new methods should be introduced into the curriculum of basic professional education.

However, we have referred to the growing and pragmatic evidence that many new methods are adopted by people learning from their contact with those who can 'approach' implementation of the innovation: 'new methods spread through contagion not conversion'. If this is true of the first two phases of the diffusion process why should it be different for those adopting at a later stage? The very first people to adopt an innovation are those most ready to learn and change; and they need evidence of the value of an innovation from people they know, and who have direct experience of implementation. Why should we assume that later, less receptive adopters will change through less credible witnesses to the value of the new methods?

Implications for change management:

- Managers, and other agents of change, need to

identify those who already practise in the required way, and those who are the most keen to develop the new way of working.

- Reorganisation, *if* required, should *follow* not lead practice changes.

- All staff need to review their current ways of working by exposure to feedback, and evaluation of the organisation's and their performance.

It has long been recognised that change requires 'unlearning' old ways and that this involves 'loss' (Marris, 1974). People will experience a period of incompetence, or de-skilling, as they are in transition from one approach to their work to another stage (Smale, 1987). A 'banking' approach as referred to in chapter three ignores the evidence of much experience of adult education and the diffusion of innovations research; people will interpret messages in accordance with their own assumptions and beliefs, which may or may not be the same as the communicator's. Innovations not entirely dependent upon precise technology will always be subject to varying degrees of *'reinvention'*, described by Rice and Rogers (1980) as *active attempts to give meaning to innovations in a local context*. This particularly applies to innovations in social work and community care. Indeed it has been argued that the very nature of working in partnership with the people in the community demands that such reinvention takes place, not only to meet the idiosyncrasies of local needs and resources, but also because local people will be involved in the choice of services (Smale and others, 1988). Griffiths advocates a similar approach:

> 'The aim must be to provide structure and resources to support the initiatives, the innovation and the commitment at local level and allow them to flourish; to encourage the success stories in one area to become the commonplace of achievement everywhere else. **To prescribe from the centre will be to shrivel the pattern of local activity.'**
>
> (Griffiths, 1988 p. iv, emphasis added)

During the first two phases of the diffusion process individuals make a significant contribution. When it comes to widespread adoption of new policies or methods, there are large numbers of people involved and, inevitably, limited resources.

It can be tempting to replace genuine 'product champions' with formal role carriers within agencies, notably trainers and managers, and to shortcut the process of learning from adequate 'role models' by using training packs and other tactics for large scale training. These strategies are sometimes successful in producing widespread change when it is a matter of building on existing practice or putting a new gloss on continuing old customs and practices. Readiness to adopt the new method or practice is the key variable in the success or relative failure of training tactics.

However, when innovations:

- are complex;
- do not fit in with or add on to existing practice;
- require a high degree of reinvention to meet local circumstances

it is necessary to draw on the persistent energy of significant change managers - change agents and product champions - and to mobilise the collaboration of sympathetic opinion leaders and role modelling of early adopters to carry the innovation out into the mainstream of practice.

During the early 1990s in the UK, the call for greater collaboration and partnerships in the Children Act, probation reforms, and many of the changes required to implement the National Health Service and Community Care Act: all involved innovations of this order. The call for multi-agency young offender teams and greater agency collaboration will require similar changes. The supply of the right people, and senior management's willingness to identify and use them, are crucial variables in the rate at which services can be reformed.

In Phase Three many of the activities outlined in Phases One and Two will need to be continued. Often the cutting edge in the mainstream adoption of innovations is organisational development. Permitting change in a marginal, innovative team requires little organisational development, but adopting new practices throughout an agency may require anything from change in some procedures to total restructuring. But we argued in chapter one that what we might call 'knee-jerk restructuring' as a reaction to policy changes is no substitute for *managing* changes in practice. There is insufficient evidence to support a belief that any particular form of organisation will dictate the methods used by, or the professional behaviour of, front line staff. Structural change should follow practice changes being designed to facilitate new methods and practices.

Developments will need to take place at different levels during Phase Three. *For managers, introducing an innovation into the mainstream activities will include:*

- undertaking an analysis of innovation to assess the factors which may encourage or discourage acceptance: understanding the factors that are likely to affect the rate of adoption, what it has got going for it and what in the organisation will cause resistance to change generally, or to the specific innovation;

- where the innovation involves second order change, managers should work out how this changes their own *behaviour* in their relationships within and/or without the organisation, and begin to act in a manner that is consistent with, or *is* part of, the change;

- identifying the people involved or affected: consider the relative benefits and drawbacks of the innovation for them;

- identifying product champions;

- identifying facilitators or gatekeepers;

- creating an awareness of the need for change, not by argument or prescription but by exposure to the problems that precipitated the innovation;

- giving management backing to product champions;

- reducing disadvantages perceived by those involved: at least bringing those people into discussions early on to give them a chance to modify and adapt innovation to suit local needs and circumstances;

- entering into negotiations between management, staff and other partners on changes in roles and expectations, job descriptions and other matters as appropriate, paying particular attention to the customs and practices which may inhibit change.

Time is crucial. Getting an innovation accepted, reinvented to match local circumstances, and then implemented, can be a long slow process - *there is no substitute for continuing effort over long periods of time.*

This list of activities is a daunting agenda for any manager and it may or may not make the task seem more achievable to add some of the dimensions Handy refers to in his standard reference on *Understanding Organisations*:

'• *be prepared to allow the recipients to adopt the final strategy (that which one adopts, one can easily call one's own ...)*

• *accept the fact that the good initiator/leader/change agent gets no credit but must let others boast of success*

• *be prepared to accept a less than optimum strategy in the interests of achieving something rather than nothing.'*
(Handy, 1981)

Just as managers may need to identify 'product champions', so product champions themselves, or other change agents, will need to:

• identify managers likely to 'facilitate' the process of change and 'open gates';

• identify gatekeepers;

• win over gatekeepers;

• search out others promoting the same idea: support for innovators is crucial to increase the power of change agents (as discussed under Phase Two).

Just as managers need *time*, so do any other agents of change. *Getting an innovation accepted and adopted by others can be a long slow process, and different aspects of major, complex innovations are likely to develop at different rates.*

For central policy organisations, and other change agencies which want to spread new methods across organisational boundaries, many of the activities in the first two phases will need to be continued.

Other major activities will include:

- publication of policy documents and guidelines;
- consciousness raising events such as conferences and articles in the trade press: these are a first step in drawing attention to the need for change;
- clear expectations of policy and signposting plans for implementation;
- supporting and initiating appropriate training;
- further development and dissemination of training materials;
- widespread dissemination of data-based directories of innovatory practice to identify networks of experienced practitioners and those with 'hands on' experience of innovation;
- consultancy to teams and wider organisations: team building focusing on changes in practice, redistributing roles and tasks within teams and across teams and organisational boundaries;
- organisational development work: an examination of the relationship between new practice and the organisation's structure (for example decentralisation and devolved resource management) to increase user participation in service planning.

Phase Four

Bringing together product champions, the early and late majorities: innovators, managers, trainers and staff. By this stage the mainstreaming of innovation is not the delicate task of protecting new shoots but that of giving sustenance to a plant that already has roots. Activities of the first two phases will be dropping away while the Phase Three tactics will be spreading towards the more reactionary, or more probably 'neglected', corners of the organisation.

Managers must now take direct responsibility for making sure that what was the innovation is being maintained by operational units and ensuring that those not already complying do so. The 'new' method is now the 'status quo', to be protected from slippage into previous, still organisationally or personally convenient, methods of work. By this time methods, their management and organisation are being consolidated, having been reinvented to fit changes in circumstances.

Many of the shortcomings of the 'new method' will be evident by this time and the seeds of its obsolescence germinate. The more innovatory spirits within the organisation will be working on the next solution or innovation, or on other problems. Managers will have to be making judgements about which of these deserve bootlegging time and which are the innovations to be adopted next.

Phase Five

Managers, trainers, consultants and 'laggards'. As we have said, some 'laggards' will be maintaining old practice because the system has not properly involved them in communication about the innovation. We should heed Rogers' warning that individuals often carry the blame for system communication problems, and change managers should investigate how much they know of the identified problems and the proposed solutions before assuming that they are stubborn opponents. Where this is the case then the activities above need to be applied to them in their situation.

If they prove to be stubborn opponents taking only the past as their point of reference, or acting only out of self interest, and they are sabotaging progress in defiance of management, then they have to be removed from the path of the development.

But we should beware that this is done for the right reasons and not for comfort or convenience. Some people seen as resisting an innovation are the product champions of alternative ideas. As we have seen not all change is progress, not all growth benign: they could be the only ones that are right not to change. We need to be confident that they are not a source of alternative problem solving that might prove to be a valuable resource for the organisation. Remember the dynamics of innovation and deviance are very similar: both challenge the status quo. Similarly compliance, and conformity, with elements of underlying opposition, can look like a convergence of ideas and the adoption of new ideas and practice. Motivation is the key difference: not just obvious, overt behaviour. Judging the difference and taking appropriate action is at the heart of effective management.

There is a need here, as there has been throughout all the processes we describe, to return to basics. Who sees what as a problem, and who sees what as an appropriate solution need to be asked all over again.

But just as some changes are adopted because all change is seen as progress, there are those who assume that things should always stay the same. Or there are those who want to change, but cannot see how they could possibly achieve it. This book cannot address all the dimensions of the inter-personal and psychological problems involved in these observations. However, we can note that work with individuals and organisations stuck in obsolete ways of working is more appropriate activity for consultancy than mainstream management and staff development. Organisations can get stuck in habitual patterns of interaction that prohibit change. The very fact that they are 'habits' may put them beyond the immediate understanding of participants. Eraut (1994) has drawn attention to the significance of tacit knowledge in professional development, and the part it plays in maintaining old ways of behaving. If a person is not aware of what they think and know, or if parties to a relationship take for granted certain ways of relating, then they are far less amenable to change. An outsider can sometimes see what others constantly overlook. They can also ask about, and so cause to be articulated the things which insiders have long since assumed that everybody knows, and yet all have 'forgotten'.

Although the ability to operate from this 'outsider' position is essential to solve intransigent organisational problems, it is also central to being an effective change agent or change manager. This dimension of change management and the skills involved in being an effective change agent are discussed in the next three chapters, Part Four.

The Skills of Change Management

Introduction

Managing change is not like walking across fixed ground. It is more like swimming in water. You could be in a calm pond where you are the only source of ripples, or in an easily crossed small stream, or perhaps a large river with many currents making it difficult, if not impossible to arrive at the point on the bank you had hoped to reach; or you could be swimming in the sea where any ripple you might make will seem insignificant compared to the waves around you. It might still be possible to keep alive and even arrive at your destination, but if you have far to go it will require planning, stamina, knowledge of all the elements, good timing of your journey and the help of others.

To have a clear idea of what to do is one thing: to be able to do it another. Throughout the preceding chapters you may have been saying: 'well that's all very well, but *how* do you find out what people really see as the problem' or '*how* do you negotiate with people who want things to change in a different way' or '*what* do you do to convince people that change is necessary even though they want things to stay the same'? So far the book has attempted to indicate all the things that have to be done, the different people that need to be identified and persuaded to behave in a way that is consistent with the implementation of particular changes. Part Four attempts to fill some of the gaps: to describe in general terms the skills involved in working with the people involved. We will do this by describing two interrelated areas of activity:

- *Understanding social situations - chapter nine*
- *Working with other people - chapter ten*

and through a discussion of:

- *The change agent's position - chapter eleven.*

But first it is important to discuss some general issues about managing change as they apply to the development of the change agent's skills.

General Issues Concerning Books, Skills and Practice

Throughout this book we have described the complex processes involved in managing changes in practice. At no time have we suggested that there is any evidence to support the idea that all you have to do is to get staff, managers and others whom you want to change to read a book about what they could do, be it a text such as this or a procedures manual.

There are severe limitations on how helpful any document can be in helping you to do any skilled operation. Piano playing manuals are of limited value, just as a good set of jokes will not turn anyone into a good comic. Approaches to managing change require skill as well as ideas to be implemented. There is always the danger that the best possible set of plans never get implemented, just like the piano in our house never sounds right. We have the right ideas about piano playing but lack the skill. Changing the piano is tempting but will not make much difference. This is stressed here not just to describe the limitations of this, or any, book, but to remind you that the 'to know is to act differently fallacy' is an easy one to fall into when developing your own skills, just as it affects the ability of staff to implement change that requires them to behave differently. Piano playing can only be learnt and developed through constant practice; through feedback - both from your own listening and from knowledgeable others; through coaching; and through understanding the underlying theory of the music you want to play. The skills you need staff to have to implement change are likely to be developed in the same way and so also are your own change management skills.

But a good set of jokes may promote a great performance for a good comic just as a text on piano playing, especially a book of exercises, might help a pianist develop technique. It is significant that the people who gave us the most positive feedback on the working edition of this book were many of the innovators and managers whom we had worked with as they developed their innovations and we developed the ideas in the book. For them the book made the implicit and the intuitive, explicit and then deliberate and planned. We have found that some people learn best from the written page, while for others the book has been most helpful after they have engaged in their practice with the questions detailed in the companion volume *Mapping Change and Innovation.*

These chapters, like their predecessors, are a synthesis of our own experience of working with successful change agents and change managers and with relevant research. A full discussion of change agent skills would be a huge task beyond the scope of these chapters. Such a review should include disparate areas such as organisational behaviour, leadership studies and other areas of group and personal change such as family therapy, group work and individual psychotherapy and counselling. The brief description of the change manager's skills provided here is intended to provide further information about how to act when managing change.

We have stressed here and in *Mapping Change and Innovation* that the plans that you draw up to manage change can only be made in your own particular circumstances. The same is true of how you should set about negotiating with others to release resources; or joining others in an alliance; persuading those who are neutral but whose co-operation is vital; and beating the opposition. All these activities have to be carried out by you changing your behaviour appropriately over time. Change is best managed through your own innovations in your own management thinking and through your own collaboration with other key players.

Most of us will have, to some extent, change management skills, for all of us are more or less successful agents of change in many aspects of our lives. But just as the professional musician has to learn fairly commonplace musical skills to a very high level, so the professional change agent has to be especially good at managing change. When you have finished Part Four you may want to revisit chapter eight to identify the different staff development modes appropriate for the skills that you decide need to be developed by members of your change management team. You may decide that you need to find somebody who can 'show' some staff what they need to do to implement changes in practice, or arrange for them to be 'contaminated' by a 'virulent virus'; while others will need their consciousness raised about new possibilities ahead of any detailed investigation into their development needs. As in all things there will be a convergence (or divergence) of ideas and knowledge: staff learning styles and current skills and knowledge should be the starting point, not an imposition of the skills required for the new task or method of work.

We have seen that in any situation there are many significant actors through whom a person will be attempting to progress an innovation. If we took a simple attitude toward the skills of the change agent we would be in danger of repeating the fallacies that we pointed out in the first chapter. Specifically we would be acting as if an individual identified as a charismatic individual were the only key person crucial to change. We want to stress here that we are not taking that view. Some change agents will lead from the front, and may well be seen as charismatic by others. But others will work effectively with a lower profile. *The essential skills in managing change are about getting others to behave in an appropriate way:* to get gatekeepers to give access to the resources they guard, to encourage product champions to put in the essential energy to carry through changes in all their complexity and so on. *To be good at managing change you do not always have to have all of these skills and attributes yourself, but you do have to be able to engage with those who have them and mobilise their persistent effort for your cause.*

We discussed in chapter three the limitations on what can be expected from any approach or model for managing change, and the issues involved in the context of change in chapter seven. The effective change manager can increase the chances of success by planning to do those things which have been identified as crucial to changing practice. One way of doing this is to use the analysis of the Innovation Trinity to map the people and plan the actions required to manage changes. But no manager can control all the variables and the processes involved. Gardeners do not 'make' plants grow and sailors don't 'make' the wind that drives their boats. They both achieve what they do because they understand the natural forces and use them to achieve their ends. They may not reach their goals by doing all the right things, for the forces of nature are certainly greater than any power that they are able to exercise. So it is with policy makers, managers and practitioners of change.

A sailor setting out to cross an ocean will get charts and as much information about currents and weather as possible, and then plot a provisional course. Each day, if not more frequently, the boat's position will be identified and the course corrected accordingly in the knowledge that the elements will have played their part in determining the actual course being followed. Failure to understand what is happening will at best hinder a successful voyage, at worst cause disaster. So it is with managing changes in practice and service delivery, where the basic area of activity concerns understanding social situations and the relationships between the key people involved.

CHAPTER NINE

Understanding Social Situations

This includes the ability to understand the situation that you are in and how it unfolds over time; the ability to think through problems and see alternative solutions and to plan and think through all the steps involved in the processes of change; and to understand and help change relationships. Under this heading we can identify three areas of skill and knowledge:

- *Thinking through problems and solutions*
- *Thinking through action and identifying consequences*
- *Understanding relationships.*

1. THINKING THROUGH PROBLEMS AND SOLUTIONS

We all employ to some degree two dimensions of thinking through problems and their solutions:

- *Imagination, creative thinking and problem solving*
- *Planning action and identifying consequences.*

These are described here to further illustrate the work of the change agent.

Imagination, Creative Thinking and Problem Solving

Watzlawick and his colleagues use the following exercise to illustrate the need to think in unconventional ways to solve certain problems. You may like to try the task they set:

Look at these nine points and taking a pencil join them up with four straight lines without taking the pencil off the paper.

We will return to the problem later.

Imagination and creativity have been identified as an essential dimension of problem solving and the management of planned change in many fields. Social work writers have stressed its centrality in the complex processes often involved in front line practice (Heus and Pincus, 1986; England, 1986; Goldstein, 1973; Smale, Tuson and Statham, in press). These and other writers point out that the very nature of social problem solving at a local level requires creativity, for it cannot and should not be prescribed from outside of the social situation involved. For example Weissman writes:

'...creativity is important because social workers deal with the highly complex problems of both people and society, currently possess a less than adequate body of professional knowledge, and operate in what often is a turbulent and changing environment. The standard operating procedures often just will not do. Creative solutions are vital.'

(Weissman, 1990 p. xv).

It is relevant to repeat the words of Sir Roy Griffiths referred to in previous chapters from his *Agenda for Action* which provided the foundation for the welfare reforms that have dominated practice through the 1990s in the UK:

'The aim must be to provide the structure and resources to support the initiatives, the innovation and the commitment at local level and to allow them to flourish; to encourage the success stories in one area to become the commonplace of achievement everywhere. To prescribe from the centre will be to shrivel the pattern of local activity.'

(Griffiths, 1988 p. iv)

This assumes that creative problem solving and innovation of services to match changing local needs and the different views of local service users was seen as fundamental to reforming community care. Sadly, evidence of the wisdom of this statement is found more in his prediction of central prescription shrivelling the pattern of local activity, than in encouraging local success stories.

The use of creative thinking and imagination is also endorsed in the diffusion of innovations literature. Roberts and King researched how 'policy entrepreneurs' initiated innovative public policy. In an interesting study of a sample of activists in the field of public policy innovation, the authors argue that the change agent has to have a capacity for imaginative, divergent ways of thinking:

'We found evidence that not only did policy entrepreneurs broker ideas, but they also invented them. One entrepreneur....was described in the following way...'just phenomenal. He is very creative...He can come up with a comparison or critical question that jars your sense of the 'givens'..."

(Roberts and King, 1989)

They also found that it is important for innovators to have the imagination to seek out and notice novel solutions:

'Sources for the policy entrepreneurs' ideas were many and varied. As brokers of ideas they 'scanned the environment' in search of ideas, patterns, or models that could be applied to education from other policy areas.'

Creative Thinking and Changing Assumptions

The need for some measure of creative imagination is identified in several ways in the literature on innovation and the effective management of change. In chapter two we pointed out that all innovation is to some extent a confrontation of the status quo: a challenge of the conventional wisdom. As we saw when discussing the adoptability of an innovation, some will be compatible with existing ideas and ways of working while others will involve a more radical shift in thinking. In the scientific world, and increasingly in the management literature, these different ways of thinking are referred to as paradigm shifts. This refers to new ways of making sense of the world: of seeing a problem and its potential solutions from a different set of assumptions or within a different framework. It is a shift of the same order as changing from believing that the Universe has the Earth at its centre, to recognising that it is but one planet orbiting one sun in a host of others; or seeing social class as a god given order, or the consequence of people's decisions and actions. The key issue here is that the shift from one perception to another is not a continuous development but a discontinuous leap. The change from Newtonian physics to Einstein's theory of relativity is a classic example of such a paradigm shift. Like most paradigm shifts it marked a breakthrough in thinking. It was necessary to make sense of information that could not be accounted for by the conventional theory of the day, and once made it helped to make sense of previously insoluble problems. Luckily many change agents are effective without having access to Einstein's intellectual capacity, but it is important to foster the ability to see problems and their solutions in new ways, to turn the insoluble 'facts of life' into understandable problems with potential solutions.

The distinction between first and second order change implies that the change agent needs to be able to imagine, or envision, fundamentally different alternative relationships between people from those that maintain the status quo. It will be necessary to do this confidently *despite* the pressures to see situations only in the conventional or 'normal' way. Remember many relationships are maintained because they have become an unquestioned part of habit: of custom and practice. The suggestion that they could be different is often enough to make the implicit explicit, the unconscious conscious. This typically both opens up the possibility of change and threatens the stability of those who rely on these taken for granted relationships. It is not surprising that the response to a suggestion of the possibility of different relationships in such situations is greeted with something akin to being the first to present evidence that the Earth is round.

Imagination for the manager of change is not just cognitive or perceptual skill. It is manifest in the capacity of people to invent their own new ways of behaving, and their capacity to find new ways of feeling about others and themselves. Such thinking and action is a recurring theme in texts concerned with the management of change. For example the following description by Kanter of 'kaleidoscopic thinking' is her analysis of the creative imagination at work (Kanter, 1991). She argues that:

'The first essential skill (of change management) is a style of thinking, or a way of approaching the world, that I have come to call 'kaleidoscope thinking'...Kaleidoscopic thinking.... involves taking an existing array of data, phenomena, or assumptions and being able to twist them, shake them, look at

them upside down... thus permitting an entirely new pattern and consequent set of actions to take place.'

Although imagination is typically seen as a personal quality, it is also one which can be enhanced by education, training, and by working in a creative environment. But as stressed in the discussion of 'mapping the people', change managers will also need to identify those innovators, product champions and early adopters who have more imagination than others and a greater capacity or compulsion to envisage alternatives to the status quo.

The 'kaleidoscopic thinking' Kanter describes as a 'skill', actually involves appropriate attitudes, talents, values and behavioural repertoires. It also involves a range of identifiable cognitive skills: the ideas of lateral thinking, brainstorming, visualisation and reframing. Some people will think like this naturally, while others will contribute by following a lead taken within a change management team.

Kanter tells the story of the chief executive who enacted 'kaleidoscopic thinking' by constantly disrupting the orthodox working of his top management group through a series of dramatic and theatrical events, such as organising a parade of elephants carrying inspirational messages on their sides. Such examples illustrate how a 'style of thinking' is a complex interweaving of personal attitudes, skills, theories about the nature of change, and specific strategies and tactics for change. It is misleadingly reductive to describe such behaviour as a 'skill'. It implies a unitary and easily identifiable individual quality, which is an oversimplification although not necessarily untrue.

It may be easy to accept that creative thinking is involved in 'inventing' new solutions and seeing problems in a new way. But why the elephants? Why would such a stunt be anything more than a stunt, a way of drawing attention to something?

The Illogical Steps in Changing Thinking

There are some messages that you can get across by rational argument. These typically involve new information, or a new solution that is based essentially on shared assumptions with the person or people you are communicating with, that is within the same status quo, the same paradigm. For example a senior manager might argue that the market has changed and the company needs to update its products, or a social policy maker may change policy to meet changing circumstances within the same values as the old policy.

But what if a senior manager or policy maker, or a middle manager or practitioner wants to communicate a different set of assumptions upon which a new form of business should be based; what if they want to change the nature of the organisation's business and the value base upon which it operates? Then communication needs to be different. Rational, logical argument will have its place but something more is needed. It may be time to consider using elephants.

There is an old joke about a man who stops and asks for directions to be told that: 'If I were going there I wouldn't start from here'. If we are working on different basic assumptions then communication is often experienced as difficult, even perverse or mad. Cross cultural communication is also fraught with difficulties for the same reason: words and sentences can be translated but the whole set of assumptions that make up the context of the conversation can be different, making the exchange of ideas very complex. Listening to most discussions about religious or even political beliefs will illustrate the futility of rational argument as a change agent strategy. The key issue here is that if I have one set of basic beliefs that are very different from yours, it is unlikely that logical argument can help either of us *to see things differently*.

The phrase *'see things differently'* is significant. It implies that a different order of perception is required, a move from 'argument' to 'visualisation'. This is exactly what may be necessary for such shifts in thinking - perhaps literally looking at the problem from a different angle, the way that Galileo went to the top of the Leaning Tower of Pisa to demonstrate that stones of different weights fall at the same speed.

Betty Edwards (1979), in her helpful book *Drawing on the Right Side of the Brain,* illustrates how people can develop their imaginative thinking and actions. Specifically she describes how those who have not been good at drawing can indeed improve their sketching ability if they can learn to use the side of their brain, in right handed people normally the right hemisphere, that governs such ability. Drawing on brain research she has developed teaching methods that she claims enable people to release abilities that have lain dormant. Watzlawick (1978) also referred to this body of research to discuss 'the language of change': the ways in which therapeutic communications can indeed help people change entrenched patterns of behaviour and their perceptions of their world.

This is of course a complicated area of research and only the essentials need concern us here. The human brain is composed of two hemispheres which have different complementary functions. Originally through observations of people who had experienced brain damage and latterly through much more sophisticated procedures, researchers have been able to ascertain what many of these different functions are. In a right handed person (the functions are typically reversed in left handed people) the *left, opposite hemisphere is the dominant side of the brain*. Its major functions seems to be to translate what we see and hear into logical, analytical coding. It is the side of the brain that is dominant in language, in making calculations, in rational thinking: it is the 'verbal' side of the brain. By contrast the *right hemisphere is subordinate.* Its functions are very different. It specialises in the holistic understanding of complex relationships, patterns, and structures. It is this part of the brain that helps us to understand and grasp the whole Gestalt, the immediate recognition of the totality on the basis of one essential detail, the way we can recognise a person from a few words of their voice. With its grasp of whole ideas it is this side of the brain that holds our fundamental beliefs, although it is probably the left hand hemisphere that works to provide a rational system of beliefs and put them into words.

To put it crudely the right hand of the brain sees the joke, while the left hand will be able to work out why it is funny. If we relate the brain to computer language the right hand brain takes care of all the analogic communications - it reads the icons; while the left side of our hand brain makes the digital calculations and functions more like the word processor or calculator itself. The healthy brain in a normal person relies on both sides of the brain, both sets of functions, to make sense of the world and act appropriately.

The typical language of the left, dominant side of the brain is the language of rational argument, digital communications. The right side of the brain, and this is the connection to 'drawing on the right side of the brain', can use analogic languages to communicate: cartoons, caricatures, jokes, aphorisms, physical demonstrations, illustrations, drawings and diagrams. Digital thinking describes the detailed processes involved in building up information bit by bit, for example the process of logically setting out an argument or mental arithmetic. By contrast, the use of diagrams, cartoons, metaphors, aphorisms and jokes can instantly communicate whole meanings that it would take many 'digital' words to describe. Many signs make use of such communication: think how much more effective it is for a shop to display no smoking and no dogs signs rather than a list of conditions.

Deliberately or intuitively, when a writer uses a diagram they are attempting to get over the whole of a concept that it might take pages to explain. Like a joke, the whole meaning is often *lost* in such explanation. Watzlawick (1978) describes how this loss could be caused by the reader's digital brain dismantling or at least processing the elements of the whole before it can be grasped. It is as if a metaphor, a cartoon, or some other analogic communication jumps directly over this typically dominant side of the brain to communicate the whole to the right hand side. It is not by chance that great teachers such as the founders of the world's great religions have told stories and parables rather than communicated in logically argued, detailed theology.

From this analysis we can perhaps understand why Newton grasped the idea of gravity by seeing the apple fall, or why Galileo is remembered on the Leaning Tower of Pisa and why Einstein's image of the falling man gave him the insight that it did. The message is that to communicate a whole set of different assumptions to another person, a new paradigm, it may be no use arguing with them. It is much more likely that you can communicate effectively by using metaphor, or a 'picture' of a different way of seeing the problem and its possible solutions.

Gareth Morgan (1985) describes the difficulties experienced within organisations when there are unspoken assumptions held about the implicit meanings and attributions surrounding each separate manager's metaphors about what organisations are supposed to do and how. In discussing organisations as political systems with pluralistic approaches to power bases and vested interests, he differentiates between 'unitary', 'pluralistic' and 'radical' metaphors of how conflict is responded to. Each conceptual frame of reference or approach leads to a different approach to managing people and dealing with conflict. Unitary approaches seek to minimise conflict and see formal authority as the only place power should reside: a 'do as you are told' approach. Pluralistic managers acknowledge the vested interests and seek collaboration and resolution as a healthy response to conflict, and conflict can be an important source of innovation leverage. In the radical metaphor, the organisation is seen as a battleground with vested interested parties at war with one another and a 'fight to the death' approach to conflict is frequently adopted: 'us' and 'them' debates persist with little room for collaboration.

We noted above that new scientific paradigms come about when a new observation cannot be explained by the conventional wisdom. In our experience bringing new people into a situation can have the same effect in social problem solving. The service user's voice introduced into professional discussions of service delivery has often caused such a shift in thinking, and therein lies its power, its threat to the status quo, and its challenge to conventional wisdom and conventional sets of relationships.

What about the elephants? They may have been a brilliant analogic communication, like the story of Archimedes getting into his bath and realising that his body displaces an equivalent amount of water. If the metaphor conveys an image of the idea then it can work as a communication of a whole set of assumptions, hopefully the way that the contrast between flat Earth and round Earth thinking conveys the idea of a paradigm shift. If the analogic communication does not do this, it can still draw attention to those who might otherwise not take notice of the way that the elephants shocked the chief executive's staff. But they might not do more than this. We can probably all think of memorable television adverts without remembering the product, just as there is no information about the message communicated in Moss Kanter's example. All we remember is the elephants, which suggests that it was just a stunt. *Like any communication, analogic language has to be understood by the intended recipient of the message if there is to be a convergence of understanding.*

We can now return to Watzlawick's exercise. The solution looks like this:

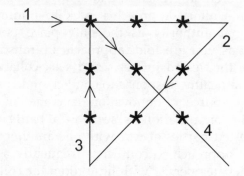

Most people doing this puzzle start, and many persist, by attempting to draw the four straight lines by drawing the lines within an imaginary box bounded by the eight outer points. This is of course impossible. It is only when the drawer moves outside this assumed box that it is possible to solve the problem and draw the four lines without the pen leaving the paper. (Many of you will have 'seen' this and found the explanation irritating because it is 'unnecessary'.)

When we are attempting to solve difficult problems and introduce complex innovations we often need to try to work outside of the boxes that we construct in our own minds: our own tacit assumptions about the world around us. By using metaphor and illustrations we can also help others to see a problem from a different perspective and challenge their own assumptions. When looking for new solutions to problems it can be an advantage to recruit people who see problems from different perspectives, who already live outside the boxes we have in our minds. The capacity for this dimension of imaginative thinking is endorsed by Kirton (1976), who has argued that:

'Everyone can be located on a continuum ranging from an ability to 'do things better' to an ability to 'do things differently', and that at the latter end, the innovator end of the

continuum, the innovator is seen as: 'thinking
tangentially...approaching tasks from unsuspected angles...'

It is worth noting that the Palo Alto Mental Research Institute group, who have had such a major impact in rethinking individual pathology and family relationships, included Watzlawick, a mathematician, Weakland, a chemical engineer, Beavin, a communications expert, as well as mental health professionals. The original team was led by Gregory Bateson, an anthropologist who had spent a significant amount of time studying the behaviour patterns of otters!

The need for creative thinking in problem solving has been stressed. Now we will turn to the need for left brain thinking, and describe the need for the kind of more rational, digital thinking required of the effective change agent. But first we need to stress a major point.

Throughout this book we have argued that *different innovations have to be managed differently. This discussion about the two hemispheres of the brain is another essential component of this difference.* We have stressed that *to arrive at a convergence of ideas by challenging some people's assumptions, or introducing them to an alternative paradigm from the one they base their thinking upon, requires analogic communication.* But it is also true that concerning some innovations *some people in your situation will share your assumptions but not yet see the problem, or its solution, the way you do. For your ideas and theirs to come together in a shared understanding will need a joint review of the evidence, and rational argument, the use of digital thinking.* This is also likely to be true of negotiations with those whose assumptions have been different also; even where there is a complete conversion to another paradigm, the details will still need to be worked out and negotiated.

2. THINKING AND PLANNING ACTION

Implicit in the MCTI approach is the need for rational planning to help you to find your way around what is often an irrational world. Other writers on the management of change and the diffusion of innovations have also stressed the need for rational planning while recognising the importance of people's feelings and the complex aspects of the unfolding of our lives (Domoney and Eno, 1996).

Gerard Egan, for example, who is particularly well known for his model of counselling, has also written on wider processes of change, and the skills required of the change agent (Egan, 1985). He draws a distinction between frameworks that include:

'...submodels, methods, and skills all related to designing, running, and assessing a system or subsystem....which presents the logic underlying a well-designed and well functioning system plus an understanding of why this logic so often goes away... and frameworks which are more to do with solving problems and planning development and change.... which provides the logic of a step-by-step process of problem management, system development, or organisational change.'

He argues that:

'These two models together with the methods and skills they entail provide a framework for the working knowledge and skills change agents need to do their work.'

(Egan, 1985 p.4-5)

In the subsequent elaboration of this framework, Egan addresses the change agent's underlying theory in use, personal attributes, skills and a range of specific strategies and tactics. In doing so, Egan identifies both some of the conventional ways in which social systems need to be thought about, and provides a model which is itself a product of such conventional, linear, digital thinking.

Many models of the change process clearly imply the capacity of the change agent to have such linear, systematic cognitive and behavioural abilities. For example, Pearson in an article on nurses as change agents draws upon systems theory and identifies a 'ten part procedural list to form as systems model for problem solving'. Major elements in this list require the kinds of thoughtfulness identified. For example:

'Step 1: Define overall needs, purposes and goals......
Step 3: Weighing the constraints versus the
capabilities and resources .....

Step 7: Analysing the options......
Step 10: Evaluating the effectiveness of a decision
            act...'

(Pearson, 1985)

Kirton (1976) makes a distinction between the adaptor and the innovator, which parallels that made here between thoughtfulness and imagination. Skinner comments:

*'The adaptor is an individual who works best **within an existing framework or structure**. He/she is characterised by precision, reliability, efficiency, prudence.....*

*At the opposite pole on this 'basic dimension of personality' is the innovator, who is most comfortable **outside the constraints of existing rules**. The innovator is seen as undisciplined, thinking tangentially, approaching tasks from unsuspected angles.....'*

(Skinner, 1989, emphasis original)

This is to frame the capacity for imagination and thoughtfulness in mutually exclusive personality types. Whether or not there really are 'personality types' in the way described, or whether they are social constructions, the main issue is that the change agent clearly needs to be able to draw upon both aspects of personality, depending on the nature of the issue being addressed and the stage of the change and innovation process.

Another way of putting this is simply to say that the personal characteristics identified by Kirton as those of the adaptor are particularly crucial for first order changes; and those associated with the innovator, are particularly necessary for second order change processes. Given that the transactor has to be able to distinguish between these different orders of change and act appropriately within each mode, then he or she will require to integrate these two sets of 'personality variables'.

Literature on the diffusion of innovations provides an analytic framework which a middle manager as change agent can use in thinking about the process of innovation which he or she may be promoting. The work of Everett Rogers provides a linear, 'rational', critical path model of the process of diffusion and adoption which, while it should not be used as a 'blue-print' to be followed slavishly, provides a model of the kind of linear, digital, flowpath thinking which may be necessary at particular points of a change process.

For example, Rogers identifies a 'sequence of change agent roles', which is actually a linear model of the process of problem solving and change:

'1. To develop need for change....
2. To establish an information-exchange relationship..
3. To diagnose problems...
4. To create an intent in the client to change...
5. To translate an intent to action...
6. To stabilise adoption and prevent discontinuance...
7. To achieve a terminal relationship...'

(Rogers, 1995 p.337)

Being willing and able to think through the steps necessary in a process of change, and being able to analyse the implications for action of each of the steps, requires a capacity for thoughtfulness about the task.

The work of Van de Ven and his colleagues (1989) lends further support to and elaborates on this dimension. Their focus is primarily on the 'middle manager' as change agent in the broad sense discussed previously:

'..the local innovation manager and the participants directly engaged in developing a particular innovation, and the investors or top managers in the organisation housing the innovation.'

(p.663)

Their focus is on innovations that consist of:

'...a purposeful, concentrated effort to develop and implement a novel idea that is substantial, technical, organisational and marked by uncertainty; that entails a collective effort of considerable duration; and that requires greater resources than are held by the people undertaking the effort.'

(p.664)

Their general emphasis on a 'purposeful' process of development and implementation of innovation is essentially an emphasis on the possibility of coherent, linear programmes of change which can be analysed, thought about, and understood in orthodox causal steps:

> 'Innovation managers should develop realistic scenarios of likely courses of action....The key point of our recommendation is not so much one of having an arsenal of strategies prior to launching development: instead it is developing and honing the skills of strategy development, which in turn are much the same as those required for adaptive learning.'
>
> (Van de Ven et al, 1989 p. 671)

These researchers go on to describe how in the process of change considerable complexity can be generated by the interaction of a few relatively simple developmental processes, and go on to recommend that:

> 'Restricting and simplifying developmental activities to the core innovation idea decreases cost and time to implementation...'

In short, for change to have a chance of succeeding, the change manager needs to be able to think through a realistic and limited sequence of steps, and be able to think through, as they occur, all the influences which will be tending to make the innovation process spiral into unmanageable complexity.

Similarly, in their discussion of policy entrepreneurs Roberts and King, analysing the 'problem-defining' stage of innovation, write:

> 'It was not enough for the policy entrepreneurs to challenge the givens and trade in ideas in the abstract. To ground their ideas and make them more compelling, they needed to present their ideas as solutions to particular 'problems' in the political context.'
>
> (Roberts and King, 1989 p.311)

The presentation and grounding of ideas as solutions to particular, publicly identifiable, problems constitutes the hard work of thinking through relatively detailed, linear action plans expressed in a form recognisable to those involved in carrying the ideas through.

Roberts and King go on to say:

> '...at the micro level, in an analysis of their activities over time, we found the policy entrepreneurs to operate more strategically, more deliberately, with greater conscious planning and orchestration......There seemed to be a logic that intentionally guided action and its consequences...'

(Roberts and King, 1989)

They go on to quote the rule of thumb of one such change agent, which includes such nostrums as:

> 'Know where you want to end up and don't lose sight of where you are headed...'

MCTI as a 'Rational Model' for Managing Change

The model for managing innovation identified in the earlier chapters can itself be seen as a planned , linear, step by step set of statements, but which will require a degree of imagination to understand as a whole and to be able to use in any particular change process.

However, to the idea of a linear, step by step process we add two main areas of caution. First, we argued in chapter seven that we need to be looking at all the consequences of our interventions and not just the implementation of the innovation. Second, life does not unfold as a step by step, rational, linear process. We argued in chapter two that we should beware that innovations are not typically adopted in such a way. Throughout the text we have avoided the word 'model', preferring 'approach'. This has been done to try to avoid an illusion that you can use the Innovation Trinity, or the other sections of the book, in a step by step way to manage change. We are acutely aware that the logic of laying out a book in a sequence of chapters means that to some extent the medium communicates an order even where it is not intended. In practice you, the reader, may come into the process of managing change at any one of the stages that are implied in this book. Perhaps this can be clarified with two contrasting diagrams that we have used in the development phases of our work.

The MCTI approach can be summarised in the following diagram. The different overlapping levels of activity are represented by interlocking triangles.

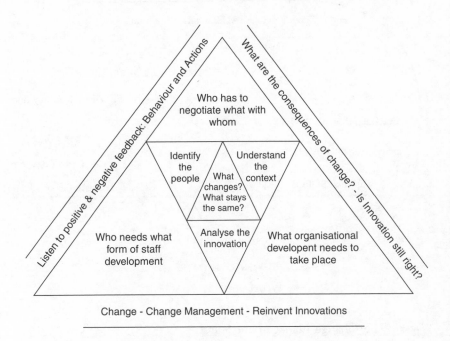

Fig. VI: The Innovation Triangles

Seen in this way each layer of triangles represents *a level of activity*, not a stage of development. Because you cannot write about everything at once, they appear in the book in sequential order. In practice you have to be engaged in all of these levels of activity most of the time, even if you think about them in order. Each of the levels has been discussed in previous chapters and are summarised again in chapter twelve.

The triangles summarise all the activities but perhaps give too neat and too mechanistic a picture of the processes. In practice, the processes look much more like Fig. VII, as action at each level causes the change agent to return to other levels of activity. For example, discovering new key players will mean that the change agent has to reconsider who sees what as a problem. These overlapping activities will be returned to, not as change agents 'go back to the beginning', but as they reconsider the basic questions as they spiral through time and get into interactions with new people.

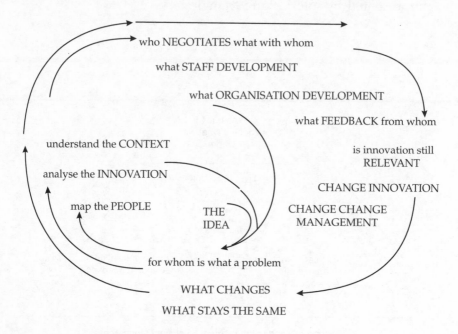

who NEGOTIATES what with whom

what STAFF DEVELOPMENT

what ORGANISATION DEVELOPMENT

what FEEDBACK from whom

understand the CONTEXT

is innovation still
RELEVANT

analyse the INNOVATION

CHANGE INNOVATION

map the PEOPLE

THE
IDEA

CHANGE CHANGE
MANAGEMENT

for whom is what a problem

WHAT CHANGES

WHAT STAYS THE SAME

Fig. VII: The Change Management Spiral

With any particular change you might enter into this spiral at any particular point. It would be convenient, logical and rational even, if we always started managing change by identifying the problem and its potential solutions. But often practitioners, front line managers, and even senior managers and agency directors have an innovation prescribed, whether they see themselves as having the problem it sets out to solve or not. We suggest they have to set out to work at all of the levels described with the key players in their situation if they are to manage change effectively. *Where you start in practice is an accident of time and place, but you do not have to perpetuate such accidents all the way through your change management.*

Some of you reading this will wonder why this section appears so late in this book. The most common feedback from the working edition and earlier drafts was to find a paragraph or two marked with the comment: 'This should come earlier in the text'. Unfortunately many different paragraphs were so marked leading to the conclusion that it should all be said in the first chapter. On reflection it underlines the point made in this book's introduction: 'We are all at different stages in the process of managing different changes, and in different places in the development of our thinking. Until we write the interactive computer version of this text enabling you to start with your questions, we are stuck with our limitations in presenting the text in a coherent way, even if it suggests reality has a neat sequence to it that proves not to be there'.

This discussion of the relationship between theoretical order and practical reality is perhaps an appropriate place to move on to the next issue in understanding social situations: understanding relationships. In doing so we change gear from leading with a discussion of skills and abilities to offer some useful ways of making sense of complex social interactions. This prefaces the theme of the next chapter on working with people.

3. UNDERSTANDING RELATIONSHIPS

There are many ways in which change agents may understand the social situations that they work in to bring about change and it is beyond the scope of this book to attempt to summarise them. We have found that certain ways of looking at relationships between people are particularly helpful in approaching change in social situations, and unravelling social problems precipitated and perpetuated by relationships between people. Readers are referred for a full discussion to the work originating at the Mental Health Research Institute in Palo Alto and the work of Watzlawick and his colleagues that have been referred to throughout this text (Watzlawick and others, 1967, 1974). Consistent with this way of thinking about human systems, we have found three patterns of interaction particularly helpful to change agents wanting to change relationships that perpetuate orthodox practice so that new innovatory ways of working can be adopted (Smale and others, 1992). These are common patterns of behaviour in the interactions between people in all kinds of situations. They can be seen in both benign or problematic relationships in many contexts including organisations, families or community groups and in the relationships between them. Understanding them helps to identify some of the strategic interventions which need to be made to bring about the changes in key relationships often required to change practice. They can also help us to understand how many social problems are perpetuated and how change agents might act to make a difference (Smale, Tuson and Statham, in press).

The three key patterns are:

- *Self fulfilling prophecies*
- *Self defeating strategies*
- *Mutually defeating interactions.*

We will see that each of these patterns takes into account both the perception, ideas or expectations of participants and the behaviour that it involves, and so can be used to make sense of all kinds of situations.

Self Fulfilling Prophecies

Definition: A self fulfilling prophecy is a prediction about the future, particularly future behaviour that is true only because the prediction has been made and subsequent behaviour brings it about.

Merton's (1948) original example described the demise of The Last National Bank. The bank starts the day as a solvent institution but a rumour is spreading in town that the bank will fail. This prophecy leads people to act, and they rush to the bank to withdraw their deposits. Until they accepted the prophecy the bank was safe, but when they believed it, and acted on their belief, the prophecy became true: the run on the bank drained its resources and the bank failed.

The distinction between a *self fulfilling prophecy* and that of accurate prediction is crucial. For a prophecy to be self fulfilling it is crucial that without the formation of the prediction or expectation, the predicted outcome would not have come about: in Merton's example, the bank would not have failed. Any self fulfilling prophecy operates at three levels or stages:

- the expectation or prediction is formed;
- action is taken based on this expectation;
- this behaviour then brings about or significantly contributes to the prophesied outcome.

For a person or people to bring about a self fulfilling prophecy, it has to be possible for their behaviour to influence the outcome of events. Thus self fulfilling prophecies are likely to be a significant factor in social relationships, but have no effect on the weather: preparing for battle might precipitate a war but putting on a raincoat will not lead to rain.

We have known about the significance of self fulfilling prophecies in human affairs for some time even if we have not always acted upon the insights that they give to changing relationships. The evidence supporting their existence is impressive and comes from very diverse fields. Barber (1969) demonstrated that interpersonal expectations are a crucial dimension in so called hypnotic states. Goldstein (1962) and Smale (1977) have illustrated the importance of expectations in helping relationships. Rosenthal's influential work *Pygmalion in the Classroom* describes the impact of teacher expectations in pupil performance (Rosenthal and Jacobson, 1968). Rosenthal (1966, 1978) also carried out a series of studies demonstrating the importance of expectations in interviewer bias in a wide range of research situations. These studies have their critics but in at least one area, placebo medicine, the power of expectations in relationships is completely accepted. Shapiro (1971) pointed out that the history of medicine is 'the history of the placebo effect', and that only in recent times has there been any certainty that medical procedures and cures are more than placebos. The power of the placebo is clearly based on the expectations of those involved and their subsequent behaviour. Its significance is so firmly established that no drug trial would be considered adequate without double blind procedures designed to counter the effect of patient and health professionals' expectations of treatment.

Brown (1996) and Moss Kanter (1992) describe the 'Pygmalion effect' as a change manager skill, which operates within the change management people-relationships.

'It is day to day managerial empowerment, recognition and trust that leads frontline workers to work in a similar way with their service users. Sometimes called a 'Pygmalion effect', it proposes that what management expects is what management gets. If frontline workers are not performing well it is more often because the expectations are unclear or the

frontline workers feel that their managers are uninterested. This managerial ability to create positive and trusting relationships with people inside and outside of their teams, as well as with service users and other colleagues, is a core feature of well functioning teams. Where it is present, you know that there is a leadership and service development ethos present, and where it is absent, it is frequently because the key manager has not shown interest, care or integrity, has not communicated recognition or invested in the frontline people, and is not interested in changing things to improve or develop their service.'

(Brown, 1996 p.119)

We suggested that although the existence of self fulfilling prophecies has been established, relatively little use has been made of this understanding to bring about positive change. The goal of the scientific establishment has typically been to try to irradiate the impact of expectations on relationships. Double blind drug trials, where neither the patient nor the medical staff treating them know who is receiving placebos and who is receiving the 'active' ingredient under study, is the classic example. This is understandable since the goal of such studies is to isolate the truly effective drugs from the generic effects of receiving treatment. However, those of us engaged in problem solving in social situations should consider how we might maximise the placebo effect (Smale, 1977). This line is pursued here but first let us look at the other related patterns of behaviour found in social relationships.

Self Defeating Strategies

The analysis of self fulfilling prophecies raises a significant question: *why are some people's prophecies fulfilled even when they do not 'want' them to be?* That is, when the person's behaviour, based on his expectations, defeats his goals. This is behaviour which we refer to as a *self defeating strategy*.

Family relationships, as children pass through adolescence, can often provide clear examples of such patterns. Here established expectations of parents move from being accurate predictions of how the young person will behave, to becoming obsolete and only true because the holder behaves in a way that precipitates the expected behaviour from the other person. Parents can persist in expecting their 'child' to still behave as a child when the latter feels like being grown up but regresses to fit the parental expectation. Of course the opposite also happens as the parents and young person see-saw round each other, and the parents treat the latter as an adult only to find that they are feeling like being a child: a reaction that can fulfil the stereotype of adolescents always being difficult sometimes perpetuated by parents assuming that they will get it wrong so ceasing to try to get it right - and thus further increasing the likelihood of getting it wrong, which only proves them right. It may also prove 'right' the young person's expectations of parents as overbearing, authoritarian and increasingly indifferent adults.

In many families the adolescent will become free of the obsolete parental expectations by persisting with the new behaviour until their parents' expectations change. Leaving home may be necessary for all parties to adjust to new perceptions and to establish new behaviour patterns. In many societies ritual rites of passage have been adopted to enable a smooth transition into new role relationships.

Similar disturbance, but with different levels of emotional charge, can be expected when second order changes are attempted in any relationship. The trick is to get changes in expectation and behaviour synchronised. But in practice there will often be disruption as one, then the other, person relapses into habitual behaviour or obsolete expectations of the other person's, or their own role. Where a new relationship is introduced, or even imposed from the outside, then considerable uncertainty will be experienced, as people literally do not know what to expect of each other or how to behave themselves, as they struggle to find a new relationship. Change will be extremely difficult where expectations are firmly held, such as in deeply held stereotypes of other people, and where behaviour is so habitual that all awareness of it has passed into the person's tacit understanding of the way the world is.

Conflict is a natural part of such transitions involving constant adjustments in behaviour as people revise their expectations of each other. Dissonance often escalates into problem proportions where a person holds unshakeable expectations, or persists in obsolete behaviour. A person who expects all people to be untrustworthy, is unlikely to trust others enough to establish mutual trust in their relationships: feedback from others that they are in fact trustworthy is typically distrusted. Stereotypes of other people typically involve entrenched expectations of their behaviour. Thus where young people are expected to be hostile and alienated they are avoided; where boys are expected 'to be boys' loutish behaviour may go unchecked.

What we see is that the current pattern of the relationship is held in place by a combination of socially constructed expectations and what has become habitual behaviour. To change this pattern may involve changing expectations and behaviour: change the latter without the former and one, and then both, parties are likely to slip back into the old established pattern. Getting both to change behaviour, and both to change the underlying expectations, may prove extremely difficult. This is especially so if one party wants to maintain the status quo, the way that the storms of adolescence are increased if parents are determined to halt or slow the process of their child turning into an adult; or for themselves to change from a parent into a prospective grandparent, or lonely older person.

These examples begin to illustrate the range of levels at which self defeating strategies can operate, and the significance of emotion, perception and habitual behaviour in their operation. It is commonly acknowledged that a person has to control his or her feelings, and move beyond 'subjectivity' if goals are to be attained. It is also recognised that this control, and the inability to voice concerns and conflicts, can sometimes present problems in themselves: self defeating strategies are one of the main ways in which, often very implicitly, the solution to a problem itself becomes the problem.

Mutually Defeating Interactions

When people, be they individuals, groups or organisations, get into a situation where both or all parties are fulfilling their expectations by provoking the reaction in the other that they do not want, they could be said to be taking part in a mutually defeating interaction. We can illustrate such patterns of interaction, and consider how difficult change agency can be, by reflecting on such processes in social work and social care organisations.

Social work and social care organisations exist to help people in a variety of ways. Some, especially children, are referred to improve their chances of a healthy and normal life: to enable them to be included in the community where they run the risk of social exclusion. Yet the very process of becoming involved with a social work or social care agency can stigmatise such children and their families and actually promote additional problems, despite the best intentions of all concerned: in short, being a 'social services client' can become a badge for the socially excluded. The thrust of social welfare legislation in the UK such as the 1989 Children Act is to prevent children from being 'received into care'. The family preservation movement in the US is also evidence of widespread awareness of the potential harm caused by such help. One of the problems that workers face in attempting to help people is the potential conflict between what they have to do to release resources and how they work towards the reintegration, the inclusion of individuals and families who may be excluded by the mainstream of society. This can be briefly stated as the tendency to build up a pathological picture of a person or family in order to pass eligibility criteria so that services can be released. This process often means building a pathological label for these people in the short term. But in the longer term this is diametrically opposed to the goal of depathologising people so that they can be reintegrated into mainstream society.

The pathological labelling process is a self defeating strategy operated by welfare agencies who have to limit their resources to 'the most needy'. In doing so they make it all the more likely that workers label their 'clients', which in turn makes it all the more likely that people will behave towards them *as if* they are pathological; which in turn makes it all the more likely that the labelled people will reciprocate and behave in the way expected, especially if they adopt the image of themselves increasingly being portrayed by others. When all parties are perpetuating self defeating strategies they are in a mutually defeating interaction (Smale, Tuson and Statham, in press). Managers introducing change convinced that people are 'resistant' to it may like to reflect on this example, and how the self defeating pattern can be repeated as they struggle with tactics designed to 'overcome resistance'.

Understanding how self fulfilling prophecies, self defeating strategies and mutually defeating interactions operate can lead to a clear analysis of the unintended outcomes of change agent activity, particularly where our attempts to help people further entrench them in their role as 'problem people': *where our intervention to include them confirms them as socially excluded people.*

The self fulfilling prophecy, the self defeating strategy, and mutually defeating interactions are all constructs intended to help us understand social situations in preparation for intervention. Their main value for the change agent is the insight they can give into what to do to introduce change in these patterns, often essential for introducing second order changes in relationships.

Behaving *as if* Predictions are True: Contingency Planning, Openness and Trust

In the above text two small key words appear that are crucial in the management of changing relationships: they are *'as if'*. The philosopher Viahanger (1935) was the first to draw attention to the significance of behaving 'as if' something were true. To drastically oversimplify his argument in discussing determinism, he says that even if it were true that all our actions were predetermined by causal factors in the past we would still have to behave 'as if' we have free will. The key issue in changing relationships is to recognise that self fulfilling prophecies, and so self defeating strategies and mutually defeating interactions, are perpetuated when a person or people behave 'as if' their expectation is true: 'as if' the prophecy is fact, and then their behaviour can influence the outcome.

These processes can be seen in the formation of some contingency plans, when the plan is prematurely implemented on the assumption that it will be required: when people slip straight from thinking *what if* it happens, into *as if* it is happening. By definition contingency plans should be implemented when the contingency has occurred. But they are sometimes implemented prematurely because the prediction of the problem is believed to be a certainty, or because the threat from the problem is so great that people feel they must act rather than wait: they feel they have to get their retaliation in first.

Formal and informal organisational structures, as well as habitual patterns of relationships in families and other social networks, can be created which generate the expectations that fuel mutually defeating interactions. There are always ways of describing outcomes of particular sequences which justify each other in a viciously circular way, such that each actor's 'success' justifies the rationales of the other actors. The manager referred to in previous chapters who wants to devolve responsibility but continues to act in his habitual way is in practice behaving 'as if' decision making had to be centralised, even though his decision is to decentralise decision making.

Such behaviour in key relationships may well be difficult to spot by people who are themselves part of such interactions; hence our stress below on *marginality* as a crucial dimension of the professional change agent's repertoire: to act as someone who can be both 'outside' enough to see what is happening, while also 'inside' enough to be able to influence the problem perpetuating behaviours of the people involved. We can see how an involved person able to see different people's perspectives in these examples also begins to see different approaches to the problem: begins to work 'as if' different expectations could be true.

Entrenched mutually defeating interactions typically feature issues of trust and mistrust. We will see that change agents or practitioners and managers wanting to manage changes in practice need to be able to establish trust in others as they work with them from a third party position to change complex patterns of behaviour. This activity will often include reframing their expectations and helping them to try new behaviour. This means working with participants to see if alternative expectations are possible and to behave 'as if' what they wanted to happen will happen, rather than assuming their fears are inevitably real and that the status quo is inevitable or the only alternative to chaos. This involves modelling alternative behaviour and helping rebuild the possibilities of trust. Thus the aim is to establish an environment within which more open communication can take place, to allow the testing out of assumptions and expectations and experimentation with new behaviour. We will continue the discussion of these issues in the next chapter, 'Working with other people'.

CHAPTER TEN

Working With Other People

This chapter includes a discussion of the need for change agents to develop their ability to hear what others say, to identify what others see as problems in the status quo and how they would set about solving them. It looks at the skills involved in working with the people on your changing maps: selling ideas, negotiating changes in behaviour and persuading people to release resources. It will be argued that it is essential that as a change agent you can listen and see, hear and observe feedback so that you can recognise the consequences of your own actions and that of the other players in the situation. All the time it is stressed that *you are working towards a convergence of ideas and actions so that the innovation can be reinvented to meet the problems that require change in your situation*. The skills involved are those required to avoid a divergence of opinion or strategy that may channel resources and energy into different directions. Key areas covered include:

- *Understanding people*
- *Working with other people's ideas*
- *Working with feelings*
- *Commitment.*

UNDERSTANDING PEOPLE

Towards the end of one of the workshops involved in the development of the MCTI approach a senior manager said that he found many of the ideas useful and they certainly helped him make sense of what went wrong in his organisation. But he doubted if it was a practical approach for him to adopt. He pointed out that to use this approach and map all his staff as suggested would be extremely difficult; as he said: 'to apply this approach you would really need to know your staff'.

Understanding the people involved in change, and those effected by its consequences, is central to using the Innovation Trinity to plan change and the whole MCTI approach. Finding out how others see problems and their potential solutions is the foundation of the approach. It is essential for deciding what should change and what should stay the same. It is the only way that you can deliberately engage in forging the convergence of ideas required for new ideas to be implemented. Similarly analysing the nature of the innovation involves both understanding the values held by key people and underlying the proposed changes, and how relationships can be changed where required. The discussion of the third dimension of the Trinity, the context within which change is taking place, also highlights the need to appreciate and use the force provided by the people moving in the same direction and how to steer around those who are obstacles.

The Managing Change Through Innovation approach is not so much about management by objectives as management by consequences: the goal is not just to implement change per se but to solve the problems you have and achieve the things you need to achieve. We will return to this theme in the final chapter but stress here that the ability to hear and act on feedback is essential for the effective change agent.

Given these activities it is then not surprising to find that in many different fields the ability of the change agent to understand how others are thinking and feeling is seen as the foundation for effective practice. Thus we see *empathy, the ability to demonstrate that you have heard and understood the other person* stressed as an essential change agent skill in disparate fields of personal and organisational change. For example, building on the work of Carl Rogers and others, it has been continually stressed in the fields of counselling, psychotherapy and other approaches to individual change (Truax and Mitchell, 1971; Egan, 1994; Bergin and Garfield, 1994) or as a key dimension of effective family and group interventions (Gurman, Smith and others, 1986; Bergin and Garfield, 1994). The ability to hear and act on feedback is at the heart of contemporary ideas of the 'learning organisation' (Senge, 1990; Beckhard and Pritchard, 1992), and has been stressed in other influential management books (Peters and Waterman, 1982). Indeed it is at the heart of the 'customer' or 'user centred' approach to running all kinds of enterprises.

In chapter four we saw that an innovation was more readily adoptable if it fits in with the views and assumptions, with the existing values and experiences of those being introduced to a new idea, product or form of practice. Everett Rogers (1995) points out that:

> '...the transfer of ideas occurs most frequently between two individuals who are similar, or homophilous. Homophily is the degree to which two or more individuals who interact are similar in certain attributes, such as beliefs, education, social status, and the like.'
>
> (Rogers, 1995 p.19)

He goes on to point out that:

> 'One of the most distinctive problems in the diffusion of innovations is that the participants are usually quite hetrophilous...(the opposite of homophily...degree to which two or more individuals who interact are different in certain attributes).'

Refining these propositions includes *empathy:* defined by Everett Rogers as *the ability of an individual to project into the role of another.* He says that:

> 'More effective communication occurs when two or more individuals are homophilous, unless they have high empathy. **Hetrophilous individuals who have a high degree of empathy are, in a socio-psychological sense, really homophilous. The proposition about effective communication and homophily can also be reversed:** effective communication between two or more individuals leads to greater homophily in knowledge, beliefs, and overt behaviour.'
>
> (Rogers, 1995 p. 19, emphasis original)

Rogers bases these conclusions on research both on early adopters and on change agents. Early adopters were found to have a higher degree of empathy with those they adopted ideas from than with later adopters. Research on change agent empathy comes from a variety of situations including studies carried out to evaluate the impact of training in interpersonal skills for nurses introducing family planning in different African countries. We should note that the work reported on by Everett Rogers is not concerned with therapy or counselling where the term empathy is perhaps more common currency.

The analysis of self fulfilling prophecies, self defeating strategies and mutually defeating interactions in the previous chapter assumes that you can indeed identify what a person's expectations are and discern the pattern of relationships underpinned by them. Throughout the basic level of the MCTI approach we have stressed the need to find answers to the questions about who sees what as a problem, who sees what as a solution. We cannot escape the need for empathy.

We can see that the managers may or may not know the staff that they are working with or understand their situation. But it is clearly essential that they have to have the ability to get to know them, and exercise it, if they want to be effective change managers.

'If People Do Not Hear You, Listen More'

Throughout the innovations workshops we have worked with people struggling to 'get their message across' to their colleagues and their bosses. They usually found it helpful to try to listen more to them, although some felt that they were working with people who were ideas deaf and allergic to appropriate action. A key issue in the convergence of ideas is the ability of the change agent to recognise and, when necessary, to learn the language, the assumptions and values that others think in. As a change manager you are not engaging in these relationships to win an argument, to prove that you are right. Such struggles are divisive. The goal is to change practice and avoid a divergence of ideas, and to create a convergence of thinking and action. This is done through listening to people so that you can recognise where their thoughts can be related to your own ideas and to those of others.

Throughout the book we have stressed the need to reinvent innovations, to repeat the process of their development, rather than attempting to simply adopt other people's solutions to your idiosyncratic problems. The point has been made succinctly by Allibrand and Benson (1980) in their study of training for rural change agents in the Third World. They argue that:

> 'Efforts to shortcut the development process by finding 'peasant-proof' modernisation methods have been largely unsuccessful.'

They go on to say:

> *'Frankly, we feel it is high time for change agents to **listen** more and **talk** less........Rural change agents should be concerned with the immediate specific needs of their clients.'*
> (Allibrand and Benson, 1980, emphasis original)

These comments come from an evaluation of change agents' efforts and reinforce a theme throughout this book: the crucial issue is the resolving of the problems the innovator sets out to provide a solution to with the innovation. We will return to this in the final chapter. Here it should be underlined that the effective change agent will be monitoring the impact of interventions on their situation throughout, for all the reasons referred to above but also to understand people's reactions to their change management, so that this can be changed where necessary, and so that the impact of change can be judged as appropriate. To do this it is essential that as a change agent you can listen and see/hear and observe feedback, so that you can recognise the consequences of your own actions and that of the other players in the situation. In short, empathy is essential to monitoring change management, both in the sense of understanding people's thinking and their feelings, and understanding their role.

To this discussion of empathy I would add that we have to strive to understand and communicate in the analogic as well as the verbal and non verbal languages. We have to understand the kinds of signs they use and we might need. We have to understand their metaphors and stories. This will help us understand when, if ever, it might be a good idea to use elephants. As we have said before, for all its perception of radical difference from paganism part of the success of institutional Christianity was building Christmas on the Winter Solstice.

WORKING WITH OTHER PEOPLE'S IDEAS

Three dimensions of the complex issues involved in working with other people's ideas will be discussed briefly here:

- *Leadership*
- *Other-centeredness, and*
- *Sociability: collaboration and maintaining dffective relationships.*

Leadership

Before discussing some of the dimensions of leadership that relate to change management we need to beware of the danger of perpetuating the charismatic individual fallacy. It is all too easy to take an individualistic approach to events. It may be good enough for tourist guides to say that King Henry VIII built Hampton Court or that Lincoln built the White House, but a change manager needs more specific and accurate information.

This raises the complex issue of 'what is leadership?' This is discussed in some depth in John Brown's companion volume to this book, *Chance Favours the Prepared Mind* (Brown, 1996). Here we will confine ourselves to a few comments to illustrate more dimensions of the skills used by change agents and change managers. John Brown's definition of leadership is as follows:

'Leadership is about creating the circumstances in which high performance teams can become committed to changing and constantly improving their service delivery.'

(Brown, 1996 p.68).

He is writing from his position as a manager, a team leader, in a social services department in the UK, an organisation, like most, with a hierarchy. Some people are then put in management positions which assume some form of authority or leadership over others. From this position Brown addresses the questions about what these people should do. However, he also discuses the literature that questions simplistic notions of all 'leadership' being invested in only those people with organisational authority. Thus he says:

'What we refer to as 'leadership' is the interaction and shared communication about direction, change, and service delivery improvements between those who have the positional power and authority to respond to change proposals and those who deliver the service.'

(Brown, 1996 p.70)

He follows Adair and others (1985), seeing:

'...leadership being about influence, consultation, persuasion, support and guidance where the key task is to get results from a highly motivated team.'

(Brown, 1996 p.74)

Brown illustrates the benefits of adopting change manager skills within an ordinary supervisory position. Common issues to respond to will be:

- *Seeing conflict as constructive and a catalyst for change*, adopting a pluralistic metaphor of organisations and teams, and always promoting convergence and collaboration rather than winning and losing.

- *Always promoting self-questioning in teams and individuals*:

  Why are we doing this?
  Why does it have to be done this way?
  Does it work?
  Is there a better way of doing this?
  Should we be going this at all?

- *Having integrity and trusting those that work for you*, encouraging the workers to be critical of both their supervisors, and the current team status quo.

- *Recognising downward dependence.* As in the Henry VIII built Hampton Court example, change managers and team leaders need to recognise that *they* don't change anything and that changes cannot be forced. Commitment has to be *given* to new practice and downward dependence recognises that the team leader, co-ordinator, manager is relatively powerless in the absence of worker support.

- *Seeing the leadership role as a people-developer.* It is important to recognise that people and team development must be highest on the priority list of managers. At the same time, it is fundamental to adult learning principles to recognise that people learn themselves: it is not something that is done to them.

- *Seeing commitment as a precious gift that is rarely given away lightly.* Commitment is given by individuals when the change task is one that convinces them. When conventional wisdom talks of leaders 'getting them committed' there is a misunderstanding of the relationships involved, which attempts to place responsibility for gaining team enthusiasm and individual commitment on to the person occupying the leadership role. This is a fallacy. Often the best thing a leader can do is get out of people's way and keep their mouth closed and their ears open. Commitment is given as a gift, not stolen by Machiavellian or charismatic people in power (Brown, 1996).

Brown's discussion of leadership focuses on the manager (Brown, 1996). In this book we are referring to *any* member of staff, whether professional practitioner, manager or care worker, who sets out to be an innovator or 'product champion' of a particular change in practice. This will include those who are in a formal position where they can, and arguably should, bring about change. We are also addressing teams of innovatory workers who have decided that they want to work in a different way. The material presented here is also relevant to, and has been used to good effect by, senior managers and policy makers wanting to mainstream innovations in their departments, just as it is relevant to policy makers wanting to introduce changes in practice to the system they make policy for.

The effective change agent, or change manager, whatever his or her formal position in the organisation, will be working up, down and across the organisation, and with people both inside and outside it. Over the years we have come to distrust the 'bottom up - top down' distinction concerning the location of the initiative for change. Those at the top of an organisation need to work with bottom up innovations just as those at the bottom need to use the initiatives, the policy and resources of those at the top. Both will need to work with and mobilise the resources of people outside of their organisation where they have no formal authority or 'position' at all. This is what understanding the context of change in your situation is all about (chapter seven). The mapping processes described in chapter three and detailed in the companion volume *Mapping Change and Innovation* deliberately avoids referring to organisational roles or levels. Indeed they attempt to encourage you, for example, to look for actual gatekeepers of the resources that you need for the innovation that you are working on. *All individuals are the gatekeepers of their own resources of time and effort:* do not assume that gatekeepers are only those with formal organisational authority. Let us then look at some of the aspects of leadership that are relevant to change agents, without assuming that they are attached to a particular organisational role.

Leadership, Vision and Change

In discussing the basic steps in the process of managing change in chapter three we said that we had found that most of the successful innovators that we had worked with had a clear vision of what kind of service they wanted to deliver.

There is considerable discussion of 'leadership' in relation to innovation, and within this, there is a frequent emphasis on 'visionary' and 'transformational' leadership. (See, for example, Manz and others, 1989; Beckhard and Pritchard, 1992.) These ideas clearly imply that those exercising such leadership have the imaginative ability to develop their own vision of how things might be or should be. A 'change-master' skill identified by Kanter is:

> *'...the ability to articulate and communicate visions... People leading other people in untried directions are the true shapers of change... this second change-master skill can be called 'leadership'.....this kind of leadership involves communication plus conviction, both energised by commitment.'*
>
> (Kanter, 1989)

Several different qualities and skills are rather unhelpfully lumped together here, and we will return to some of them below; but nevertheless, the capacity to imagine, to envision, is seen as underlying many other behaviours.

In a similar vein, Beckhard and Pritchard (1992) write:

> *'The leaders of the organisation must have a clear vision of the desired end state of the entire system, including such*

dimensions as its business, its organisation, and its ways of working.'

(p.4)

This approach might now be seen as conventional wisdom, with most management writers emphasising the central importance of strategic vision encapsulated in the organisation's 'mission statement'.

Kanter, like many writers in this field, frames this quality of vision and leadership as essentially individualised - this is self-contradictory since leadership is by any definition an interactive or *interpersonal* event, not an individual one: for there to be leaders there must be those that are led. Having the vision may be the essentially individual dimension of this 'change-master' competency, but interacting with others in a way that is perceived as them being led - the implementation of the vision - is essentially the *interpersonal* dimension or leadership. We might remember that the most effective form of leadership has been said to be where the leader tells people to do what they would have done anyway!

Egan presents an elaborate model of the change process, and the skills of the change agent within which he identifies three different kinds of leadership task:

- professional technical leadership
- managerial leadership, and
- transformational leadership.

Of the latter he writes:

'Such leaders usually have a larger vision of things than the other members of the organisation, institution, or community...'

(Egan, 1985 p.203)

An analysis of Bob Geldof's success with Live Aid offers a particularly interesting study of visionary leadership and the importance of imaginative abilities. It is particularly relevant to us here to recognise that, to begin with at least, he lacked, or perhaps we should say 'was free of', a formal organisation. This enables us to see some of the change agent issues without assuming that they are attached to a role within a particular organisation. In his study, ***Bob Geldof and Live Aid: The***

Affective Side of Global Social Innovation, Westley (1991) writes:

> *'In terms of personal background, the early life experiences of visionaries provide them with, at the very least, a core of intense preoccupation with a vocabulary of images which can be used, like templates, to organise and give meaning to adult forms of such preoccupation. This is true of all people, but visionaries with their particular symbolic capabilities are particularly adroit at the use of this kind of symbolic metaphor.'*

A methodologically sophisticated empirical analysis of the personal characteristics of 'champions' of specific technological innovations across a range of companies concludes among other things that:

> *'...the findings suggest that fundamental components of a champion's capacity to introduce innovations successfully are the articulation of a compelling vision of the innovation's potential for the organisation...'*
>
> (Howell and Higgins, 1990 p.336)

To have a vision for the organisation, or clear idea of how practice could be done, may well be a necessary requirement for those leading change but in our experience it is not enough. In chapter two we also pointed out that many of the innovatory practitioners and managers we worked with also took their values and vision literally and acted upon them. They may have been enshrined in mission statements to be framed and put on the wall of executive offices and made into posters for the corridors, but more crucially they were also a working set of values applied to every day problem solving. Indeed the commitment to solve key problems seemed paramount. However, we should remember Watzlawick's warning that there is no idea more lethal than a belief that the final solution has been found. In our experience it is perhaps more important that people are committed to solving certain problems and applying benign values in the process. This leads us to consider other attributes of the effective change agent.

Other-centredness

How often do we hear cynical judgements of managers who

are said to be only making changes to benefit their careers? Whether or not this is a true perception of cynical behaviour is not important for our purpose here. What is significant is that, true or false, such perceived motivation is commonly seen as a good enough reason for not collaborating with the proposed changes, irrespective of their intrinsic merits.

The evidence from a range of literature is that the change agent clearly needs to communicate that his or her prime concern or interest is with the needs, interests and concerns of the people being worked with, as against the interests of the change agent or the change agency. This can be summarised as the capacity of the change agent to be 'other-centred' in his or her professional relationships. This is potentially complex, particularly in the situations in which many managers in all fields and front line social work and social services staff commonly find themselves, of mediating between conflicting parties. Being 'other-centred' here entails being able to tune into several conflicting individual perspectives, and the relationships between them, without being seen to be taking sides in unhelpful ways.

In his discussion of the change agent, Everett Rogers writes:

> '....local change agents empathise with their clients, and give priority to client's problems. In fact change agents are often personally liked by their clients to the extent that they seek to circumvent bureaucratic rules...Change agent success is positively related to a client orientation, rather than to a change agency orientation.'
>
> (Rogers, 1983 p.319)

Rogers' work on the diffusion of innovations is exemplified in the situation of the professional change agent seeking to diffuse a particular technological innovation, for example birth control in Asia, to a clearly identified 'client' population or target system. This is sometimes a different situation from that of a middle manager or practitioner seeking to get a team of staff to take on a new way of working. The latter may have more organisational constraints to contend with, and Rogers (1983) acknowledges that early editions of his work have been criticised for lacking an analysis of organisational behaviour. The opposite is often true of most management writers, who look almost exclusively at internal organisation factors. For example Kanter (1985), Peters and Waterman (1982) or Senge (1990) are primarily concerned with management strategy and internal organisational dynamics. This means they tend to fail to recognise that many innovations spread through organisational boundaries and that it is the overall social network of staff that is important, not just their intra-organisational lives. Nonetheless the need for the manager-change agent to be essentially 'other-centred' remains crucial in all of these situations.

Allibrand and Benson (1980), in their study of training for rural change agents in the Third World quoted above, underline the need for change agents to work with the immediate problems of the indigenous population. Their argument against 'peasant proof innovations' underlines the need for change agents to avoid what is essentially self-centred thinking. Just as it is useless for us to adopt other people's solutions to their problems unless their problems and circumstances are identical to ours, so it is useless for others to have our solutions imposed upon them.

A major practical implication of an 'other-centred' orientation is that the capacity of the change agent to be able to listen to those with whom he or she is working cannot be assumed to be present. It is often assumed to be happening when it isn't; and assumed to be a relatively simple task which everyone will naturally do when, in fact, effective listening may be more the exception than the rule. Everett Rogers, for example, reminds us that:

> '*Change agent empathy with clients is especially difficult when the clients are very different from the change agents.*'
> (Rogers, 1995 p.342)

We have found that the opposite is also true. In interactional skills training for social workers and supervision skills development with managers, we found that the interviewer familiar with the interviewee's problems sometimes made serious mistakes. This happened when the manager or worker jumped ahead of the other person, assuming that they already knew what they were going to say based on their own experience of the problem or situation. They thus failed to hear and so empathise with the other person's own experiences.

The fundamental, core issue of the need to rediscover problems, recognise their idiosyncratic significance and the need for constant reinvention, is illustrated in Dr David Riley's work. *By listening to localised problems and frustration about getting something done, or there being something wrong in the situation, the change agent or change manager gathers information and perceptions in collaboration with others* (in the gestation period, see chapter five), *a process of gaining consensus and commitment to doing it some other way.*

Riley (1997) describes an excellent practical example of using listening and local data gathering approaches 'to the *process* of the diffusion of innovation' when applied to a public health and community development initiative in Wisconsin. Having successfully introduced a pilot programme for 'latchkey' after-school childcare in one area of Wisconsin, he began a 'simple linear' or 'solutionist' approach to the state-wide dissemination of the successful pilot. He encountered a range of indifference and resistant responses, in which each locality or community simply said to him that they did not accept that the 'problems' from another area of Wisconsin had any relevance for their area of Wisconsin - a classic 'not invented here' response.

It was only when he altered his strategy from a simple linear approach to one of locally-based convergence, collaboration and reinvention *in every single community or town*, that people began to see that there was a problem in *their* area and the commitment to solution-generation began. Riley had to literally reinvent the data collection to highlight the problem in each single town before there was any acceptance for the solutions that were available. Even then, he himself had to accept that there was a need for each town to modify and tailor the existing solution to their own local needs. He had to help them to reinvent the problem before he could introduce solutions. The success that was achieved, having moved away from a simple linear or solutionist approach, bears testimony to his comments that:

> *'I had not heard of anything like this before, and nothing in my graduate training had prepared me for this factory-like way of replicating the same research again and again. My departmental peers were also a bit mystified at first. Was this*

real research? I was finding basically the same results in each community, so why didn't I just publish it and go on with the next topic? The answer to this question implied a redefinition of the researcher's role and audience. Of course I knew what we would find in each new community, but the community did not, and they each had to find out for themselves. They did not believe that research conducted elsewhere was relevant to their town. In some cases, local leaders (such as school administrators) told us they were politically unable to advocate for after-school programmes until we created a public demand, which they could then answer. In such cases, we acted as a catalyst and probably hastened a process that would have taken some additional years otherwise.

One might say that instead of diffusing knowledge, I was diffusing the knowledge-generation process, teaching community members to be their own researchers.'

(Riley, 1997)

Here we see the combination of listening and other-centredness, in this instance a recognition that his knowledge is irrelevant. It is the knowledge of others that is important.

Others, writing about the world of industry and commerce, underline the crucial importance of these dimensions of change management. For example, Moss Kanter provides another perspective on the importance of listening, which itself can only come from a basically 'other-centred' disposition in the change agent, when she writes:

'Thus active listening to the information circulating in the neighbourhood is really the first step in the generation of an innovative accomplishment, and information is the first power tool.'

(Kanter, 1985 p.218)

Another level of 'other-centredness' and the ability to hear the communications of others is evident in the study of Bob Geldof and Live Aid. Bob Geldof writes of switching on the television as a diversion from his own worries about a recently produced record:

'I saw something that placed my worries in a ghastly new perspective. The news report was of famine in Ethiopia. From the first seconds it was clear that this was a horror on a monumental scale....I felt disgusted, enraged.......To expiate yourself truly of any complicity in this evil meant you had to give something of yourself...'

(Westley, 1991)

Geldof's description clearly conveys a capacity for 'other-centredness', both in the sense of being able to hear the communications of the television programmes, and also in the sense of moving beyond his own preoccupations and concerns in order to act in an 'other-centred' fashion. Clearly anyone seeking to promote change at either the global scale which Geldof sought, or the micro level scales of the average organisational middle manager or practitioner, will require some minimal capacity for the same attitudes and behaviours.

A major study on the training of change agents conducted in the 1970s involved bringing together a conference of academics and expert practitioners and getting them to identify levels of agreement on general propositions about the nature of change agency. Two propositions which received the highest proportion of agreement as essential to the effective change agent were:

'The user's need is the paramount consideration in any planned change activity';

and

'User initiated change is likely to be stronger and more long lasting than change initiated by outsiders.'

(Havelock and Havelock, 1973)

These statements are expressions of the importance of an essentially 'other-centred' orientation required of the change agent. The fact that this might appear more complex for many managers and practitioners who have to attend to several 'users' with possibly conflicting perceptions of their own and each others' 'needs', simply underlines how crucial it is for the change manager or change agent to be able to maintain such an orientation.

Sociability: Collaboration and Maintaining Effective Relationships

There is a common stereotype of the innovator as an oddball, somebody who is thinking in their own world and out of step with others, the eccentric 'nutty professor' or 'mad inventor'. There is perhaps some truth in these ideas concerning inventors and very early adopters: remember the Peters and Waterman quote about the trail blazers being the people up ahead with the arrows in their backs, and the analysis of innovation and its kinship with deviance. However, in our experience effective change managers combine their willingness to step out of line and challenge the conventional wisdom with an ability to work collaboratively, even if this is restricted to a team of like minded pioneers. More frequently though, the effective change agents we have worked with have good social skills and are motivated to form partnerships and coalitions with a wide range of disparate people.

Change agents work with and through other people. We will see in the next chapter when we discuss 'marginality' that they need to be capable of sufficient independence to be able to function in a third party position relative to key relationships, organisations and social networks of people. However, it is also crucial that the change agent is able to develop a range of ways of joining with, and working alongside, other people. They need to be able to do this in a wide range of configurations including individuals both in the same organisation and outside, and including both subordinates and superiors; groups of different sizes, whole communities, organisations, networks and so forth. The negotiation of convergent understandings discussed previously is essentially a social process, and thus requires in the transactor a general capacity to engage effectively with other people.

Evidence from a diverse range of literature supports this view. For example Kanter identifies 'coalition building' as the first of several interpersonal and organisational skills. She writes:

'Though the literature on organisational politics has emphasised one-on-one relationship building, my research moves the emphasis to the coalition. What makes people effective in organisations is the ability to create a whole set of

backers and supporters, specifically for projects of innovative activities, that helps lend the power necessary to vitalise these activities.'

(Kanter, 1991 p.58)

Collaboration is seen in this context of developing innovations and managing change in large companies and commercial organisations as an element in a change strategy. Within this strategy there will be a range of tactics in relation to the development of particular coalitions. For example, Kanter (1985) describes 'an attractive young woman' who proved to be a highly effective 'change master':

'She brings others into projects; she works with peers and people below to make them feel included. She creates multiple relationships...'

Weissman's study of entrepreneurship in social work concludes that:

'While all entrepreneurs need interpersonal skills, the social entrepreneur is probably more dependent on such skills than his counterpart in business. Although both business and social entrepreneurs must be adept in dealing with people, the social entrepreneur needs to be especially well-versed in organisational and governmental politics and processes.'

(Weissman, 1990 p.132)

Being 'well-versed' here does not just relate to an intellectual understanding of such processes - it refers to all that is involved in the social activities of:

'... 'making deals'. In the political arena, this activity may involve....obtaining sponsorship of key supporters.....getting officers to authorise projects and allocate staff....reach agreements with other program managers, and so forth.'

Such activities require the change agent to be able to work in lots of different ways with lots of different kinds of people, that is to be fundamentally sociable.

Kanter identifies a second 'interpersonal skill' which she characterises as team building:

'Once a group of supporters has been generated, it is time to get down to the actual project work. Now the next interpersonal-organisational skill comes into play - the ability to build a working team to carry out the idea.'

(Kanter, 1991 p.59)

In this she seems to be using the same definition of 'team' as referred to throughout this book: a team is a group of people related to each other to complete a task. Essentially then we are talking here about overlapping collections of people within and across organisational boundaries and not just the 'teams' that constitute part of many organisations structures. John Brown (1996) has discussed issues to do with organisational team development and the management of change and development of innovations in some detail in his companion volume to this book.

In his study of Live Aid, Weissman (1990) identifies that a crucial feature of Bob Geldof's success in mobilising the Live Aid appeal was his familiarity with the international network of people involved in the pop music industry, and his ability to use these relationships, to generate a snowball of commitment.

Everett Rogers concludes from his extensive review of the literature on innovations that:

'Change agent success is positively related to the extent that he or she works through opinion leaders....The time and energy of the change agent are scarce resources. By fostering communication activities upon opinion leaders in a social system, the change agent can hasten the rate of diffusion.....In fact, after the opinion leaders in a social system have adopted an innovation, it may be impossible to stop its further spread.'

(Rogers, 1995 p.354)

As well as the 'economic' argument for working through opinion leaders, the need for this is also a function of the need for the change agent to be able to remain in a third party position. The opinion leader is, so to speak, the person in the client network who is just over the fence from the change agent, but well connected in the client territory, and through such links the change agent can both be sufficiently involved and sufficiently independent.

Roberts and King in their study of policy entrepreneurs discuss the practical tasks of linking up innovators, developing and maintaining support networks, and bringing together practitioners and researchers, as part of the change agent's task. They write:

> 'The policy entrepreneurs tended to organise themselves into a group of individuals....(they) usually met once a week and...regularly kept in contact by telephone... 'Informed others' would be invited to sit in....Forums to discuss their ideas ranged from informal ones such as public speaking engagements, university courses, leadership development programmes...Our respondents also cited the policy entrepreneurs' telephone calls, personal contacts....and special meetings that brought together national education 'experts' with state and local political and educational leaders.'
>
> (Van de Ven et al, 1989 p.313)

These policy entrepreneurs/change agents engage in highly complex and enriched social relationships as part of their ways of influencing the situation and providing support to and challenging themselves and others in the change process. Some of the rules of thumb developed by one of the subjects of their research included:

> 'Change never comes through consensus. Get the key leadership to back your idea and 'the pack will rush to follow'...Get the elite involved...Destabilise the opposition by co-opting one of the ...establishment groups.'
>
> (Van de Ven et al, 1989 p. 313)

Our own experience of working with innovators has certainly endorsed the crucial significance of diffusion networks - we called them practice exchange networks - in supporting and sustaining innovators and innovatory teams. These people were typically relatively isolated in their own organisations and received much information as well as essential support from these networks. It follows from this that change agents and innovatory managers need to be good networkers. Indeed Rogers (1995) concludes that the cosmopolitan nature of innovators and early adopters is a key personal characteristic.

In their study of leadership and innovation Manz and others (1979) examine the process by which a new chief executive, who was installed against the wishes of a newly acquired company, sought to 'join' with the organisation. They write:

> *'This leader spent a great deal of time and energy initially both trying to assimilate the style of the acquired organisation and coming to understand the rhetorical vision of the community. He did this through intensive and constant personal communicative involvement with the entire staff....'*
>
> (Manz et al, 1989 p.620)

An essential element of the change process he was managing consisted of intensive, face-to-face contact with staff, crucial for actually understanding the perspectives of those with whom he had to work in order to bring about the necessary changes.

These are all examples of the change agent deliberately planning to work through and with other people, and through their relationships with those who the change agent seeks to influence: that is, **the change agent requires the cognitive, attitudinal, and behavioural abilities to work socially, in many different ways**. One of the ways that the change agent needs to work is to be able to work with, rather than avoid recognition of, the feelings of key people that will be aroused by the process of change.

WORKING WITH FEELINGS

Change agents and change managers should anticipate having to manage changing feelings throughout the innovation and change processes. Those initiating change often experience intense excitement during the initiation of innovation; frustration and conflict in the middle period as they work out the details of implementation and work with all the key people involved; and satisfaction mixed with loss on the implementation of a long held goal. We have seen throughout this book, and specifically in chapter five, that many people will experience loss for very complex reasons which need to be understood by the change agent. These changing and conflicting human emotions represent some of the most difficult management problems for those leading innovation and change. Managers will have to manage their own feelings, and that of their collaborators as well as those of staff 'on the receiving end' of change, if they are not to become destructive forces in the path of change, and in the body of the organisation. Angle and Van de Ven sum up some of the feelings typically associated with innovation and change thus:

> 'Innovation participants often experience euphoria in the beginning, frustration and pain in the middle period, and closure at the end of the innovation journey. These changing human emotions represent some of the most gut-wrenching experiences for innovation participants and managers.'
>
> (Angle and Van de Ven, 1989)

Self in the Sea of Change Revisited

In chapter five we discussed the need for change managers to understand the complex feelings of the people involved. Specifically we referred to the need for them to understand the sources of their feelings beyond the fact of the possibility of change. Thus we discussed three interrelated dimensions of people's reactions and suggested three questions:

1. *Are they active or passive?*
2. *Does the innovation change their identity?*
3. *Do they perceive themselves as winning or losing?*

As a change manager you will rely on your own observations and knowledge of the staff around you to discover the answers to these questions. Clearly if your map has many people on it, some of whom you have very little contact with, you will rely on the observations of others. There is however no easy escape from having to know the key people in the process, and finding out more about them through negotiations within which you demonstrate your ability to empathise with them. If your organisation has a good performance review system, then some of this information will be there in skeletal form; just as you will be aided by managers and colleagues who have closer relationships with key people inside and outside of your own organisation. But we have commented before that innovation and change, like putting antifreeze in an old car, has a way of finding all the leaks in the system. If you do not know your staff and have no system for doing so, you have further areas of innovation to engage in.

We have seen that a key feature is the impact of the innovation on the identity of those involved. This is an area where you might consider if you do have to change job titles where they clearly relate to professional identities. We should note that there is nothing sacred about professionalism per se. But such identities are typically hard won. Dismissing them can feel like ignorance of their meaning or an attack on the value of the study and effort involved in qualifying. This is an area where you may consider what can stay the same, and what needs to change; and if it has to change what it will mean to whom. I am not suggesting that you follow those companies that 're-engineer' and in the process demote most of the remaining managers but inflate their titles to 'executive director of...' Such tricks are easily recognised and such cynicism will breed distrust at a time when you need commitment and trust most.

To recognise the meaning of change involves an understanding of people's underlying values as well as what they might say about a particular change. In our experience the most difficult aspect of these discussions in many organisations is their indirectness. For example staff will often challenge a change because of what they assume to be the initiator's motivation and the consequences for them. Thus a change in working practices might be seen as requiring a move in accommodation and be introduced as a cost cutting exercise. In many organisations staff will say they think the innovation will not work, rather than admit to being afraid the cost cutting might extend to losing their posts. The problem is that cost cutting exercises are sometimes introduced as service developments. Here we can see that 'working with people' and especially their feelings requires trust. Trust is a two way process and we would reintroduce a theme from the discussion of self fulfilling prophecies in chapter nine. You cannot 'make' people trust you, but if you behave 'as if' they can trust you and 'as if' you can trust them, a chain of understanding may be invoked and a divergence of thinking and action avoided. We will return to the issues of trust and change agent authenticity in the next chapter.

Change, Loss and Gain, and Timing

What follows is a very brief attempt to describe some of the key issues that change agents need to consider when they are working with others to manage change. Writing about these issues underlines the limitations of a book such as this, discussed at the beginning of Part Four. To write specifically about the sensitivity and timing required to handle loss is like explaining how to tell a joke. But just as no change agent should overlook these issues because they are difficult and often painful, so no book on managing change should ignore them because they are complex to describe and because other media are required to develop your expertise.

Attention was drawn to the need for people to mourn the losses involved in many changes in chapter five. It was also suggested that gains typically follow losses. Kanter's work on the acute disruption involved in major reorganisations was referred to and her warning to managers quoted:

> 'Issue number one in managing a difficult transition smoothly is to allow employees to mourn the past, to grieve over their losses...The second key to commitment building during the restructuring process is getting the survivors excited about the future - offering positive vision to compensate for their loss.'

The use of career counselling and pre-retirement courses was referred to for those situations where staff are likely to lose their jobs. But the change manager will need to be able to help people through less dramatic changes. Timing is the essential ingredient to add to empathy and time itself. Grieving takes time, and the time it takes varies enormously.

The processes of change are a minefield of people's feelings. One of the problems with mines is that what you see on the surface belies what is under the water. We have seen that the meaning attached to a change may be unexpected and cause greater confusion and loss than anticipated. Similarly the impact of a loss is often compounded by previous bereavement and delayed grief can surface when triggered by relatively minor loss (Murry-Parkes, 1986).

Although we said that change managers do not have to become bereavement counsellors, arguably their job should be confined to helping those with particular problems caused by loss. All change agents will not only confront loss: they will often set out to cause it. This places a responsibility on them to understand how they can respond constructively and deliberately. The first step has to be the open acknowledgement of the fact of, and potential problems associated with, loss.

Beyond this, generalisation becomes increasingly difficult, since reactions to loss and change are both individual and derived from the culture the individual is part of. It is easy to suggest, as Kanter does in the above quote, that it is necessary to pass from grieving to recognising gains and building commitment: but when? Sensitive timing, empathy and trust are essential if these situations are to be worked with effectively. Empathy, particularly the ability to read feedback from interventions intended to be supportive, will inform timing.

The following diagram describes in an over simplified way some of the dimensions of these processes, to help you map those involved. It has been modified from a diagram tried and tested on pre-retirement courses, but the features are essentially the same for many major transitions. Like the other suggestions in this book and its companion volumes, it is a guide to your own map making. And like all maps, any that you make will be only a map, and easy to plot a route on; as opposed to the territory, which will require considerably more effort to journey over.

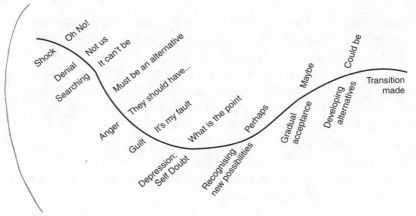

Fig. VIII: Reactions to Loss and Change (from GS Consultants, 1997)

Channelling Energy: Time and Commitment

The key to many of the fallacies described in chapter two is the fallacious assumption that there is some natural force at work driving change. The research is clear that people's actions, or lack of them, and decisions, even if made by default, are crucial to the course of change. Product champions have been found to be crucial in many studies because they are a vital source of energy. The commitment of these key people is literally the force which drives change. Plants grow through photosynthesis; sailors can sail because of the wind; objects fall to the ground because of gravity: innovations are introduced because people make a series of decisions and behave differently and the ideas that make this happen are passed on to others because people act. They put energy into making the changes happen. Without this energy the most brilliant human inventions would, and perhaps have, stayed in the mind of the inventor.

This perhaps seems obvious enough, but it often seems to be overlooked since many managers rely on passing on the word in the form of statements, procedures, guidelines or instructions to implement policy. Ideas, including these in this book, cannot be tested by reading them alone: they have to be acted upon, and the consequences of the actions evaluated before you can know if they work. But before we explore some of the relevant literature on commitment, we should stress that commitment cannot be applied practically without reference to time: *'There is no substitute for persistent effort over time.'*

We hope the reader will agree that it is worth repeating this statement: it is one we have found ourselves saying often. Over the last few years we have been engaged in a series of consultancies with colleagues in the US wanting to develop a community based practice or patch approach to social work practice and social services delivery (Martinez-Brawley, 1993; Adams and Nelson, 1995). We have found these colleagues ready to adopt innovations with enormous energy and commitment, so much so that we became concerned that their eagerness to bring about major changes rapidly would lead to unrealistically high expectations.

As we saw in the last chapter when discussing self fulfilling prophecies and change, all the evidence suggests that unrealistically high expectations will fail. In this context unrealistic expectations meant setting out to introduce changes that could not be achieved in the given time scale. Community based practice or patch requires the development of many community relationships between formal, professional helpers and informal, voluntary sources of support and residents' own social networks. Such relationships take time and have to grow in ways that are natural to the cultural values of the people concerned. We constantly found ourselves saying 'there is no substitute for persistent effort over time'. *Many innovations involving changing relationship between people have to be grown; they cannot be transplanted fully fledged, let alone engineered and brought in or prefabricated and moved around.*

Time presents us all with problems. If we were building any kind of structure, or running any kind of manufacturing operation, we would have to use time effectively. We would carry out a critical path analysis to enable us to plan each operation appropriately so that we would not have the roofing materials and labour on site until the walls were built and so on. Unfortunately many of the innovations that we are engaged with in the human services fields, and this is true for other fields also, involve innovations in the way that people think and behave rather than in more measurable physical activities. The analysis of the nature of the innovation and comparison with the adoptablility criteria will help this process. But such attempts to set realistic time scales are not yet commonplace.

Instead we live in a world where time scales are set by funding cycles. Typically three year deadlines are set to introduce and evaluate a new form of practice. In the fields of social policy the deadlines appear to be even more random, with the beginning of a financial year being a common target, revealing the absence of any realistic estimate of how long tasks will actually take. The change manager who seriously wants to change practice, to solve the problems that the innovation attempts to solve, will need to be realistic. You will recognise that funders and policy makers, like other gatekeepers, have their own views of the world and that you will have to work towards a convergence between your perception and theirs. It is then not surprising to find that time and commitment are often put together in the literature.

COMMITMENT

Kanter writes:

> *'Leaders of innovation persist in an idea; they keep at it. When I examined the differences between success and failure in change projects or development efforts, I found that one major difference was simply **time** - staying with it long enough to make it work.'*
>
> (Kanter, 1991 p.57, emphasis original)

Such quality of persistence or commitment may have many dimensions, and there will be many personal and contextual factors affecting why someone persists with an innovation through all the vicissitudes of the change process. However it is also a crucial personal quality, according to several of the literature sources.

In their argument for the central importance of organisations to become 'learning organisations', Beckhard and Pritchard (1992) write:

> *'A learning mode can only become part of the basic culture of the organisation if members of the top and senior management are personally committed to making the organisation operate in this way.'*
>
> (p.18)

Everett Rogers identifies 'factors in change agent success', including the generalisation that:

> *'Change agent success is positively related to the extent of change effort in contacting clients.'*
>
> (Rogers, 1995 p.379)

This seems very like Kanter's 'persistence'. Clearly there are personal attributes in this - qualities of stubbornness for example, belief in the innovation being promoted and loyalty to the people for whom the innovation is seen to be of value. There are strategic and tactical dimensions - who to contact and how; as well as a skills elements - the skills to communicate effectively with those who are contacted and so forth. However, underlying such factors is a basic commitment to the task which helps keep the change agent going and on track.

A study of the change process in two residential homes for elderly people concluded that:

> *'Achieving change in residential care does not necessarily entail the introduction of an external catalyst. An Officer in Charge with a brief to change, **active commitment**....can fundamentally alter the ethos of a home.'*
> (Potter and Wiseman, 1989 p.47, emphasis added)

As previously argued, it is important to remember that the process of innovation is essentially interactional, and that focusing on the attributes of individuals can be misleading. In this respect the Minnesota studies emphasise the contributions of commitment from a range of people involved in the innovation process. One of their concluding recommendations is:

> *'First, have not only a powerful innovation sponsor, but also an effective process facilitator who is committed to continuing with the adoption process, particularly when difficult hurdles and setbacks arise.'*
> (Angle and Van de Ven, 1989 p.687)

As with any personal quality, the change agent's capacity for commitment may conflict with other qualities equally necessary to the process of change. For example, there has been some discussion in the literature on the extent to which an innovator should allow or resist the efforts of others to change or modify the innovation being promoted. The conclusion of one study is that:

> *'The change agent has an obligation to protest vigorously any modifications in the innovation that would compromise its effectiveness.'*
> (Glasser and Backer, 1977 p.130)

This presents several problems for innovations in the human services areas. While it is easy to agree that modifying an innovation to the extent that it is useless or harmful would be a mistake, we have also stressed the need to avoid the trap of the false and dangerous: that you have discovered the final solution. Although we stressed in chapter three that we need to identify 'what stays the same', we did say that this is only relative to what we want to change now: eventually, inevitably, many if not all these innovations will pass. The convergence of ideas that will take place suggests that most ideas, even the way that technological hardware is used, will be modified. How else is technological progress to be made? The suggestion that the change agent seeks to achieve convergence does not imply that you give up your belief in the best solution for the problem: the best innovation. It suggests that you will, either deliberately and explicitly or accidentally and implicitly, enter into negotiations about what to do. We would suggest that there is always a higher commitment to solving the problems concerned and that this is essential, and overrides commitment to any one particular solution.

A change agent who was committed to finding solutions rather than a specific innovation was Bob Geldof. In his study of Live Aid, Westley says:

> 'While at times his personal style was off-putting, his integrity and commitment were rarely questioned.'
>
> (Westley, 1991 p.1014)

More likely what is described as 'off-putting style' was in fact a dimension of Geldof's commitment to the task, which inevitably may have been greater than many of those whom he worked with, and who would have experienced such commitment as unreasonable demands, inability to compromise and so forth.

A high capacity for commitment to the innovation or process of change is identified in a study of entrepreneurs in social work. The author writes:

> 'Two characteristics that all entrepreneurs appear to share are exceptionally high levels of energy and a single-minded dedication to purpose...The financial, regulatory, political and bureaucratic barriers often seem endless, frustrating, and sometimes insurmountable, particularly for social services ventures dependent on the public sector. Only the most dedicated social entrepreneurs can stay the course.'
>
> (Weismann, 1990 p.132)

Wright, in a study of the process of change in a district general hospital, concludes from this experience and from the wider literature that:

> '...the main sources of support to the change agents themselves and the pre-requisite skills.... (included)....Physical and psychological stamina, patience... Clear sense of commitment to the job/perseverance...'
>
> (Wright, 1985)

Finally we need to comment on 'channelling' commitment, using the energy of others. It is common to see change as a struggle, even a battle between those for and those against. A popular way of analysing this is taken from Kurt Lewin's force field analysis (Lewin, 1951). In its simplistic form this involves drawing up a list of all the people for and against the proposed changes. We used to find this helpful but limited. It encouraged us to feel comfortable in a 'them and us' way but it failed to differentiate between the many different positions that people were in. It also tended to make it harder to understand 'them' and to recognise the legitimacy of their perceptions from the positions they are in. It worked against the idea referred to above: 'if they do not hear, you need to listen more'. It implied that force needed to be met with greater force.

We have found it more helpful to map all the people involved, identifying the role they play in relation to the innovations you are concerned with, as described in chapter four and the companion volume to this book *Mapping Change and Innovation*. This is partly because identifying all the parts played by the different players gives more useful guidance to the change agent about who they have to do what with. But it is also because increasingly we have found obsolete the idea that change can be constructively pursued by using a model where force is met with force. During the course of the workshops we used a judo metaphor, explaining that understanding the context was all about identifying the different forces in the system and using them through alliances to gain momentum for your own innovation. Now we suggest that the idea of convergence should be uppermost in our minds. Thinking systematically about the negotiations and changing relationships involved in our changing maps we can perhaps see how we could be trying to construct win-win, rather than win-lose relationships.

Those who think that this is over idealistic can consider the later work of Charles Handy (1994). Writing about current and future industry and commerce he refers to what he calls 'the Chinese contract'. He derives this name from an anecdote he introduces to illustrate his point about the negative response of a Chinese businessman to the idea of a written contract. Why, reasons his would-be partner, does Handy need a written legal document? If the contract is truly to the benefit of both parties then it will hold because it is beneficial, and not need the force of law. To his way of thinking the need for a legal document suggested that he was being taken advantage of and that the contract was not really to his benefit. Handy argues that all good contracts are mutually beneficial. This has implications for the role of the change agent: the need for those managing change to be 'honest brokers', which will be discussed in the next chapter.

CHAPTER ELEVEN

The Change Manager's Position

Who Are the Change Agents or Change Managers?

During the development of this approach we negotiated entry into several organisations to work with staff at all levels on the management of change. In all of these discussions we said that we wanted to work with staff in the department who were leading change. On some occasions this produced a discussion within the directorate team about which staff were expected to lead change. Team leaders, it was suggested, or perhaps service managers, certainly principle officers with a service development brief 'should' qualify, but frequently the knowing looks around the table suggested that some of these were the last people likely to be leading change. Thinking that 'product champions', by definition, make the most enthusiastic change agents, we suggested that they thought in terms of individuals or groups of staff they knew to be very keen to develop a form of practice, or aspect of service. It was becoming clear that to some we had suggested something counter culture: the identification of individuals by their particular characteristics related to, but also independent of, their job.

Some of the senior managers present had no trouble with this and readily suggested individuals, or teams, they knew to be pioneering new forms of practice. Others were not sure they wanted to identify particular people without reference to their job descriptions. Some thought it would be wrong to do so, over personalising what should be organisational roles. Of these some felt that it was wrong to single out particular staff, fearing that it might be divisive. Others clearly felt uncomfortable because they did not know enough about their staff to know who the 'product champions' would be. In other organisations there were also managers who felt that we should only work with staff whom they saw as resisting change, since they felt that others would be good enough at managing change and all development activities should be targeted on the staff who were a problem for the organisation.

All of these organisations were in the process of introducing policy changes embodied in two major Acts of Parliament governing their work. All were going through major reorganisations: some in response to the Acts, some for other reasons. Many were anticipating major further reorganisations because of imminent local government boundary changes. Yet despite this sea of change, some found it difficult to identify 'people leading change in practice and service delivery' in their departments.

We addressed in chapter two reasons why some of these organisational changes would be seen as different from innovating in practice. It remains a curious fact though that neither of the Acts referred to intended to provoke a major reorganisation of local authority departments. But they did intend to reform practice. This underlines the tendency, discussed in Part One, of managers assuming that all change involves reorganisation. However, here we are concerned with who, in this situation, is identified as 'leading change'. To some extent all managers were appropriately identified as leading change, but most of these were said to be 'doing it because they had to' and so did not qualify as 'product champions'. This, of course, suggests that these organisations had significant problems, or were even in serious trouble, attempting to implement change that very few people wanted to lead.

To 'mainstream' major changes in practice requires a significant body of product champions: people committed to the changes and with the energy to push them through. If we reflect on the classic diffusion of innovations curve introduced in chapter four we can see that these S-shaped curves illustrate how a few people take up a new form of practice or a product, but for the bulk of a population to adopt it requires sufficient numbers of early adopters for them to copy. The researchers refer to the critical issue of gathering momentum (Rogers, 1995; Angle and Van de Ven, 1989). Typically in the public sector policy-led changes are defined as 'reforms', presumably with intentional pro-innovation bias. Our impression has been that throughout the many organisations we have worked with since the reforms were made official policy by the Acts, few have had such a body of product champions in post. Some of the many reorganisations that have taken place have been born of attempts to arrive at such a situation.

The identification of key people such as product champions or opinion leaders for the different aspects of the reforms, and the deliberate mobilisation of their efforts, is rare: it is as if we do not want to recognise our lawns when we have wholesale change to grass on our minds. The MCTI approach which suggests the identification of such people, indeed the mapping of all the key players so that their resources can be mobilised and managed, is counter culture for some, maybe many organisations. It is more accurate to say counter culture with many people in many organisations. It is true, as the MCTI approach predicts, that if you map all the actual people in your organisation or social situation you will be able to differentiate between them around a particular innovation. You will be able to identify who is an opponent and who is a product champion; who is a gatekeeper and who a collaborator. There will be different people in these roles for different innovations and they will not fall neatly into job descriptions.

This is true even with cultural innovations such as managing changes by identifying individual innovators, teams of product champions, gatekeepers and so on, instead of mechanistically seeing people only in terms of their jobs descriptions and formal role: that is adopting a process of managing change such as the MCTI approach. You will recall the definition of innovation in chapter one: for any form of practice, technology or product to be an innovation it only has to be new to the people it is introduced to. As with all 'innovations', as opposed to original inventions, identifying people by their individual stance on an aspect of change will be a new idea for some and natural, intuitive practice for others. Mapping the people helps you to identify who needs to change and who needs to stay the same.

We addressed many of the activities involved in implementing national policy-driven changes in practice in Part Three. We will return to the problems confronting senior managers attempting to identify appropriate change agents to do the job later in the chapter. But first I want to say more about the location of change agents in the organisation and discuss key issues related to their position in relation to others in the organisation.

The Location of Change Agents

It was not surprising to us to discover change agents and

product champions from all levels of organisations and with many different job descriptions. We have based the MCTI approach on the research cited in this book and our development work over several years with innovatory practitioners and managers involved in national and international professional networks. We said at the beginning of the book that many of these people innovated despite their organisation, and that understanding the social processes of deviance, whether labelled 'leadership' or 'delinquency', helps understand the processes involved for all who confront the status quo.

During the development phase of our work we have worked with people at all levels of their organisation: from the home care worker determined to develop a twenty four hour home care service, to the directorate introducing new information systems. It is clear that innovators, change agents or change managers are placed at all levels in their organisations. In chapter four we defined the change agent thus:

> *'Change agents are those 'formally or informally employed to implement innovation or to introduce new methods to others' (Rogers, 1983). The broad scope of this definition and the widespread emphasis on the need for a person, or people to consciously manage the 'process' of introducing an innovation has led us to use this term throughout the text, sometimes using 'change manager' interchangeably with 'change agent' to avoid constant repetition. We have made the assumption throughout that you the reader are wanting to manage change, that you are a change agent or change manager.'*

Because you, the change agent or change manager, may come from any formal position in the organisation you will need to work up, down and across the organisation, and with people both inside and outside it. *All individuals are the gatekeepers of their own resources of time and effort* and will need to be negotiated with to use their resources in the desired direction. We recognise that some people have far more formal power and authority than others, and that by definition those with power can do more than those without it. We also recognise that some people have a greater responsibility than others for initiating or implementing changes in policy. But, as we have said before, 'bottom up - top down' distinctions about change are illusions: almost all changes may, or may not require both. You will need to map the people involved in your particular innovation to identify who needs to do what. Typically those at the top of an organisation need to work with bottom up initiated innovations, just as those at the bottom need to use the initiatives and resources of those at the top. Both will need to work with, and mobilise the resources of people outside of their organisation where they have no formal authority or 'position' at all.

We recognise that you may or may not be defined as a change agent in your job description, but also guess that this will neither stop you if you really want to change things within your sphere of influence, nor be enough to motivate you on its own. We are even more confident that putting it in your job description will not turn you into a product champion for all innovations. Whatever it says in your job description, you are likely to be a product champion of some innovations and in opposition to others (think of increases in pay or the opportunity to do more of your favourite work activity on the one hand, and reductions in pay and benefits on the other). We are then all likely to be change agents who will want to manage change appropriately in certain circumstances.

This presents us with a difficulty since the literature about to be reviewed has drawn on the work of researchers looking for particular characteristics of the 'change agent', as if they were a special category of individual. This has echoes of the leadership discussion in chapter ten. Here we saw that we can look at the characteristics of 'leadership' or the 'characteristics of leaders'. Along with many contemporary writers we recognise that the search for 'leader' characteristics has proved illusive but 'leadership' is more identifiable. For example, studying the leadership qualities of Hitler when he was an art student or corporal in the army would produce less useful information than attempting to understand the relationship between him, his ideas and the people he led, their ideas and needs.

CHANGE AGENCY, CHANGE MANAGEMENT CHARACTERISTICS

Throughout Part Four of this book we have been looking at the skills, attributes and knowledge of the change agent to illustrate how the tasks set out in the body of this book can be effected. To take this process a step further we will discuss characteristics associated with taking up the role of change agent or change manager. The central dimension of this role has been mentioned before: it is the change agent's ability to be both an integral part of the organisation, and yet also able to be detached sufficiently to understand what is happening around you. It is about being a party to different relationships and the ability to act as an honest broker between people to help them change those relationships. It is about what we have called 'independence' or 'marginality'.

Independence or Marginality

The change agent continually needs to be able to occupy a relatively independent, 'third party' position in relation to the individuals and networks of people with whom he or she is working. The capacity for this has been described elsewhere as 'marginality' (Smale and Tuson, 1988; Smale, Tuson and Statham, in press). This means being able simultaneously to participate in the activities involved in promoting change in partnership with other people, while also being sufficiently independent to be able to observe the ways in which those interactions are proving helpful or unhelpful, and which includes reflection on your own behaviour. This quality of independence has cognitive, attitudinal, emotional, and behavioural dimensions.

Everett Rogers' work is primarily focused on the process of diffusion of specific, often technological, innovations in which the change agent is often, but not always, seen as a necessary linkage between a formal change agency organisation and its 'clients'. Of this he writes:

> 'As a bridge between two differing systems, the change agent is necessarily a marginal figure with one foot in each of two worlds.'

> (Rogers, 1995 p.336)

Rogers sees being a marginal figure as a problem for the change agent, which it is. But it is also essential, since the change agent needs to be able to enter and move comfortably in the two worlds, representing each to the other, and this can only be done if he or she is able to be relatively independent of both at different points in the change process.

In many change situations, of course, particularly those in which social workers and their managers are involved, the staff member who is the change agent will be 'linking' far more than just two 'systems', and often some of these will be in conflict with each other. Consequently, the change manager will have an even greater need to be able to think and act independently of those with whom he or she is working, while at the same time remaining sufficiently involved to be able to hear, understand and negotiate with the other people involved.

This quality of independence can result in the change agent having a particularly rough ride. For example, in a study of 'entrepreneurs in social work', the author writes:

> 'In a few cases, social services entrepreneurs are not professionally credentialed... 'Mavericks' whose ideas or approaches fall outside orthodox professional practice can be the source of substantial innovation. Unfortunately, these individuals have a difficult time having their work accepted by others.'

> (Young, 1990 p.130)

The author goes on to discuss a particular example of an innovative agency simultaneously prospering and under critical attack. We should note that this has echoes of Peters and Waterman (1982) and their observation that 'you can tell the pathfinders - they are the ones up ahead with the arrows in their backs'. We need to recognise an important distinction here. We saw in chapter two that pilot projects may be an excellent way of developing an innovation because you can put a wall around the workers and let them focus on their exclusive task. But we also argued that they can be completely counterproductive to the diffusion of that innovation to the rest of the organisation: indeed a potent form on inoculation. So the bloody minded inventor or 'maverick' may be a brilliant source of ideas which counter the conventional, but their worst advocate.

The effective change agent does not go around proving all others wrong but developing a convergence of thinking between potentially or actually competing ideas: the innovation and the status quo, or alternative innovations. But this position is also uncomfortable. 'Marginality', in the sense we are using it, is as if to say 'I am one of you, but only to the degree that I can also be one of them'. The marginal, independent change agent will do this to bring about a sufficient convergence of ideas and practices for the new form of practice, the innovation, to be reinvented so as to be relevant in local circumstances. We are acutely aware that the line between taking up a marginal position and being marginalised is a thin one, and not within the exclusive control of the change agent, since it is others who marginalise us.

The Minnesota Management of Innovations Project researchers, in different ways, also identify the need for the change agent to be able to act independently through retaining a third party position, despite all the pushes and pulls which would tend to influence the change agent towards support of the status quo. Identifying a range of ways in which people in organisations become blind to the need for change, precisely because of the capacity of humans to adapt to changing circumstances, they argue that:

'...mechanisms can be put into place for redirecting and jostling the attention of organisational members so that subtle changes and needs will be noticed.'

(Van de Ven et al, 1989 p.669)

By these 'mechanisms' they mean primarily people who, because of their independent position relative to the members of the organisation whose attention needs to be 'redirected and jostled', can actually see the need, and are able to act. 'The management of attention' described here will always require someone to be in an independent and marginal position to those whose attention needs to be challenged/redirected/ expanded, because by definition *they* will not notice that something needs to be noticed.

Gareth Morgan (1986) calls this form of cognitive self-imprisonment being 'locked inside Plato's Psychic Cave'. In the metaphor, prisoners are chained inside a cave, and can only see dancing shadows from the light of a fire on the wall on the other side of the cave. They cannot see the cave entrance. After a while they give names and meanings to the patterns of these shadows, as if they had a life of their own. When one of the prisoners escapes and discovers that there is a much wider array of life beyond the cave, he cannot return to the previous state because his psychic understanding has shifted. When he also returns to the cave and attempts to communicate with those who are still prisoners, he discovers that they cannot 'see' what he means and they exclude, label or marginalise the new knowledge.

The analogy is similar to one developed by Rosabeth Moss Kanter (1985) to explain the invisible walls that exist between sections of a segmentalised organisation, and what gets done to prevent wider networking. It also helps to understand the 'not invented here' phenomenon, and also the 'need for reinvention'. David Utterback (1996) similarly identifies commercial versions of the phenomenon: companies which are 'locked into' previously successful products. But it is the 'locking into them' which prevents them from the more radical 'next steps' that they need to take to remain competitive. He illustrates this by contrasting a number of companies but, as an example, he highlights how one of the earlier typewriter manufacturers could have made or taken the huge leap in technology that they would have had to make, to become industry-leading computer manufacturers.

The nine point exercise introduced in chapter nine is an elegant example of 'cognitive self-imprisonment' or the 'invisible walls' we put around problems and so cut ourselves off from possible solutions.

Attribution theory suggests the need for 'marginality' too. Given our propensity to attribute causes of success and failure differentially depending on what is in our interests, then we have a permanent need for someone or some organisation to be in a position to challenge these attributions. This will require the characteristics of marginality: being sufficiently close to be heard, but also distant enough to maintain some independent viewpoint.

We have already drawn attention to the strong interconnections between leadership and effective change agency. Leadership studies are a significant literature source for change managers. For example, a recent overview of management and leadership theory which is consistent with our approach to the change agent argues that:

'....under many circumstances, leaders have no option but to rely on themselves as a source of event meaning. To do otherwise is to risk becoming a pawn in the hands of one's role set...Management of oneself could be seen as the central element in the process of leadership. It may be, as we have argued, that leaders need to listen to and negotiate with their sources of event meaning, but still more importantly, they need to know when to listen to them and when not to.'

(Smith and Peterson, 1988 p.160)

Managing the ways in which other people define the situations in which the change agent is involved, that is what Smith and Peterson call 'event management', clearly requires the capacity for independent thought and action - to be able to think and act differently to that which is expected by one's 'role set'.

This literature refers to the independence of the change agent, but we have also referred to this dimension of the role as *'honest* broker'. Throughout the book we have drawn attention to the need for the change manager to be able to establish trust between themselves and others. At one level this is very basic to any kind of change. All change provokes some degree of anxiety. The outcome of any action, particularly something new, is unpredictable, a risk. This is why so many people want evidence that a new idea will work, overlooking that they have no evidence that the status quo works; or even where they have evidence that conventional practice fails. They want some insurance, or reassurance that there is no risk or that it is minimal. *Would you accept the offer to take a risk from a person you do not trust?* This leads us to consider our next important dimension of being a change agent.

Authenticity

It is a necessary implication of some of the other characteristics discussed in Part Four that the change agent has a capacity to be his or her own person and does not simply identify with existing custom and practice or the role expectations of others. The unequivocal recognition of Bob Geldof's 'integrity', quoted earlier, is an example of the potential power of, and necessity for, a high degree of authenticity in the change agent.

When entering into negotiations with others to arrive at a convergence of ideas we are not talking about compromise at any price. We have stressed that there will be opponents. If no deal can be made with opponents then the change agent will have to find a way round them, and win any competition there may be for resources. In all the transactions undertaken to achieve change in the desired direction, there is a need to be honest and straightforward with people about the organisational constraints the change agent works with. It is equally important to be honest with your agency about the perceptions and experiences of the people in the community with whom you work. *A major way of maintaining a destructive status quo is to maintain the fiction that it works well.*

Authenticity and Consistency

It is crucial that the change agent *genuinely* listens to others, and does not simply feign to do so while continuing to pursue his or her own agenda. The recurring cynicism of staff who believe that 'consultation' is an empty exercise and that senior managers have already made up their mind is all too often perpetuated by reality. Straight and honest communications require a degree of self-awareness in the change agent so that unwitting self-deception, and incongruence between actions and beliefs, are noticed and dealt with. This general capacity can be understood as the need for the change agent to be *authentic* in his or her professional relationships.

The need for such authenticity is identified in several ways in the literature. For example Everett Rogers, in a discussion of the use of aides and paraprofessionals, writes:

*'One of the particular problems often encountered with aides is **inauthentic professionalism**, the process through which an aide takes on the dress, speech, or other identifying marks of a professional in his or her field...But such inauthentic professionalisation destroys the very hetrophily-bridging function for which the aides were employed.'*

(Rogers, 1995 p.354)

Van de Ven and others (1989) assert that:

'The innovation team leader bears the chief responsibility for maintaining a sound relationship with those who control

resources. Perhaps the key to this relationship is unambiguous mutual expectations, more often achieved in theory than in practice....A key to developing a clear set of mutual expectations is the development of trust.....The subordinate's openness and candour seemed to be the key to developing a senior's trust.'

(p.689)

Being open and honest in communications with others requires that the person values such behaviour in himself and others, and thus has an essentially honest, candid attitude. Of this they write:

'It is equally important for the innovation manager to know him or herself. Innovators are often mavericks, fitting the classic description of the entrepreneur who is not comfortable with authority relationships. This type of personality has been termed 'counter-dependent' by personality psychologists. We believe it is incumbent on innovation team leaders whose propensity is towards counter-dependence to be aware of this and to take whatever steps are necessary to curb overt signs of this predisposition.'

(Van de Ven et al, 1989 p. 689)

Allibrand and Benson, in their discussion of training for rural change agents in developing countries, underline the importance attached to the self-awareness which is a concomitant of authenticity when they write:

'To a great extent the training programme will be a personal growth experience for the trainees: they will be challenged to confront and contemplate their social attitudes and values. They will be encouraged to undertake personal growth risks and to experiment with new interaction approaches... Inasmuch as a change agent's main resource is the power to effectively use his or her personality as a tool to educate and advocate...'

(Allibrand and Benson, 1980)

The issue of authenticity arises too at the organisational level, although it is still true that we are talking about the qualities and behaviours of individual people. Van de Ven and others write:

'One often hears organisational maxims such as 'here we let people fail', which indicate an espoused organisational rule that one should not stifle innovation by making people wary that they have only one chance to make it. Yet our experience in MIRP has been that this maxim is not always operative...On the contrary, we have seen instances where innovation team leaders whose projects floundered are stigmatised as losers.'

(Van de Ven et al, 1989 p.692

This introduces a new dimension of trust. In the opening paragraphs to this section we asked: **Would you accept the offer to take a risk from a person you do not trust?** Reflecting on our own experience and the above quote we would also suggest that the following variation on the question is relevant: **Would you take a risk working under this manager?** In our experience we found that so many people would have to say no to this question that we recommended in chapter four that a key person or people to identify on your maps are 'minders': 'someone in a senior management position who supports you when the going gets tough'.

Authenticity then is not just applicable to the change agent. For the climate to be right to foster innovation it helps if authenticity runs through the organisation. If senior managers of organisations do not 'practise what they preach', that is are inauthentic, then it will not be possible for the organisation to develop the levels of trust required for good enough communication and clarification of expectations. Beckhard and Pritchard write, for example:

'The most important single instrument for ensuring that learning and change take place is the set of positive and negative rewards that are demonstrated by management behaviour. If the stated values and priorities are not consistent with the behaviour of the leadership, the change will not stick.'

(Beckhard and Pritchard, 1992 p.15)

Discussing the dilemmas of participation, Kanter identifies some of the complex ways in which managers of organisations fail to be authentic or practice what they preach. She writes:

'Participation is something the top orders the middle to do for the bottom......participative activities are initiated because

someone at a high level directs others to get involved in task forces, set up teams, or to treat their subordinates differently...It certainly appears that leaders are not modelling the behaviour they want others to adopt.'

(Kanter, 1985 p.244)

Reflecting on the discussion in chapter five about orders of change and the 'be spontaneous binds' that managers can place on staff and the examples of 'empowerment' and 'devolved decision making', we can see that more than poor role modelling is at stake in these situations.

Authenticity and Feeling

The capacity for authenticity, and in particular the capacity to use other personal resources authentically, is closely interlinked with the place of emotion and feeling in the process of innovation and change. Much of the literature, because it consists of generally post-hoc academic analyses of human interaction, can imply a picture of change which is essentially behavioural and cognitive, and thus minimise the factor of emotion which, in a person, links behaviour and thought. We addressed some of these important issues in chapter three and elsewhere. We should stress that genuine emotions are also powerful motivators of change. Westley (1991) is very clear about the role of emotion in Live Aid. He writes of Bob Geldof:

'By his sensitivity to the power of visual imagery and sound and his ability to combine the two, he mobilised a group of consumers, whose identification with the youth culture spanned national boundaries, but whose institutional power was negligible. By blatantly engaging them through the effect created by music and channelling that effect and solidarity toward the famine relief....'

(Westley, 1991 p.1032)

We have seen that the traditional literature on loss and change, for example the work of Peter Marris, similarly identifies the place of emotion in processes of change and innovation, but much of the contemporary literature rather understates this dimension. Authenticity, of course, requires that the transactor's behaviour is not seriously inconsistent with his or her feelings, and thus requires a degree of self-awareness, and an ability to take a third party position in relation to oneself.

Who Are the Best Change Agents to Implement New Policy?

In the introduction to this chapter we described our experience of finding many organisations very short of product champions to lead what were seen as major changes in their organisations. Here we return to the specific issue of identifying the best 'change agents' for management led practice change. In Part Three we suggested that managers leading change need to target their efforts carefully. If you are a senior manager faced with too few product champions and limitations on your own efforts, what should you do? In mapping your situation you were invited to identify 'opinion leaders' as well as the other key players. We said that:

> '*Opinion Leaders* are those people within an organisation or profession who have an influence on the methods used by others. These are the people whose status or personal prestige causes others to see them as models of good practice. The relationship between these people's approach to practice and that of product champions can be crucial. Ideally opinion leaders will be recruited as product champions but where this is not possible the change agent or change manager's negotiations will have to produce a compromise or bypass the influence of opinion leaders.'

Drawing on their own research and that of other communication experts from the last twenty years Larkin and Larkin, writing in the Harvard Business Review, conclude that:

> '*Despite research showing that frontline employees prefer to receive information from their supervisor - the person to whom they are closest - companies continue to depend on charismatic executives to inspire the troops. Why doesn't this work? Because frontline supervisors are the real opinion leaders in any company. Senior managers must discuss a change face to face with supervisors, who will pass information along to their subordinates. Communication between frontline supervisors and employees counts the most*

toward changed behaviour where it matters the most: at the frontline.

(Larkin and Larkin, 1996)

In our experience senior managers in the human services in the UK are more likely to rely on formal organisational communications and reshuffling staff than the 'huge rallies, rousing speeches, videos and special editions of the company paper' that the authors suggest that US corporate leaders should stop engaging in. But their recommendation is entirely consistent with the mapping approach to managing change summarised in *Mapping Change and Innovation* and the steps described in more detail in Part Three of this book.

If we reflect on the descriptions of the discussions with the directorate members we can see that they were all at least partially right. What the senior manager has to do is marry identifying individual product champions, and opinion leaders, with directing their efforts to the formal role holders in the organisation that are most likely to effect the practice they espouse. For many areas of practice this will mean focusing on front line supervisors and managers. We see these staff as the keystone to practice in many organisations. They stand between management and staff in a naturally marginal position. It is less clear that many senior managers enable them to be appropriately independent.

PART FIVE

Conclusions and Overview

'Beware of those who rip up the lawn to turn the whole garden over to grass.'

This warning has been used to draw attention to the tendency to change too much, destroying examples of good practice by managing change in an insensitive, unsophisticated way. The metaphor was also used to draw attention to the need to identify 'what needs to stay the same' as well as the more usual change management focus on 'what needs to change'. This chapter reflects on the important question of time. In doing so it touches on what to change, and where to look for the best innovations? It suggests that the real challenge facing change managers of the future may be the need to go backwards as well as forwards, to make real progress rather than just to promote new innovations or change for its own sake.

In this chapter I will also underline the need to learn how to go beyond management by objectives and develop management by consequences. This includes a discussion of the use of feedback in guiding change management and the next round of developments. This is followed by a brief summary overview of the whole approach, addressing the fourth level of analysis of the MCTI approach: feedback and changing change management.

I will also reflect upon some of the wider lessons learnt during the process of working with many different people on the management of change. I will briefly return to our understanding of the context of change to suggest that *time* is a major issue in considering the changes we should attempt to make. But first it is necessary to revisit some of the fallacies described in chapter two and the usefulness of recognising that introducing innovations and the management of change are essentially problem solving activities and not ends in themselves.

CHAPTER TWELVE

Conclusions, Consequences And Time

Revisiting 'All Change Is Progress'

We started this work with a pro-innovation bias. Our goal was to develop an approach that helped change managers achieve their task, not to suggest what should or should not be changed. We have, however, learnt the increasing importance of warning against such a pro-innovation bias. We are constantly reminded of the crucial importance of the basic questions: *what changes; what stays the same?*

We have come across many examples of good practice dismantled by accident. This may seem strange, even incomprehensible to the outsider. Inside large organisations it is common enough. Any change is likely to provoke unintended and unwanted consequences. Managers struggling with major reorganisations are bound to cause these effects and compound problems by obscuring the impact of their previous actions with the next round of structural change. It is common to find that the parts of the organisation dismantled by accident are those that are taken for granted. Like many taken for granted relationships they are often crucial to our well being. In social services organisations, for example, we have come across several departments unexpectedly needing to organise new duty systems. Somehow they presumed that the duty system would carry on regardless of major staff relocation. In the health service we find professionals continually need to reassert the values of the relationship between staff and patients as they are unintentionally displaced by new technological procedures and equipment.

The past is full of ideas and practices that work. A classic example is the work of Lisbeth Schoor (1989), *Within Our Reach: Breaking the Cycle of Disadvantage*. Evaluating a series of projects mounted in the US during the 1980s she reported, as her title suggests, that many of the problems of the most disadvantaged children in the communities of that country could be tackled effectively. However, a few years later she reported that not only have many of these innovations not been repeated: many of them have not even been sustained where they had been developed (Schoor, 1993).

It has become fashionable to see innovation and change as synonymous with progress, to the extent that only the new can be a viable solution. However, our experience has led us to stress that innovations should not be adopted, change not made unless we are clear that it is a solution to a priority problem. To find new inventions and other innovations we tend to look at contemporary fashion, and the increasingly fashionable so called 'cutting edge' of progress. But to find the best solutions to present and future problems we need to:

- identify and sustain what works now;
- review what worked in the past;
- invent and adopt better forms of practice, service delivery and products;
- understand as many consequences of our actions as possible;
- innovate in our approaches to management to:
  ◇ sustain effective problem solving, and
  ◇ match management behaviour to the nature of the innovations introduced.

We cannot afford to adopt innovations just because they are the latest idea and meet all the criteria that make them easily adopted. They have to be good solutions to the problems we need to solve, without causing more harm than good.

The inevitable challenge to all change agents is that they have to be prepared to confront the status quo. One consolation is that they may see themselves at the cutting edge of progress. The next generation of change agents may have to be prepared to be unfashionable as well.

Change: For Better, or Worse?

Not all growth is good: cancer springs from the same well that produces the healthy body. We recognise the need to understand and cure cancer and increasingly check unexpected growth for malignancy. There are many who are challenging what they see as the eventually self destructive race of technological change and economic growth. But it is yet far from routine to check changes to see if they are wanted in all the places they are applied, let alone explore if they are harmful. We need to become as sophisticated as the best oncologists in recognising when change is healthy and when it is malignant.

A major problem confronting change agents at a local level, and those concerned with many social problems at a policy level, revolves around one person's progress being another's disaster. New solutions can often unravel the established solutions to old problems. The status quo is typically a set of solutions to past problems, just as we see when considering the plight of endangered species: the wolf, for example, is now threatened with extinction but its eradication in Britain did originally solve some people's problems.

People benefiting from change are often not the same as those suffering from the consequences. If others suffer the consequences of change, is it perhaps expecting too much altruism to assume that those who benefit might change their view of change? This dilemma often arises from a narrow management by objectives approach where change managers focus only on a particular goal and its achievement: on a problem and its immediate solution. The implementation of a particular innovation may ignore many of the consequences. Such a mind set may never recognise the many consequences that follow when 'they' lose their jobs in a reorganisation, when 'they' lose their way of life to make way for a dam, when 'they' lose the environment they love to make way for a new road. The reader may feel that these observations have been drawn from unfortunate and maybe pessimistic examples of change, and that the many benefits of innovations are overlooked. However, I suggest that there are two implications of such an analysis that hold for all effective change management:

- the need to tread carefully, to look for all the consequences of our actions and to be prepared to change those actions based on the feedback received; and
- the need to be realistic about time.

Toward Management by Consequences

Success is not to be found in simply getting an innovation adopted, be it the implementation of policy changes or the development of new practice. The key issues are:

- *does it solve the problems that it sets out to solve;*
- *does it precipitate unwanted consequences; and*
- *is it still relevant to current circumstances by the time it is actually being implemented?*

All actions have a range of consequences, some desirable, some undesirable. Undesirable consequences, such as pollution following new industrial processes, have to be tackled with new innovations in their turn. Not all unintended consequences are bad. 'Windfall profits' from a new product being used in ways not imagined by inventors are common. Many major innovations are by-products of the intended invention: examples include the possibility of houses having many rooms following the development of the central chimney, the many inventions of the alchemists even though they failed to make gold, the microwave oven as a by-product of experiments to help air crew survive ditching in the sea and many many more (Burke, 1978).

What is important for the change manager is that they evaluate what actually happens as a result of their interventions and not just the narrow area of goal achievement. There are a range of different consequences to look out for:

Desirable .... *Undesirable*

Anticipated .... *Unanticipated*

Direct .... *Indirect*

You will see that undesirable, unanticipated and indirect consequences tend to go together just as do their opposites. Change managers should be warned that it is often not possible to separate the desirable from the undesirable consequences: the advantages of nuclear power come with the risks.

New industrial technologies are no longer judged simply on their efficiency and effectiveness in achieving narrowly defined goals. Their impact on the environment has also to be taken into consideration. The management of change and innovation should be a reflective and a self reflective process: it should include monitoring the impact of the innovation on people; and also monitoring the consequences of the management process itself. If a method does not work, an innovation is called for to replace it. If the innovation does not have all the desired consequences then it will need to be reinvented, or replaced in its turn by a new innovation.

It is beyond the scope of this book to enter into all the issues involved in evaluating the outcomes of our interventions. But we cannot escape the strategic imperative to argue for the need to consider a far wider range of feedback than formal, orthodox evaluations would typically involve. The current move from focusing entirely on 'inputs' (are we doing what we think we should do) to evaluating 'outcomes' (are we achieving identified targets) only takes us one step down the path towards effective management.

Understanding how the changing world is unfolding and the consequences of our actions, our interventions, is a crucial next stage in our ability to manage change effectively. This is perhaps the skill of the great entrepreneur: understanding the trends in changing events, recognising their opportunities and knowing how to respond. The title of John Brown's companion book reflects this position: *Chance Favours the Prepared Mind*.

This will be a difficult step to take because of the complexity of all the factors involved: how is the world changing, what impact are your interventions having, what are the consequences? Evaluating outcomes, especially without attempting to identify precise relationships to inputs, seems, by contrast, deceptively simple: never mind about what you did; have you achieved your targets?

If we apply the criteria for evaluating adoptable innovations, described in chapter six, we can immediately see that management by objectives, and a focus on tightly defined outcomes, is adoptable. By contrast the complexity of management by consequences will make it a slow innovation to be adopted. All we can say is, beware: adoptable innovations are not effective, simply adoptable. H.L. Mencken has said:

'There is always an easy solution to every human problem: neat, easy and wrong.'

Feedback and Further Action

Throughout this text it has been stressed that the management of change is not a straightforward linear process, with research or an assessment at the beginning, followed by action and then evaluation and then further implementation if evaluations are positive. However, we have also described this approach to managing change in a reasonably conventional manner, warning that this should not be interpreted as indicating that the MCTI approach to managing change is just a step by step approach. We see this clearly in the circular relationship between feedback and further action.

From taking the first steps in discovering who sees what as a problem, through discussing people's training needs, on to identifying the consequences of all interventions, the change manager will be picking up feedback from people about their reaction to change and the way that its introduction is being managed. In chapter five particularly we described the different elements that are likely to influence people's reactions, and so their feedback to change. For example we stressed that the consequences of change are quite different for those who feel in charge, with 'their hands on the rug', from those 'standing on the rug' as it is whipped away from under them.

It is important to recognise that 'feedback' comes from all forms of communication, from verbal responses, to people's silent behaviour. Caution is always required about interpreting the motivations behind what people say and do. Open discussion is to be encouraged wherever possible. Remember the process of adopting new ideas is one of convergence of ideas and practices, a synthesis of the current with the new. The chances of success in managing change will often depend upon promoting convergence and minimising divergence, and this is difficult when communication is not open and frank. All change means stepping into the unknown, and trust in change agents is a key dimension to success and, again, dependent upon open negotiations and communication.

In one of the companion volumes to this book, *Mapping Change and Innovation*, I suggest that it is important for change managers to continually return to the maps they make of the key people directly and indirectly involved in change. This will guide you to three aspects of this essentially pragmatic approach to managing change, summarised as follows:

- *Do more of what works - less of what provokes hostility.*
- *Work with allies - do not put all of your energy into 'overcoming resistance'.*
- *'Resistance' and 'hostility' are negative feedback: change the way that the innovations are being introduced or change the innovation.*

If the way in which changes are introduced has undesirable consequences, that too has to be replaced by a different way of introducing innovations.

We have repeatedly found that when unanticipated people prove to be in the path of change unintended consequences often arise. It has been suggested that the maps drawn in the early stages of change management should, like medieval maps, have spaces marked 'here lie dragons'.[2]

It cannot be overstressed that we should monitor the adoption and adaptation of innovations in terms of their effectiveness as a response to the original problem they attempted to solve, and current issues. They should not be assessed just in terms of how well they are adopted. Adoption success, the fact that change has taken place, is not progress.

And Now? Start Again

'Well at least it passed the time.' 'It would have passed anyway.'

(Waiting for Godot)

If you have been attempting to manage change while you have been reading this book many things will have happened, with or without your help or hindrance. Had you started out by 'mapping all the people involved', your maps will be changing

---

[2] Margo MacLellan, Personal Communication.

as people leave and join, as well as through your own discoveries. The innovations that make up the component parts of your managed change will have been reshaped and adapted, in as much as you and others have been able to fit them into your human environment and change the environment to accommodate them. Now it is time to ask the final set, or is it the first set, of questions:

- *How are today's problems best solved?*
- *How are your goals achieved?*
- *For whom is the new status quo a problem?*
- *Who wants change and for what reasons?*

Final Summary of the Managing Change Through Innovation: MCTI Approach

This approach to introducing new forms of practice and managing change was summarised in chapter nine using the following diagram. The different overlapping levels of activity are represented by interlocking triangles (the triangle being a symbol for change). The levels, and the particular questions that require to be answered to develop your own map for managing change, are described further in *Mapping Change and Innovation* (Smale, 1996).

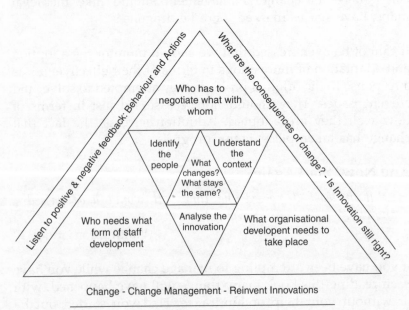

Fig. IX: The Innovation Triangles

The inner triangle represents **LEVEL ONE: WHAT CHANGES - WHAT STAYS THE SAME.**

This fundamental level of work (which corresponds to the material covered in Part One of this book) looks at: identifying the changes to be introduced and the component innovations; considering the relationship between the proposed innovations and the problems they attempt to address. Change managers work out 'What needs to change' and 'What should stay the same' by asking 'For whom is the status quo a problem' and 'Who sees the innovation as a solution'. We all know that everything changes over time, but this awareness does not always help in practice. The change agent needs to understand the relative rate of change. To be precise, we need to identify: 'What needs to change relative to what should stay the same'.

The three triangles round the centre describe the second level of activity (corresponding to the analysis in Part Two of this volume):

LEVEL TWO: THE INNOVATION TRINITY. This is the core of the approach. It looks at how change managers can plan change by:

- *Mapping the people: to identify all the key players*
- *Analysing the innovation: to plan appropriate action and time-scales*
- *Understanding the context: to use it to your advantage.*

The three outer triangles describe:

LEVEL THREE: NEGOTIATIONS, STAFF AND ORGANISATION DEVELOPMENT. Working at this level (described here in Part Three of the book) will help you to identify the negotiations that need to take place and who needs what form of staff training and what organisational development should take place. Part Four of this book discusses the skills involved in change management. The concluding chapter, chapter twelve, discusses the fourth level of the MCTI approach. This is summarised in the outer border of the triangle, which contains the key dimensions of:

LEVEL FOUR: FEEDBACK, CONSEQUENCES AND CHANGING CHANGE MANAGEMENT. Throughout we have stressed that this is not a step by step model. Managers and practitioners using this approach will not complete level one and then proceed neatly on to level two, and so on. There is a logic to such a sequence, and that is why they have been presented in this order. But 'real life' is often much more complex than such elegant logic.

In this final chapter we have said that at the end of the process of implementing, or more precisely reinventing the innovations, or even long before this time, the change agent will need to start the process again. In chapter nine we presented an alternative diagram because the triangles give too neat and too mechanistic a picture of the processes. This diagram, repeated here, attempts to describe how action at each level causes the change agent to return to other levels of activity. For example, discovering new key players will mean that the change agent has to reconsider who sees what as a problem. These overlapping activities will be returned to, not as change agents 'go back to the beginning', but as they return to renegotiate the answers to basic questions as they spiral through time.

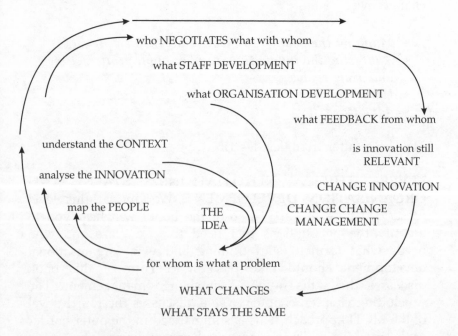

Fig. X: The Change Management Spiral

Change and Time

If you want to make real progress prepare to go slow.

As we enter into a new millennium it is worth reflecting on the context within which we are attempting to manage change, and specifically the speed of organisational and technological transformations. In the opening chapters it was argued that no approach to managing change could guarantee success: that good change management could only increase the odds of achieving desired goals.

Throughout I have stressed that no one person or group can expect to be in control of all the many factors that will affect change. In introducing the discussion of the skills of the change agent in Part Four I suggested that managing change was more like swimming in water than walking on firm ground. This metaphor was used to illustrate that the change manager was inevitably working in a fluid context, where many different forces will influence the course set and progress made. Understanding and using these forces is an essential dimension of plotting a successful course. Let us consider how fast the currents are running.

Let us assume that there is a new generation every twenty five years and that a person surviving until adulthood is likely to live until they are seventy five. Only forty such generations have passed since Jesus Christ was alive, just twenty five lifetimes ago. A person passing on their grandparents' memories to their own grandchildren would cover over one hundred and forty years. Fourteen conversations of this kind would span the whole Christian period. My father could remember when the mail was sent from Exeter to Exmouth on a coach pulled by four horses. My grandfather rode as footman on such a coach: a servant to the nineteenth century aristocracy. My father and his brothers and sisters rushed into the road to see the first motor car in their area. What will our grandchildren see? What could they pass on in a direct line of human experience? Will they think the past experience of the people they know has enough relevance to bother ?

It is understandable that the technological changes of the scientific era have been seen as 'progress'. Many problems, for many people, have been solved, holding out the promise that solutions can be applied to all problems and for all people. In this context it is understandable that the champions of change have seen those who oppose them as laggards. Of course stigmatising the opposition is often easier than countering their arguments, and it undermines the validity of their definitions of important problems and their solutions.

The Danger of Defining Change as Inevitable

Of all the technological developments and social changes that have taken place since the industrial revolution, perhaps one of the most significant changes is our view of change itself. Ancient Chinese philosophers understood that the only thing that did not change was the continuation of change (I Ching). But they were describing the natural unfolding of the forces of nature and the never ending cycles of life. For them change was inevitable, the way that you can never enter the same river twice.

Now we are confronted with different dimensions of change as our use of technology radically changes both our life styles and the environment around us. Rivers that once defined the landscape can be moved. We are constantly reminded of the accelerating speed of change. From a time only a few generations ago when technological change took place over lifetimes we have reached a point where the latest technological gadgets will pass into obsolescence in two or three years. For many the debate about 'should we change' has become obsolete: they believe that it is inevitable - a fact of life. As we have seen individuals not embracing innovations can be seen as 'laggards': people resistant to change. Indeed it is sometimes said that people 'resist change' as if this were some fundamental flaw in the human character. Countries not participating in, or failing to win the race for technological development are seen as 'underdeveloped', even if the term is modified into 'developing' to soften the negative connotation. In this slip from seeing change as something to be considered and decided upon, to perceiving it as inevitable we render ourselves powerless: you cannot change the facts of life. We have perhaps begun to believe in two of the fallacies outlined in chapter two so completely that they have become unquestioned assumptions: the fallacy that all change is progress and the anthropomorphic fallacy.

Faced with the 'inevitability of change' we have grown used to being surrounded by examples of what is seen as the obvious need to make some things worse to make them better. We move about the country resigned to the long traffic jams caused by road works to widen the roads to ease congestion. We have perhaps become so used to the wreckage caused by wholesale changes that we are numbed into a state where we no longer feel as if we have any control. Increasing technological change, the rebuilding of towns and the reorganisation of work and the workplace, have become 'a fact of life' rather than chosen solutions to perceived problems. In this there is a danger of widespread acceptance of the anthropomorphic fallacy: the belief that 'change' or 'innovations' somehow have a life of their own, independent of the decisions and actions of the people involved. 'Change' may be inevitable but particular changes and the adoption of certain innovations are not. We are reminded of Saul Alinski writing in his *Reveille for Radicals*:

'*A problem is something you can do something about. We may not know how, where, and what, but we know that eventually we can do something. The tragedy would be if we viewed a crisis as a plight; as an inevitability of life, like death; as a happening to which one is resigned. This has always been the prime task of the organiser - the transformation of the plight into the problem.*'

(Alinsky, 1989 p.209)

We can see again the usefulness of recognising that innovations are solutions to problems. Seen as solutions to problems several alternatives and options open up. People will have different definitions of the problem, different people will have alternative priorities for the problems that should be tackled and many will have different ideas about possible solutions. They do not *have* to be adopted. We have commented on the 'practical' management view that 'you cannot make omelettes without breaking eggs', and pointed out that there is a more sophisticated approach. But choices have to be made. If the shell is needed then the skill of egg blowing has to be used; if the yoke has to be separated from the egg white then the shell will have to be broken, just as it can be if the shell does not matter.

We are becoming increasingly aware of the negative environmental consequences of uninhibited economic growth.

We are also becoming more sophisticated at recognising the circular chains of causality that underlie events, for example recognising that wider roads will encourage more people to use their cars, requiring wider roads which means narrowing them with road works so as to widen them, and so on. We are increasingly recognising that one person's 'progress' may be another person's 'disaster' and that the consequences of today's change may have unbearable costs in the future. We know how to achieve many things and are beginning to recognise all the consequences of our actions and the need to pause to take stock before irreparable damage is compounded. The developing understanding of ecology, of the interconnectedness of many different aspects of life and the environment, is causing much rethinking of our attitudes towards what constitutes 'progress' (Capra, 1996; Lovelock, 1991). Many of these issues are beyond the scope of this book. But it is within this context that we are discussing the management of change and some lessons need to be absorbed by all change agents.

Appropriate Expectations

Throughout this text we have encouraged you to have realistic expectations. All the evidence suggest expectations that are too low will lead to negative consequences, while those that are too high are destined to collapse because they cannot be met as anticipated (Smale, 1975; Smale, Tuson and Statham, in press). If you do not believe that you can sail West forever without falling off the flat Earth then you will not go. If you expect to reach land in a couple of days you are most likely to turn back when it does not appear as anticipated.

The MCTI approach does not assume that you can control all the variables. I have stressed the need for understanding the way things are going and using changing events, nudging them in the direction that you want to go. But to assume that rampant change is inevitable can provoke self fulfilling prophecies on a scale far greater than the run on the bank that caused financial failure, described by Merton (1948). Some policy makers' approach to change is as if they felt that all the lawns were going to die one day so we might as well rip them all up now. More commonly perhaps they believe that other people will rip up the lawn, so they might as well get there first with the plough of 'progress'.

Reorganisation remains the taken for granted approach to changing practice and service delivery in many areas of public policy. The disruption to service delivery and the neglect of task performance are accepted as a necessary cost of change, the way road works block roads in the name of increasing traffic flow. If all organisations were roads, cone production would certainly be a leading industry. In this thinking there is a blind assumption that 'it will be all right one day', the organisation will be properly organised, the roads will be finished. But each day dawns with the introduction of another round of reorganisations.

A cynic might say that these reorganisations are a product of very low expectations: that because they predict that it is impossible to make the organisation work properly managers reorganise to provide an alibi for chaos and poor achievement. Their response to criticism would then be: 'Yes, but it will be alright when...'. However, I suggest that these cycles of activity are more often the product of expectations that are too high. It is as if we believe that we could set up the organisation in such a way that 'the system' would produce good practice, like a well designed machine does its job. These expectations can never be fulfilled and so they are abandoned when disillusionment sets in, and replaced with another grand design.

Conclusion

Changing practice takes time. Whatever the approach adopted to managing change all our experience suggests that there is no substitute for persistent effort over time. Our reflections have led us to recognise that change is difficult, and managing it complex. We also know that it is often possible, particularly where we can map a course through understanding the dynamics of our situations. To manage change as effectively as possible takes time out from the action. It may be possible to cross the ocean by trial and error. But the wise sailor spends time in the cabin plotting a course using all the available information, keeps an eye on the weather and the barometer and constantly changes tack, in response to feedback about current position and circumstances.

References

Ackerman, N.W. (1958) *The Psychodynamics of Family Life*. New York: Basic Books Inc.

Adams P. and Nelson K. (Eds) (1995) *Reinventing Human Services: Family- and Community-Centered Practice*. New York: Aldine De Gruyter.

Albrecht, T.L. and Hall, B. (1991) *Relational and content differences between elites and outsiders in innovation networks*. Human Communication Research, Vol.17 No.4 pp.535-561.

Alinsky, Saul D. (1989) *Reveille for Radicals*. New York: Vintage Books.

Allibrand, T. and Benson, D. (1980) *Training rural change agents for the Third World*. Social Development Issues, Vol. 4 Part 2 pp. 16-30.

Angle, H.L. and Van De Ven, A.H. (1989) *Suggestions for managing the innovation journey*. In Van De Ven, A.H., Angle, H.L., and Poole, M.S. (Eds.) Research on the Management of Innovation: The Minnesota Studies. Grand Rapids: Ballinger/Harper and Row for the University of Minnesota.

Argyris, C. (1970) *Intervention Theory and Method*. Reading, Mass: Addison-Wesley.

Argyris, C. (1982) *Reasoning, Learning and Action: Individual and Organisational*. San Francisco: Jossey Bass.

Argyris, C. and Schon, D.A. (1978) *Organisational Learning: A Theory of Action Perspective*. Reading, Mass: Addison-Wesley.

Argyris, C. and Schon, D. A. (1985) *Evaluating theories of action*. In Bennis, W.G., Benne, K.D. and Chin, R. (1985) The Planning of Change. 4th Edition. New York: Holt, Rinehart and Winston.

Audit Commission (1986) *Making a Reality of Community Care: Report by the Audit Commission*. London: HMSO.

Barber, T. X. (1969) *Hypnosis*. New York: Van Nostrand.

Barclay, P.M. (Chair) (1982) *Social Workers: Their Role and Tasks. Report of a Working Party.* London: National Council for Voluntary Organisations for National Institute for Social Work.

Bateson, G. (1979) *Mind and Nature.* London: Wildwood House.

Beckhard, R. and Pritchard W. (1992) *Changing the Essence: The Art of Leading Fundamental Change in Organisations.* San Francisco: Jossey-Bass.

Becker, H.S. (1973) *Outsiders: Studies in the Sociology of Deviance.* New York: The Free Press.

Beer, M., Eisenstadt, R.A., and Spector, B. (1990) *Why Change Programs Don't Produce Change.* Harvard Business Review, November-December.

Bennett, W. (1987) *Introduction to community social work.* In Beecher, W. Directory of Community Social Work Initiatives: Scotland. London: National Institute for Social Work for Scottish Network for Community Social Work.

Bennis, W.G, Benne, K.D, Chin, R. and Corey, K.E. (1961) *The Planning of Change.* 1st Edition. New York: Holt, Rinehart and Winston.

Bennis, W.G., Benne, K.D. and Chin, R. (1985) *The Planning of Change.* 4th Edition. New York: Holt, Rinehart and Winston.

Bentovim, A., Gorell-Barnes, G. and Cooklin, A. (1982) *Family Therapy.* London: Academic Press.

Beresford, P. and Croft, S. (1986) *Whose Welfare: Private Care or Public Service?* Brighton: Lewis Cohen Urban Studies Centre.

Beresford, P. and Harding, T. (1993) *A Challenge to Change: Practical Experiences of Building User-led Services.* London: National Institute for Social Work.

Bergin, A.E. and Garfield, Sol. L. (1994) *Handbook of Psychotherapy and Behaviour Change.* 4th Edition. New York: John Wiley.

Bernard, J. (1990) *Innovation in a Local Authority Social Services Department: Content, Context and Process.* Unpublished MA dissertation. London: Polytechnic of East London.

Bowen, M., (1976) *Theory in the practice of psychotherapy.* In Guerin, P.J. (Ed.) Family Therapy. New York: Gardner Press.

Brown, J. (1996) *Chance Favours the Prepared Mind: Leadership, Teamwork and Mapping Change for Human Resources.* London: The Stationery Office.

Bulmer, M. (1986) *Social Science and Social Policy.* London: Allen and Unwin.

Burke, J. (1978) *Connections.* London: Macmillan.

Butcher, J.N. and Koss, M.P. (1978) *Research on grief and crisis oriented therapies.* In Garfield, S.L. and Bergin, A.E. Handbook of Psychotherapy and Behaviour Change. 2nd Edition. New York: Wiley.

Calsyn, R., Tornatzky, L.G. and Dittman, S. (1977) *Incomplete adoption of an innovation: the case of goal attainment scaling.* Evaluation, Vol. 4 pp. 128-130.

Capra, F. (1996) *The Web of Life: A New Synthesis of Mind and Matter.* London: Harper Collins.

Carkhuff, R.R. (1969) *Helping and Human Relations.* New York: Holt, Rinehart and Winston.

Carkhuff, R.R. (1987) *The Art of Helping.* 6th Edition. Amshurst, Mass: Human Resource Development Press.

The I Ching or Book of Changes (1951) Trans. Wilhelm, R. London: Routledge and Kegan Paul.

Coch, L. and French, J.R.P. (1948) *Overcoming resistance to Change.* Human Relations, Vol 1 pp.512-532.

Cooper, M. (1992) Personal communication.

Connell, J., Kubilch, A., Shoor, L. and Weiss, C. (1995) *New Approaches to Evaluating Community Initiatives Concepts Methods and Contexts.* Washington DC: Aspen Institute.

Crosbie, D., Bennett, W., Smale G. and Waterson, G. (1989) *Disseminating Community Social Work in Scotland.* London: National Institute for Social Work: Practice and Development Exchange.

Crosbie, D. and Vickery, A. (1989) *Community Based Schemes In Area Offices*. Report to the Department Of Health. London: National Institute for Social Work.

Darvill, G. (1997a) *The Management of Work-Based Learning*. London: The Stationery Office.

Darvill, G. (1997b) *Work-Based Learning: Examples of Practice*. London: National Institute for Social Work.

Darvill, G. and Smale, G., (Eds.) (1990) *Partners In Empowerment: Networks of Innovation in Social Work*. Pictures of Practice. Volume II. London: National Institute for Social Work.

Department of Education and Science (1988). *Report by HM Inspectors on a critique of the implementation of the cascade model used to provide INSET for teachers in preparation for the introduction of the General Certificate of Secondary Education*. (360/88). Stanmore: DES.

Department of Health (1989) *Caring for People: Community Care in the Next Decade and Beyond*. (CM 849). London: HMSO.

Department of Health (1995) *Child Protection: Messages From Research*. London: HMSO.

Dewey, J. (1974) *John Dewey on Education: Selected Writings*. Ed. R.D. Archambault. Chicago: University of Chicago Press.

Domoney, L. (1989) *Directory of Community Social Work Initiatives: England*. London: National Institute for Social Work.

Domoney, L. (1992) *The Management of Innovations: Literature Review*. Report to the Department of Health. London: National Institute for Social Work.

Domoney, L. and Eno, J. (1996) *Managing Change and Innovation: A Guide to Alternative Approaches*. London: National Institute for Social Work.

Domoney, L., Smale, G. and Warwick, J. (1989) *Shared Care: Towards Developing Partnerships between Health and Social Services Staff and the People They Serve*. Final Report: HEA feasibility study. London: National Institute for Social Work.

Department of Health and Social Security (1985) *Social Work Decisions in Child Care: Recent Research Findings and Their Implications*. London: HMSO.

Department of Health (1989) *Caring for People*. London: HMSO.

Drazin, R. (1990) *Professionals and innovation: structural-functional versus radical structural perspectives*. Journal of Management Studies, Vol. 27 No.3 pp. 245-263.

Egan, G. (1985) *Change Agent Skills in Helping and Human Service Settings*. Pacific Grove, PA: Brooks Cole.

Egan, G. (1994) *The Skilled Helper: A Problem Management Approach to Helping*. 5th Edition. California: Brooks Cole Belmont.

Elizer, J. and Minuchin, S. (1989) *Institutionalizing Madness*. New York: Basic Books.

England, H. (1986) *Social Work as Art*. London: Allen and Unwin.

Eveland, J.D., Rogers, E. and Klepper, C. (1977) *The Innovation Process in Public Organizations*. Ann Arbor: University of Michigan Department of Journalism. Quoted in Rogers (1995) The Diffusion of Innovations. 4th Edition. New York: The Free Press.

Foster, R. (1986) *Innovation: The Attacker's Advantage*. London: Pan Books.

Freud, S. (1970) *Civilization and its Discontents*. London: Hogarth Press.

Freeman, C. (1972) *Report on Project SAPPHO*. University of Sussex. Quoted in Peters, T. and Waterman, R.H. (1982) In Search of Excellence. New York: Harper and Row.

Friere, P. (1972) *Pedagogy of the Oppressed*. Harmondsworth: Penguin.

Galbraith, J.K. (1991) *The Guardian*. November 20th.

Glasser, T. and Backer, T. (1977) *Innovation redefined: durability and local adaption*. Evaluation, Vol.17 pp.131-135.

Goldstein, A. P. (1962) *Therapist-Patient Expectancies in Psychotherapy*. London: Pergamon Press.

Goldstein, H. (1973) *Social Work Practice: A Unitary Approach.* Columbia, SC: University of South Carolina Press.

Goldberg, T. (1989) *From description to experiment.* In Smale, G. and Sinclair, I. (Eds.) Evaluation: Research and Management Perspectives. Unpublished Discussion Papers. London: National Institute for Social Work: Practice and Development Exchange.

Griffiths, Sir R. (1988) *Community Care: Agenda for Action.* Report to the Secretary State for Social Services. London: HMSO.

Green, R. (1989) *The Badenoch and Strathspey Social Work Team for the Highland Region.* In Smale, G., and Bennett, W. (1989) Pictures of Practice. Volume I. Community Social Work in Scotland. London: National Institute for Social Work.

GS Consultants (1997) Unpublished training material.

Guerin, P.J. (1976) *Family Therapy: The First Twenty Five Years.* In Guerin, P.J. (Ed.) Family Therapy: Theory and Practice. New York: Gardner Press.

Gurman, A.S., Kniskern, D.P. and Pinsof, W.M. (1986) *Research on the Process and Outcome of Marital Therapy.* In Garfield, S.L., and Bergin, A.E. (Eds.) (1986) Handbook of Psychotherapy and Behaviour Change. New York: Wiley.

Hadley, R., and Clough, R. (1996) *Care in Chaos.* London: Cassell.

Hadley, R. and McGrath, M. (1984) *When Social Services Are Local: The Normanton Experience.* London: Allen and Unwin.

Handy, C. (1981) *Understanding Organisations.* London: Penguin.

Handy, C. (1994) *The Empty Raincoat: Making Sense of the Future.* London: Hutchinson.

Handy, C. (1995) *Beyond Certainty: The Changing World of Organisations.* London: Hutchinson.

Haley, J. (1987) *Problem Solving Therapy.* 2nd Edition. San Francisco: Jossey-Bass.

Harris, J. and Kelly, D. (1991) *Management Skills in Social Care: A Handbook for Social Care Managers.* Aldershot: Gower.

Harvey-Jones, J. (1990) *Making It Happen: Reflections on Leadership.* London: Fontana/Collins.

Havelock, R.G. and Havelock, M.C. (1973) *Training for Change Agents.* Ann Arbor: University of Michigan.

Hearn, B. (1991) *Final Report on Community Social Work Exchange.* London: National Institute for Social Work: Practice and Development Exchange.

Hearn, B. and Thomson, B. (1987) *Developing Community Social Work in Teams: A Manual for Practice.* London: National Institute for Social Work: Practice and Development Exchange.

Henderson, P. and Scott A. with Miller, C., Smale, G.G. and Thomas, D. (1984) *Learning More About Community Social Work.* London: National Institute for Social Work.

Henry, J., and Walker, D. (Eds.) (1991) *Managing Innovation.* London: Sage.

Heus, M. and Pincus, A. (1986) *The Creative Generalist: A Guide to Social Work Practice.* Barneveld: Micamar.

Howell, J. M. and Higgins, C. A. (1990) *Champions of technological innovation.* Administrative Science Quarterly, Vol. 35 pp. 317-341.

Kanter, R. Moss (1985) *Change Masters: Corporate Entrepreneurs at Work.* London: Allen and Unwin.

Kanter, R. Moss (1989) *When Giants Learn to Dance: Mastering the Challenges of Strategy, Management and Careers in the 1990s.* New York: Simon and Schuster.

Kanter, R. Moss (1991) *Change master skills: what it takes to be creative.* In Henry, J. and Walker, D. (Eds.) Managing Innovation. London: Sage for the Open University.

Kaplan, G. (1961) *An Approach to Community Mental Health.* New York: Grune and Stratton.

Kimberley, J.R. (1988) Review of *Implementing Routine and Radical Innovations* by Nord, W.R. and Tucker, S. (1987) Administrative Science Quarterly, Vol. 33 No.2 pp314-316.

Kirton, M.J. (1976) *Adaptors and innovators: A description and measure.* Journal of Applied Psychology, Vol. 61 pp. 622-629. Quoted in Skinner, N.F. (1989) Behavioural implications of adaption-innovation: Managerial effectiveness as a function of sex differences in adaption-innovation. Social Behaviour and Personality, Vol. 17 No. 1 pp. 51-56.

Kolb, D. (1981) *Learning Style Inventory.* Boston, Mass: McBer and Company.

Kotter, J. P. (1995) *Leading Change.* Harvard Business Review, March-April.

Kotter, J.P. (1996) *Leading Change.* Boston, Mass: Harvard Business School Press.

Kuhn, T.S. (1970) *The Structure of Scientific Revolutions.* 2nd Edition. Chicago: University of Chicago.

Laing, R.D. (1969) *Intervention in Social Situations.* London: Philadelphia Association.

Laing, R.D., Phillipson, H. and Lee, A.R. (1966) *Interpersonal Perception.* London: Tavistock.

Larkin, T. J., and Larkin, S., (1996) *Reading and changing frontline employees.* Harvard Business Review, June.

Lauerman, M. (1993) *Change is not an event.* Local Government Policy Making, Vol. 20 No. 1 pp. 34-37.

Lewin, K. (1951) *Field Theory in Social Science.* New York: Harper and Row.

Law, J. (1989) *The Barlanark Project.* In Smale, G. and Bennett, W. (1989) Pictures of Practice. Volume I. Community Social Work in Scotland. London: National Institute for Social Work.

Lindquest, K.M. and Mauriel, J.J. (1989) *Depth and breadth in innovation.* In Van de Ven, A.H., Angle, H.L. and Poole, M.S. (Eds.) Research on the Management of Innovation: The Minnesota Studies. Grand Rapids: Ballinger/Harper and Row for the University of Minnesota.

London, M. (1988) *Change Agents: New Roles and Innovation Strategies for Human Resource Professionals.* San Francisco: Jossey-Bass.

Lorenz, C. (1992) *Refining the strategy.* Financial Times, February 21st.

Lovelock, J. (1991) *Healing Gaia.* New York: Harmony Books.

Manz, C.C., Bastien, D.T., Hostager, T. J. and Shapiro, G. L. (1989) *Leadership and innovation: a longitudinal process view.* In Van de Ven, A.H., Angle, H.L. and Poole, M.S. (Eds.) Research on the Management of Innovation: The Minnesota Studies. Grand Rapids: Ballinger/Harper and Row for the University of Minnesota.

Marcus, A.A. and Weber, M.J. (1989) *Externally-induced innovation.* In Van de Ven, A.H., Angle, H.L. and Poole, M.S. (Eds.) Research on the Management of Innovation: The Minnesota Studies. Grand Rapids: Ballinger/Harper and Row for the University of Minnesota.

Marris, P. (1974) *Loss and Change.* London: Routledge and Kegan Paul.

Marsh, P. and Fisher, M. (1992) *Good Intentions: Developing Partnership in Social Services.* York: Joseph Rowntree Foundation.

Martinez-Brawley, E. (Ed.) (1993) *Transferring Technology in the Personal Social Services.* Washington, DC: NASW Press.

Merton, R.K. (1948) *The self fulfilling prophecy.* Antioch Review, Vol. 8 pp. 475-88.

Mayer, J.E. and Timms, N. (1970) *The Client Speaks.* London: Routledge and Kegan Paul.

Mintzsberg, H., (1989) *Mintzberg on Management: Inside Our Strange World of Organizations.* New York: The Free Press.

Minuchin, S (1974) *Families and Family Therapy.* Cambridge, Mass: Harvard University Press.

Minuchin, S. and Fishman, H.C. (1981) *Family Therapy Techniques.* Cambridge, Mass: Harvard University Press.

Mitchell, R. (1991) *Masters of innovation: how 3M keeps its new products coming.* In Henry, J. and Walker, D. (Eds.) Managing Innovation. London: Sage for the Open University.

Monod, J. (1972) *Chance and Necessity.* New York: Vintage Books.

Morgan, G. (1986) *Images of Organization*. London: Sage.

Morris, J. (1994) *The Shape of Things to Come: User-led Social Services*. London: National Institute for Social Work.

Morrison, K., Gott, R. and Ashman, T. (1989) *A cascade model of curriculum innovation*. British Journal of Inservice Education, Vol. 5 No. 3 Winter pp. 159-169.

Mosteller, F. (1981) *Innovation and evaluation*. Science, Vol. 211 pp.881-886.

Murry-Parkes, C. (1986) *Bereavement: Studies of Grief in Adult Life*. 2nd Edition. Harmondsworth: Penguin.

Netting, F.E. (1992) *Care management: service or symptom?* Social Work, Vol.37 No.2.

Newburn, T. (1992) *Making a Difference? Social Work after Hillsborough*. London: National Institute for Social Work.

Newburn, T (1993) *Disaster and After: Social Work in the Aftermath of Disaster*. Jessica Kingsley: London.

Nicholson, John (1992) *Citizen Nicholson steps forward*. The Independent, October 13th p.21.

Nord, W.R. and Tucker, S. (1987) *Implementing Routine and Radical Innovations*. Lexington, MA: Lexington Books.

Oakley, A. (1982) *Interviewing women: a contradiction in terms*. In Roberts, H. (Ed.) Doing Feminist Research. London: Routledge and Kegan Paul.

Office of Public Management (1992) *Managing Fundamental Change: Shaping New Purposes and Roles in Public Services*. London: Office of Public Management.

Parad, H.J. (1967) *Crisis Intervention: Selected Readings*. New York: Family Services Association of America.

Pascale, R. and Atlas, A. (1983) *The Art of Japanese Management*. Harmondsworth: Penguin.

Pascale, R. (1990) *Managing on the Edge: How Successful Companies Use Conflict to Stay Ahead*. Harmondsworth: Penguin.

Payne, C. (Ed.) (1989) *Better Services for Older People: Report of a Practice and Development Exchange Project to identify how research findings can inform good practice and the issues that arise during implementation.* London: National Institute for Social Work: Practice and Development Exchange.

Pearson, A. (1985) *Nurses as change agents and a strategy for change.* Nursing Practice, Vol. 2 pp. 80-84.

Peters, T. (1985) *Passion for Excellence.* London: Fontana.

Peters, T. (1987) *Thriving on Chaos: Handbook for a Management Revolution.* London: Pan.

Peters, T. (1992) *Liberation Management.* London: Macmillan.

Peters, T. and Waterman, R.H. (1982) *In Search of Excellence: Lessons from America's Best Run Companies.* New York: Harper and Row.

Poole, M.S. and Van De Ven, H.A. (1989) *Toward a general theory of innovation processes.* In Van de Ven, A.H. Angle, H.L. and Poole, M.S. (Eds.) Research on the Management of Innovation: The Minnesota Studies. Grand Rapids: Ballinger/Harper and Row for the University of Minnesota.

Pottage, D. and Evans, M. (1992) *Workbased Stress: Prescription Is Not the Cure.* London: National Institute for Social Work.

Potter, P. and Wiseman, V. (1988) *Improving Residential Practice: Promoting Choice in Homes for Elderly People.* London: National Institute for Social Work: Practice and Development Exchange.

Potter, P. and Wiseman, V. (1989) *Champions, allies or irritants? reform begins.* Social Work Today, July 13th.

Quinn, R. and Cameron, K. (Eds.) (1988) *Paradox and Transformation: Towards a Theory of Change in Organization and Management.* Ballinger Series on Innovation and Organizational Change. Cambridge, Mass: Harper Business.

Rice, R. E. and Rogers, E. M. (1980) *Reinvention in the innovation process.* Knowledge: Creation, Diffusion, Utilization, Vol. 1 No. 4 June pp. 499-514.

Riley, D.A. (1997) *Using local research to change 100 communities for children and families.* American Psychologist, Vol. 52 No. 4 pp. 424-433.

Raines, J.C. (1990) *Empathy in clinical social work.* Clinical Social Work Journal, Vol. 18 No. 1.

Roberts, N.C. and King, P. J. (1989) *The process of public policy innovation.* In Van de Ven, A. H., Angle, H. L. and Poole, M. S. (Eds.) Research on the Management of Innovation: The Minnesota Studies. Grand Rapids: Ballinger/Harper and Row for the University of Minnesota.

Roethlisberger, F.J. and Dickson, W.J. (1939) *Management and the Worker.* Cambridge, Mass: Harvard University Press.

Rogers, C., (1957) *The necessary and sufficient conditions of therapeutic personal change.* Journal of Counselling and Psychology, Vol. 21 pp. 93-103.

Rogers, E.M. (1983) *The Diffusion of Innovations.* 3rd Edition. New York: The Free Press.

Rogers, E.M. (1995). *The Diffusion of Innovations.* 4th Edition. New York: The Free Press.

Rogers, E.M. and Kincaid, D.L. (1981) *Communication Networks: Toward a New Paradigm for Research.* New York: The Free Press/Macmillan Publishing Company.

Rogers, E.M. and Shoemaker, F.F. (1981) *Communication of Innovations: A Cross-Cultural Approach.* New York: The Free Press.

Rosenthal, R. (1966) *Experimenter Effects in Behavioural Research.* New York: Appleton-Century-Crofts.

Rosenthal, R., and Jacobson, E. (1968) *Pygmalion in the Classroom.* New York: Holt, Rinehart and Winston.

Rosenthal, R., and Rubin, D. (1978) *Inter-personal expectancy effects: the first 345 studies.* Behavioural and Brain Sciences, Vol. 3 pp.377-415.

Satir, V. (1964) *Conjoint Family Therapy.* Palo Alto: Science and Behaviour Books.

Schaffer, R.H. and Thompson, H.A. (1992) *Successful change programs begin with results.* Harvard Business Review, January-February.

Schein, E.H. (1987) *Process Consultation. Volume II: Lessons for Managers and Consultants.* Mass: Addison-Wesley.

Schon, D.A. (1983) *The Reflective Practitioner: How Professionals Think in Action.* London: Temple Smith.

Schon, D.A. (1987) *Educating the Reflective Practitioner.* San Francisco: Jossey-Bass.

Schorr, A.L. (1992) *The Personal Social Services: An Outside View.* York: Joseph Rowntree Foundation.

Schoor, L. D. with Schoor, D. (1989) *Within Our Reach.* New York: Doubleday.

Schoor, L. D. (1993) *Effective Strategies for Increasing Social Programme Replication/Adaptation.* Keynote Address, National Association of Social Workers Seminar. Washington DC, June 1993. Washington: NASW.

Seebohm, F. (Chair) (1968) *Report of the Committee on Local Authority and Allied Personal Social Services.* (Cmnd.3703) London: HMSO.

Seligman, M.E.P. (1975) *Helplessness: On Depression, Development and Death.* San Francisco: WH Freeman.

Senge, P.M. (1990) *The Fifth Discipline: The Art and Practice of the Learning Organization.* New York: Doubleday.

Shapiro, A.K. (1971) *Placebo effects in medicine, psychotherapy and psychoanalysis.* In Bergin, A. and Garfield, S.L. (1971) Handbook of Psychotherapy and Behaviour Change. 1st Edition. New York: Wiley.

Shaull, R. (1972) *Foreword* to Friere, P. Pedagogy of the Oppressed. Harmondsworth: Penguin.

Sinclair, I., Crosbie, D., O'Conner, P., Stanforth, L. and Vickery, A. (1988) *Bridging Two Worlds: Social Work and the Elderly Living Alone.* Aldershot: Gower.

Skinner, N.F. (1989) *Behavioural implications of adaption-innovation: managerial effectiveness as a function of sex differences in adaption-innovation.* Social Behaviour and Personality, Vol.17 No. 1 pp. 51-56.

Smale, G.G. (1977) *Prophecy, Behaviour and Change.* London: Routledge and Kegan Paul.

Smale, G.G. (1983) *Can we afford not to develop social work practice?* British Journal of Social Work, Vol. 13 pp. 251-264.

Smale, G.G. (1984) *Self fulfilling prophecies, self defeating strategies and change.* British Journal of Social Work, Vol. 14 pp. 419-433.

Smale, G.G. (1985) *Information Exchange: Swamp or Desert?* London: National Institute for Social Work: Practice And Development Exchange.

Smale, G.G. (1987) *Some principles of interactional skills training.* Social Work Education, Vol. 7 No. 1 pp.3-9.

Smale, G.G. (1991) *'Paradigms', 'Visions', 'Methods' and the 'Mission Impossible': Steps Toward Developing a New Practice Theory.* Discussion Paper. London: National Institute for Social Work: Practice and Development Exchange.

Smale, G.G. (1992) *RATS in the System: Reorganisation for Practice Change or for Chaos?* Discussion Paper. London: National Institute for Social Work: Practice and Development Exchange.

Smale, G.G. (1993) *The nature of innovation and community based practice.* In Martinez-Brawley, E. (Ed.) Transferring Technology in the Personal Social Services. Washington, DC: NASW.

Smale, G.G. (1996) *Mapping Change and Innovation.* London: The Stationery Office.

Smale, G.G. and Bennett, W. (Eds.) (1989) *Pictures of Practice. Volume I. Community Social Work in Scotland.* London: National Institute for Social Work: Practice and Development Exchange.

Smale, G.G. and Sinclair, I. (1987) *Evaluation: Battle Ground or Meeting Point?* London: National Institute for Social Work: Practice and Development Exchange.

Smale, G.G. and Statham, D. (1989) *Research into practice: using research in practice and policy making.* In Stein, M. (Ed.) Research into Practice. Proceedings of the Fourth Annual JUC/BASW Conference. Birmingham: BASW.

Smale, G.G. and Tuson, G. (1988) *Learning for Change: Developing Staff and Practice in Social Work Teams*. London: National Institute for Social Work: Practice and Development Exchange.

Smale, G.G. and Tuson, G. (1990) *Community social work: foundation for the 1990s and beyond*. In Darvill, G. and Smale, G. (Eds.) Partners in Empowerment: Networks of Innovation in Social Work. Pictures of Practice. Volume II. London: National Institute for Social Work.

Smale, G. and Vernon, J. (1986) *Report to the Department of Health on Dissemination of Child Care Research*. London: National Institute for Social Work.

Smale, G.G., Domoney, L., Tuson, G., Ahmad, B., Sainsbury, E. and Darvill, G. (1994) *Negotiating Care in the Community: The Implications of Research Findings on Community Based Practice for the Implementation of the Community Care and Children Acts*. Report to the Department of Health: London: HMSO for National Institute for Social Work: Practice and Development Exchange.

Smale, G.G., Tuson, G., Cooper, M., Wardle, M. and Crosbie, D. (1988) *Community Social Work: A Paradigm for Change*. London: National Institute for Social Work: Practice And Development Exchange

Smale, G. and Tuson, G. with Biehal, N. and Marsh, P. (1993) *Empowerment, Assessment, Care Management and the Skilled Worker*. London: HMSO for National Institute for Social Work: Practice and Development Exchange.

Smale, G., Tuson, G. and Statham, D. (in press) *Social Work in the Community*. London: Macmillan.

Smith, P.B. and Peterson, M.F. (1988) *Leadership, Organisation and Culture*. London: Sage.

Specht, H. (1990) *Social work and the popular psychotherapies*. Social Service Review, Vol. 64 pp. 345-357.

Stocking, B. (1985) *Initiative and Inertia: Case Studies in the NHS*. London: Nuffield Provincial Hospital Trust.

Sturges, P.J. (1992) *Comparing practice in the United States and the United Kingdom*. Ageing International, pp.15-27.

SWING (1988). *Directory of Social Welfare Information Networks.* London: National Institute for Social Work: Practice and Development Exchange.

Thom, R. (1975) *Structural Stability and Morphogenesis: An Outline of a General Theory of Models.* Reading: Benjamin.

Thomas J. (1984) *Responses to the Barclay Report: England and Wales.* London: National Institute for Social Work.

Tornatzky, G.G. and others (1983) *The Process of Technological Innovations: Reviewing the Literature.* Washington, DC: National Science Foundation.

Truax, C.B. and Mitchell, K.M. (1971) *Research on certain therapist interpersonal skills in relation to process and outcome.* In Bergin, A.E. and Garfield, S.L. (Eds.) Handbook of Psychotherapy and Behaviour Change. New York: Wiley.

Tuson, G. (1984) *Paradox and Partnership in Community Social Work.* Discussion Paper. London: National Institute for Social Work: Practice and Development Exchange.

Utterbuck, J. (1996) *Mastering the Dynamics of Innovation.* Boston, Mass: Harvard Business School Press.

Vaihinger, H. (1935) *The Philosophy of 'As If'.* London: Routledge and Kegan Paul.

Van De Ven, A. H., Angle, H. L. and Poole, M.S. (Eds.) (1989) *Research on the Management of Innovation: The Minnesota Studies.* Grand Rapids: Ballinger/Harper and Row for the University of Minnesota.

Van De Ven, A. H. and Angle, H. L. (1989) *An introduction to the Minnesota Innovation Research Program.* In Van De Ven, A. H. Angle, H. L. and Poole, M.S. (Eds.) Research in the Management of Innovation: The Minnesota Studies. Grand Rapids: Ballinger/Harper and Row for the University of Minnesota.

Waddington, C.H. (1977) *Tools for Thought.* London: Paladin.

Watzlawick, Paul. (1978) *The Language of Change.* New York: Basic Books.

Watzlawick, P. (1990) *Munchhausen's Pigtail.* New York: Norton.

Watzlawick, P., Beavin, J.H. and Jackson, D.D. (1967) *Pragmatics of Human Communication: A Study of Interactional Patterns, Pathologies and Paradoxes.* New York: W.W. Norton.

Watzlawick, P., Weakland, J. and Fisch R. (1974) *Change: Principles of Problem Formation and Resolution.* New York: Norton.

Watson J.D. (1970) *The Double Helix.* Harmondsworth: Penguin.

Webb, J. and Dawson, P. (1991) *Measure for measure: strategic change in an electronic instruments corporation.* Journal of Management Studies, Vol. 28 No.2 March pp.191-206.

Weissman, H.H., Ed. (1990) *Serious Play: Creativity and Innovation in Social Work.* Silver Spring, MD: NASW.

Westley, F. (1991) *Bob Geldof and Live Aid: the affective side of global social innovation.* Human Relations, Vol. 44 No. 10 pp. 1011-1036.

White, R., Hodgson, P. and Crainer, S. (1997) *The Future of Leadership: A White Water Revolution.* London: Ashbridge/Pitman.

Wilson T.D. and others (1978) *Information Needs and Information Services in Local Authority Social Services Departments. (Project INISS).* Final Report. London: British Library.

Woodcock, A. and Davis, M. (1980) *Catastrophe Theory.* Harmondsworth: Penguin.

Wright, S. G. (1985) *Change in nursing: the application of change theory to practice.* Nursing Practice, Vol. 2 pp. 85-91.

Young, D. (1990) *Champions of change: entrepreneurs in social work.* In Weissman, H. (Ed.) Serious Play: Creativity and Innovation in Social Work. Silver Spring, MD: NASW.

Zaltman, G.R., Duncan, R. and Holbeck, J. (1973) *Innovations and Organizations.* New York: Wiley.